Landscapes of Care

STUDIES IN SOCIAL MEDICINE

Allan M. Brandt, Larry R. Churchill, and Jonathan Oberlander, editors

This series publishes books at the intersection of medicine, health, and society that further our understanding of how medicine and society shape one another historically, politically, and ethically. The series is grounded in the convictions that medicine is a social science, that medicine is humanistic and cultural as well as biological, and that it should be studied as a social, political, ethical, and economic force.

A complete list of books published in Studies in Social Medicine is available at https://uncpress.org/series/studies-social-medicine.

Landscapes of Care

Immigration and Health in Rural America

Thurka Sangaramoorthy

The University of North Carolina Press CHAPEL HILL

We are proud to announce that this book is freely available in an open-access edition thanks to TOME (Toward an Open Monograph Ecosystem)—a collaboration of the Association of American Universities, the Association of University Presses, and the Association of Research Libraries—and the generous support of the University of Maryland. Learn more at the TOME website: openmonographs.org.

Set in Merope Basic by Westchester Publishing Services
Manufactured in the United States of America

Library of Congress Cataloging-in-Publication Data
Names: Sangaramoorthy, Thurka, 1975– author.
Title: Landscapes of care : immigration and health in rural America /
  Thurka Sangaramoorthy.
Other titles: Studies in social medicine.
Description: Chapel Hill : The University of North Carolina Press, [2023] |
  Series: Studies in social medicine | Includes bibliographical references and index.
Identifiers: LCCN 2022053982 | ISBN 9781469674162 (cloth) |
  ISBN 9781469674179 (paperback) | ISBN 9781469674186 (ebook)
Subjects: LCSH: Immigrants—Medical care—United States. | Rural health services—
  United States.
Classification: LCC RA448.5.I44 S264 2023 | DDC 362.1/042570973—dc23/eng/20221114
LC record available at https://lccn.loc.gov/2022053982

Cover illustration: Aerial view of field © shutterstock.com/Mariusz Szczygiel.

*To Gyan and Ashok for inspiring me to focus on the story that
I wanted to tell, and to all those on Maryland's Eastern Shore
who generously taught me about the intimate connections
between immigration and rural health*

Contents

Illustrations

Preface
Writing Immigration: Love, Loss, and Longing

I am an immigrant, a refugee forced to leave the only home I had ever known at the tender age of seven. My parents fled war-torn Sri Lanka in 1983 after my mother issued an ultimatum to my father: we leave together as a family, or she would go alone with her two young daughters. Weeks after the deadly riots in July 1983—commonly referred to as *Black July*,[1] the anti-Tamil pogrom that resulted in the death of potentially 3,000 Tamils and sparked the twenty-five-year civil war—the four of us met my mother's relatives in the United States. We narrowly escaped, carrying only two small suitcases and the clothes on our backs.

Although I was young when we left Sri Lanka, I have clear memories that remain. In my small village neighborhood, I remember an army checkpoint at the end of the main road. My friends and I used to play and ride our bikes down that road. We had to cross the checkpoint to get to stores, schools, and other homes. I remember being told by my parents how to behave near the checkpoint: walk straight and slow, do not make sudden movements, and if confronted by any uniformed officer, answer all questions and obey orders no matter what. This wariness became part of my muscle memory. Forty years later, my body still automatically tenses up around uniformed police and military.[2]

In the United States, I followed the Sri Lankan Civil War through stories from relatives, family friends, and the media. I heard accounts of forced disappearances, torture, and rape. I saw pictures of dead bodies, shelled homes, and flattened villages. My reactions to these stories and photographs have always been dissociative, mainly because I do not feel an intimate connection to a place that I have never been able to return to and do not have close family members who remain. I also felt alienated and traumatized by the harmful, enduring equations between Sri Lankan Tamils and death, violence, and terrorism.

At the same time, I have never felt like I belong in my adopted home, either. Growing up poor and Brown in America is not easy. I continue to experience challenges related to racism, discrimination, and being treated differently, even though the circumstances of my life have shifted drastically since my arrival. These feelings of not belonging either here or there, root-lessness, and always longing for a home that no longer exists—and perhaps, in some ways, never existed—have been with me since I was a child. But there are also moments of celebration, hope, and resoluteness, of finding community and engaging in the radical politics of being and caring, despite the challenges.

These are the perspectives I rarely see in academic books on immigration. Yet this is the intimate familiarity from which I am able to write. I am a Sri Lankan Tamil immigrant scholar from a working-class background in the United States and the first in my family to attend college. Still, others see me as what Leisy Abrego calls "out-of-place" among scholars of immigration in anthropology.[3] As a first-generation immigrant, I was expected to work on South Asia or South Asian diaspora issues. I never once witnessed my white colleagues subjected to the same expectations of working in their own com-munities. Instead, they were encouraged to work on issues affecting minori-tized and vulnerable people, often in faraway or "exotic" locales. Even when I had opportunities to work on projects that focused on the experiences and perspectives of poor South Asian immigrants living in New York City, research advisers constantly questioned my ability to conduct rigorous, objective, "unbiased" research among "my own." Others' discouragement and my incapacity to reckon with my own historical trauma of coloniality, war, and terror made me hesitant to work with Sri Lankan Tamil communi-ties, especially in the realm of health and well-being.

AS A GRADUATE STUDENT IN PUBLIC HEALTH, I learned of the discrimina-tion toward Haitians while working on a longitudinal study of those living with HIV. I spent time listening to Haitian immigrants' narratives of life in Haiti and the United States. I realized how much we had in common as we shared memories of extraordinary yet routine political violence back home and exchanged stories of personal experiences of economic insecurity and racism. Through the research encounter, we co-performed pain and suffer-ing, seeing the unseen and hearing the unspoken, moving perhaps toward what Naisargi Dave calls "the subject of intimacy and away from the self and its protective skin."[4] These modes of witnessing and accompaniment en-gendered an unwavering commitment to a moral praxis rooted in solidarity, empathy, and understanding.[5]

I continued to work with Haitian immigrants as a PhD student, explor-ing the biopolitics of HIV prevention policies and programs and their effect on the health and well-being of transnational communities. Unfortunately, a military coup prevented me from continuing my dissertation fieldwork in Haiti. As a result, I constantly worried about the safety and welfare of friends, colleagues, and interlocutors while pivoting my research to focus on Haitian communities in South Florida. During this time, white colleagues openly remarked that my U.S.-based fieldwork was "easy" and "uncomplicated" compared to theirs in more "global" settings without reflecting how such assumptions are pervasive within anthropology, a discipline rooted in imperialism and white supremacy.

As I began to publish the findings from my dissertation, I felt increasingly disillusioned with the academic inclination to focus exclusively on immigrant vulnerability and suffering and, in the case of Haitians, Black death and deficiency. A reviewer for my first book, for instance, rejected it based on a lack of "thick ethnographic description" about stigma, suffering, and blame, claiming that many Haitian interlocutors could not be considered immigrants at all without these signifiers. In working alongside others, I had witnessed and lived otherwise—in joy and despair, resistance and fear, care and abandonment. Such moments of being do not easily render themselves observable to those whose paradigm focuses on violence, pain, and silence. Even now, colleagues rarely view my work with Haitians as fitting within the pervasive narratives that dominate the anthropology of immigration. Truth be told, I have never been comfortable making it suitable for the consumption of mainly white scholarly audiences.

In a 2020 interview published in *The Cut*, writer Alexander Chee shared what he wished he had known about writing and the kind of advice he would give to young writers and those starting out.[6] "I have always asked my students to focus on the stories only they can tell," he states. "By which I mean, to watch for the vision that opens to them. To write what they never see in books. And I think that is still the advice. It still works now." I know that in writing about immigration and health, I am also telling my story and those of others like me, and in the process, I am decentering the whiteness that dominates the scholarship on immigration and rural studies.

LANDSCAPES OF CARE is an ethnography of how care becomes conceptualized and enacted in rural settings among immigrants and nonimmigrant residents. Set in the rural and politically conservative region of the Eastern Shore of Maryland, this book explores the dynamic relations between immigration, health, and rural precarity. The nearly six years of ethnographic fieldwork that inform the book began in 2013, approximately three years after the U.S. government enacted the Affordable Care Act (ACA). As a result, I trace the aftermath of the U.S. health care system's most significant regulatory over-haul and expansion of coverage since the passage of Medicare and Medicaid in 1965. I also document the repercussions of Donald Trump's presidential election and his administration's sweeping changes to federal immigration policy. Such changes include heightened immigration enforcement and de-portation, reduction of refugee and asylee admissions, and expansion of the "public charge" rule to limit green card and temporary visa applications.

The book's narrative revolves around how care unfolds amid precarity spe-cific to immigration and rural life. I find precarity a helpful concept for thinking through the intimacy of the daily struggles of living and how life is continuously being made and unmade on Maryland's Eastern Shore. As I use it here, precarity signifies the enduring vulnerability and uncertainty stem-ming from various racialized economic and social forces. Yet precarity does not signal presumed conditions about the nature of rural life or what it is like to be an immigrant. Instead, it is a point of engagement of accompanying others in their provisional and haphazard trajectories of making a livable life and how rural living practices unfold.

Such orientation centers on immigrants' and rural providers' shared con-ditions of uncertainty and disposability, how they come to embody such anxieties, and how suffering and agency transpire amid chronic insecurity. More importantly, it is a sensibility that is attentive to how immigrants do not experience these struggles alone in isolation but through their emergent relations with others and various care networks. I argue that this mutual de-pendency and care is what makes living possible under challenging times. Pre-carity allows us to ask what it means to understand living and peoples' lives as fields of intensities and durations rather than raw material for exploitation.

In light of the rapid increase in rural immigration and the difficulties commonly associated with rural areas, I explore how precarity relates to immigration and rural life, its manifestation as physical and emotional dis-tress, and how it is mediated through social relations and community coop-eration. An orientation to precarity shifts the framing of health and health care from spatially and temporally bound systems to a field of relations. Instead of focusing on health care systems, I attend to the complex forma-tions that constitute what I call a "landscape of care" on Maryland's Eastern Shore. The notion of landscape better incorporates the irregular, informal, and improvised reality of immigrants' care experiences in rural regions and many other places worldwide struggling with global migration and health governance challenges.

Finally, a theoretical and methodological orientation toward precarity allows for the broad diversity of immigrant voices and experiences living and working in rural landscapes. Often, scholarship on immigration tends to focus on particular immigrant groups, which has led to two related outcomes: exceptionalism of each group's experiences as unique or rendering all immigrant experiences the same through the framework of legality. My formative work on immigration and health illustrated how racialization—the ongoing (re)creation of new definitions, groupings, and associations between racial hierarchies and the categories they comprise—engendered Haitian and Black immigrants' social, cultural, and political marginalization.[7] Racialization is an undeniable dimension of immigrant experiences in the United States and shapes individual and community relations, health and well-being, and the politics of care. This book, in turn, focuses on the spatial, temporal, and racial logics that affect immigrant experiences in rural regions.

FIELDWORK

Although this book draws on the work I have done with Haitian and Latinx immigrant communities in rural and urban settings throughout the United States since 2000, research in rural Maryland for the book began in 2013. This ethnography moves back and forth between community health facilities, service organizations, homes, work sites, and immigrant enclaves (e.g., migrant camps, temporary housing, apartment complexes) to detail daily life and social interactions between immigrants and care providers on Maryland's Eastern Shore. Traditional ethnographic methods, including participant observation and individual, in-depth interviews, were used to conduct research that grounds this book.

Many immigrants who come to this region find work in agriculture, poultry, and seafood processing. Latinx and Haitian immigrants make up the vast majority of those working and living in the area. Some come directly from Latin America and the Caribbean, particularly Mexico, Central America, and Haiti; many others migrate from other parts of the East Coast. The Eastern Shore is considered a new receiving destination, a place without high concentrations of immigrant communities.[8] Those on temporary work visas and migrant farmworkers from Florida and other parts of the United States arrive in late spring and early summer and stay through the growing season. Migrant Mexican women who work in crab processing also follow the same seasonal employment pattern. Others, like those working in the poultry processing plants, have settled here more permanently, fashioning a life for themselves and their loved ones.

Health and social services providers are integral to the social integration of these immigrant communities. Providers featured in this book range from nurse practitioners to outreach coordinators to translators. Many providers consider themselves long-term residents of the area; a handful, however, are immigrants themselves, who settled in the region with their families. Spending time in institutions that deliver health care and social services and with providers who care for immigrants helped clarify how local policies and institutional practices affect the health care experiences of immigrants. In addition, navigating care landscapes with immigrant interlocutors helped ground my perspectives on how immigrants understand care and access essential social services in their communities. Engaging in these interactions, I witnessed firsthand how providers and institutions interacted with immigrant clients and perceived their care needs and how immigrants and nonimmigrants alike enacted and performed care work.

Initial contact and fruitful conversations with researchers and community organizers led to entry into social service organizations and health clinics and eventually into people's homes and community life. Informal discussions and formal interviews with interlocutors brought about additional recommendations from colleagues, neighbors, friends, and family members interested in telling their perspectives and stories of the landscape of care on the Eastern Shore. Interviews were conducted in English, Spanish, and Haitian Kreyòl and digitally recorded with permission for transcription, translation, and analysis.

Formal interviews and informal discussions with local researchers, academics, health and social service providers, and immigrants helped solidify analysis presented in *Landscapes of Care*. Twenty-four care providers and sixty-two immigrants participated in formal ethnographic interviews. Providers came from a broad range of service sectors, including health care (20 percent), social services (20 percent), legal services (15 percent), employment outreach (30 percent), and educational services (15 percent). Immigrant participants were mainly women (79 percent) and included those who identified as Hispanic/Latino/Mexican/Central American (n = 37) and Haitian or Black (n = 25).

Very little information exists on these communities on the Eastern Shore besides official census counts and large-scale surveys; therefore, it was essential to collect primary demographic data during the formal interview sessions. Health and social service providers also provided information about their immigrant clients and their pressing needs. They spoke at length about their daily experiences of providing care for immigrants against the backdrop of immigration restrictions and health care policy changes. Finally, immigrant interlocutors detailed their journeys to the Eastern Shore, daily life, community relations, perceptions of health and well-being, and availability, quality, and use of health care services.

CONTRIBUTIONS

Initially, I was interested in documenting the rise in immigration from Mexico, Central America, and Haiti to the area. When I set out to review the gray (unpublished) literature about immigration to this rural, isolated region of Maryland, I found little to no information on the topic. In talking with local researchers, academics, medical and social service providers, and immigrants, I heard about the challenges experienced by immigrants and nonimmigrant residents within rural health care systems. In spending time with my interlocutors, I witnessed the effects of cost-containment and profit-driven measures that had been ongoing since the 1990s.[9] Even though my research initially focused on immigration, the challenges of rural health care became a frequent topic of conversation in my field site. For many, immigration experiences could not be decoupled from issues of rural health care provision and delivery.

Providers, administrators, and local experts emphasized that increased immigration intensified issues related to health precarity in rural regions already struggling with provider shortage, high rates of uninsured populations, and limited public resources. Immigrants also noted that working and living in an isolated rural area made it difficult to obtain care and access resources. The people I worked with insisted that immigration-related issues — such as the politics of belonging, citizenship, and deservingness—were vital to understanding rural health provision and delivery. Interlocutors' demands, in many ways, rendered visible the limits of scholarly understanding of immigrant health, even my own. These exchanges and analyses, particularly interlocutors' insistence on immigration and rural health's shared conditions of precarity, guide the book's primary interventions.

Landscapes of Care interrogates the statistical and demographic portraits of immigration, often the only data available in rural spaces. As a result, it provides a more grounded understanding of the lives of individuals and communities than what has been available thus far (i.e., data captured through survey-oriented health and immigration research). This book addresses the complex relations between political concepts of rights, racial capitalist for-mations of value, and moral assessments of health-related deservingness. It also documents the epidemiological and lived implications of immigrant health.

The book's primary intervention is to move our understanding of immi-gration and health beyond the singular focus on legality and criminality and to consider the impact of race and racialization, gender, space/place, and time on immigrants and migrants' experiences of seeking, receiving, and fash-ioning care. *Landscapes of Care* examines rural precarity and the place-based, temporal, and racialized dimensions of immigrant health that remain overlooked and underestimated. Namely, it considers rural and immigrant precarity and racial inequalities as familiar, ordinary manifestations of health and health care. There are real-world implications for these insights, as im-migration, legal, and racial equity advocates seek ways to move policy and public dialogues on migration and health beyond narrow public health in-terventions and protectionist policies. This book, therefore, is written to pro-mote critical reflection, political mobilization, and social change.

Landscapes of Care also addresses critical theoretical concerns within the social sciences and public health regarding structural drivers of immigrant health—specifically, the role of immigration and health policy developments in shaping and influencing the complex care pathways for vulnerable popu-lations. Here, this book envisions public policy as one of several theoretical explanations for immigrant structural vulnerability and place-based and ra-cial inequalities in health. Rather than overlook the material effects of health care and immigration reform and the ideologies that make them seem practical, the book attends to the spatial, temporal, and racial articulations of policies as they unfold "on the ground" and shape immigrants' decisions for seeking care.[10]

Immigration scholarship has shown that immigrant integration and ex-clusion occur across organizational domains, including education and work. Yet health and health care have not been binding sites of analysis.[11] This book documents how local contexts of reception, organizational culture, and pro-vider attitudes and behaviors are critical to how immigrants experience the U.S. health care system, particularly those racialized as Black or with pre-carious legal status. Focusing on health (and rural health in particular) as an analytical domain advances what we know about immigrant and minority health more broadly. Moreover, it expands understanding of the processes and consequences of exclusion that immigration scholars want to examine globally. This book deepens theoretical debates within the scholarship on immigration, specifically how health care's organizational practices affect immigrants' sense of belonging and feelings of marginalization.

Further, *Landscapes of Care* advances our understanding of public policy's social and cultural dimensions, particularly individual perceptions and behaviors and community relations. This book analyzes how care providers' perceptions and behaviors intersect with organizational practices and national policies to produce specific, local care contexts. In doing so, it provides an ethnographic context about how recent policy developments in health care and immigration become translated across organizational and community levels. Such an endeavor is urgent at a time of great uncertainty about the future of various individuals with precarious legal status in the United States and how federal policy mandates may come into conflict with state and local commitments regarding health care, racial equity, and immigrant rights.

Recent changes to the U.S. political landscape indicate that the future of health care and immigration reform is unclear. A vital aim of this book is to attend to questions of who deserves care and the role of the state and organizations in providing health care that inevitably affects all aspects of life for immigrants, their families, and larger communities. By bringing attention to the spatial, temporal, and racial logics of structural conditions, organizational processes, and individual and community perspectives that unfold in rural settings like Maryland's Eastern Shore, this book illustrates how some proposals to cut public spending on health will have a long-term negative impact on entire communities, nonimmigrants and immigrants alike.

Landscapes of Care

Introduction

The Land That Time Forgot

Summer in Maryland means one thing: blue crabs. Every summer, residents and visitors flock to Maryland's coast to get their fill of blue crabs. Famous for its sweet, tender meat, the blue crab is an essential part of the region's culinary heritage. There are few things more enjoyable to Marylanders than sitting with family and friends, tearing into a bushel of blue crabs coated with the local seasoning, Old Bay, and washing it down with ice-cold Natty Bohs (see figure 0.1). Eating blue crabs in the traditional manner is not for the faint of heart or for those who prefer eating with utensils and white tablecloths. In restaurants and homes, people pile steamed and seasoned blue crabs in the middle of a table covered in paper. Then, using small mallets, knives, and bare hands, diners break open the hard shells and extract the juicy meat inside. It is a messy experience, one that is quintessentially Maryland.

The Latin word for blue crabs is *Callinectes sapidus*, meaning "beautiful swimmer." Blue crabs get their name from their sapphire-colored claws and are one of the most iconic species in the Chesapeake Bay. In Maryland, hard shells are steamed rather than boiled, a common practice along the East Coast and Louisiana. Marylanders insist that steaming gives crabmeat its moistness, and the flavor is best appreciated by cracking and eating steamed hard shells or feasting on soft shells.[1] However, suppose you would instead not go through the hassle of picking crab. In that case, it is easy to buy fresh crabmeat by the pound at local grocery stores or enjoy them steamed or sautéed, as Maryland crab cakes or crab imperial, or in crab soup or crab dip at any area restaurant.

In Maryland and elsewhere, eating blue crab is a communal activity and is meant to be enjoyed with family, friends, or large groups. As a result, people often experience picking crab as a pleasurable experience and social exercise. Even those who purchase fresh crabmeat at the grocery store or a restaurant rarely consider how it was processed or who picked and cleaned it. Many people forget or overlook how crab picking is a livelihood for many, mainly poor, women. For generations, African American women from Maryland's rural, maritime communities did the grueling job of picking crab for crab houses on the Eastern Shore. Today, fewer than ten crab houses are left, and the workforce is exclusively female migrant workers from Mexico.

1

FIGURE 0.1 *Crabs* by Jason Garber is used under a CC BY-NC-SA 4.0 license.

Like many other places around the world, Maryland's rural Eastern Shore has come to rely heavily on the labor of noncitizen immigrants. Yet policymakers and the general public often regard their presence as illegitimate, threatening, and a drain on national and local resources, ignoring how their "illegality" and "foreignness" often place them in positions of considerable social risk. In recent years, the national spotlight on border walls, immigration bans, the inhumane treatment of undocumented immigrants at detention centers, and the disproportionate impact of COVID-19 on immigrant farmworkers and meat processors has raised some public awareness of the plight of immigrant workers. But immigration remains an increasingly polarized issue among rural Marylanders and Americans more broadly. In Maryland, for instance, comprehensive news coverage of increasing visa caps for migrant workers, COVID-19 pandemic restrictions, and crab shortages have left many concerned about the fate of the crab industry.[2] Politicians and influential business owners have appealed to the federal government to increase the number of visas the country provides to female Mexican migrants, arguing that the H-2B temporary worker program is vital to the Eastern Shore's iconic seafood economy. These discussions on the dire need to increase immigrant labor occur in some of Maryland's most politically conservative areas, where there is strong support for federal and local anti-immigrant rhetoric and policies.

SINCE 1990, THERE HAS BEEN a steep rise in immigration to the United States. The increases are highest in rural America.[3] Some rural counties are experiencing growth rates of over 1,000 percent in their immigrant population, who have filled essential roles in the labor force and mitigated the growing decline of rural populations.[4] Yet, despite their valuable contributions to rural communities, immigrants are not necessarily treated well or openly welcomed by local residents. Often, advocates, experts, and policymakers discuss the fate of immigrants in static, oppositional terms—whether society will embrace and integrate them or reject and push them out. In rural Maryland (and perhaps much of rural America), where demographic shifts have been sudden and drastic, the lives of immigrants and rural community relations are highly complex and tenuous and challenge existing either/or assumptions about immigrant integration and exclusion.

Large demographic studies help us recognize the impact of policies on people's migration trajectories. Yet they tell us very little about how diverse structural dynamics shape rural communities' reactions to this burgeoning wave of newcomers, especially in regions without large immigrant enclaves. Survey-based work can also overlook important details related to the everyday life of immigrants and the politics of belonging. *Landscapes of Care* fills a necessary gap in the literature on immigration by attending to policies, organizational processes, and community relations ethnographically. More specifically, the book details the spatial, temporal, and racial dynamics operating at the nexus of immigration and rural health on Maryland's Eastern Shore—a relatively isolated and rural area composed of nine counties east of the Chesapeake Bay (see map 0.1). Jobs and resources are challenging to come by, and the region's physical remoteness often requires residents to travel long distances to work or obtain care. In addition, many of the available jobs are strenuous and dangerous—farming, fishing, commercial food processing and production, and logging. Work in these industries places people at risk for injury or illness. *Landscapes of Care* examines how the daily functioning of racial capitalism and white supremacy shapes the shared conditions of precarity among immigrants and rural residents. It attends to how precarity engenders physical suffering and emotional anxiety and generates powerful forms of sociality, mutual obligation, and rural vitality.[5] Understanding immigrant and rural precarity together render

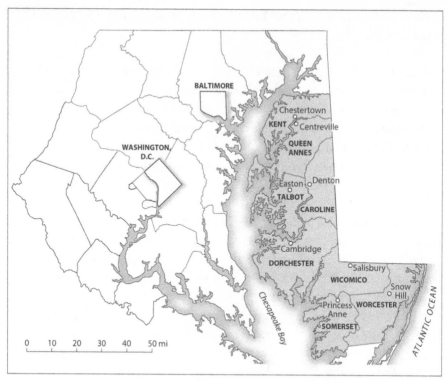

MAP 0.1 Maryland's Eastern Shore.

visible how people in rural contexts care for each other despite social discrimination, economic precarity, and an often hostile political climate. Such discussions of rural immigration focused on belonging, deservingness, and scarcity are integral to broader national and global debates on migration and health.

A Day with Elizabeth

I was nervous and excited to spend the day with Elizabeth, a nurse practitioner who runs the local mobile health unit. Her mobile team was the only one of its kind and offered care to those living in the furthest, most remote corners of the Eastern Shore of Maryland. Elizabeth and her team worked for a local federally qualified health center (FQHC), a community-based health care provider that receives funds from the U.S. government to provide primary care services in underserved areas. They operated the mobile health unit from June to August—the peak season for migrant workers in agriculture and seafood processing. I knew accompanying Elizabeth was a rare opportunity, and I felt grateful that she generously invited me on a trip to the local crab processing plants.

I agreed to meet the mobile health unit staff at the local Walmart parking lot outside Cambridge's town center so that I could accompany them to their appointments that day. Cambridge sits on the Choptank River, a major tributary of the Chesapeake Bay on the Eastern Shore of Maryland about ninety miles southeast of Washington, D.C., the nation's capital. Its waterfront, small-town feel makes it a popular destination for nature lovers, recreation enthusiasts, and history buffs alike. Initially inhabited by the Nanticoke people, English colonists violently colonized the area that would become Cambridge, Maryland, in 1684. Soon, Cambridge became a hub for the local slave trade. Harriet Tubman was born into slavery just a few miles away and escaped in 1849 with her two brothers.[6] In the following years, Tubman returned to Cambridge to help free as many as sixty to seventy other enslaved people, including those who fled the auction block on the steps of the same Cambridge courthouse I was passing by. Years later, Cambridge became an unlikely epicenter of the nation's civil rights movement, led by activist Gloria Richardson, head of the Cambridge Nonviolent Action Committee.[7] Her iconic photo, where she fiercely pushed aside a National Guardsman's bayonet with her sidelong glance at a local demonstration on July 21, 1963, sits in the Smithsonian's National Museum of African American History and Culture. Today, Cambridge prides itself on charm, history, and natural beauty. I shivered, thinking about how the courthouse was still in use today.

Elizabeth and her team arrived in a burgundy Dodge minivan a few minutes after I parked. At first, I felt confused. I expected a much bigger vehicle large enough to house a clinic office or exam room inside, but I had no time to process my surprise. Ellen, the medical assistant, poked her head out the window and yelled at me to get inside. I hopped on board the minivan in the blistering heat. The only seat available was between rattling medication cases, medical files, equipment, and folding furniture. Nevertheless, I squeezed in. We drove through stretches of farmland, tidal marshland, and mixed hardwood and loblolly pine forests, crossing over a series of bridges with panoramic views of the Chesapeake Bay, passing landmarks like St. Mary Star of the Sea and the iconic General Store. Some people from the area describe the Eastern Shore as "the land that time forgot." It was easy to see why. The sudden isolation and stillness of the landscape were disquieting, as if we had physically crossed into a different place and time. My cell phone lost its signal entirely, and I did not see a single person, vehicle, or home on our forty-minute drive.

Our first stop was a rustic restaurant on a grassy knoll. The restaurant was closed, but we were not there to dine. Instead, it was a pit stop where we got organized, notified the various seafood houses of our arrival, and secured permission from owners to set up the mobile clinic on their property. I helped the staff spread out the medical files on the wooden benches outside that were typically reserved for outdoor dining. Then, I organized the prescription medications for migrant workers who Elizabeth had seen during previous visits. The medical files were disorganized; the workers' names on the list provided by the seafood houses sometimes did not correspond to the names on the files. We did our best to match the medications to the appropriate patient files and then arranged them according to their employer. This filing system made it easier for the health team to distribute the prescriptions correctly to the women. I peeked at the medications that the team hoped to dispense on this trip. They varied, ranging from skin creams to pain relievers. Cuts, scrapes, rashes, and skin infections were common among women working in crab processing. Some women also suffered from allergic reactions to vapor, salty water, bleach, and other chemicals used in crab processing. In addition, women experienced minor injuries, chronic pain, tendinitis, and myalgia from long hours picking crabs in crouched positions.

Matching medication to patient files took over two hours—much longer than anyone anticipated. It was past noon, and I was unsure how much time we had left to visit the crab houses. Elizabeth, however, was in a cheerful mood because she secured several health visits from crab processing plant managers. We filed back in the van and drove another few minutes to grab lunch at a modest convenience store with a small deli case, ice cream counter, and a grill. In the backroom, we ate next to five older white men wearing trucker hats and smudged T-shirts. Elizabeth explained the plan for the rest of the day. I worried about how much of her schedule would get done, given that half the day had already passed. Finally, perhaps sensing my anxiety, she leaned over and told me that she needed to get the van back within twenty-four hours. Otherwise, she would pay for an extra day. Noticing my surprise, Elizabeth explained: "I use my personal credit card and then get reimbursed. Otherwise, no one would get care."

I did not have time to inquire further into Elizabeth's revelation because we were on the road again. Our first stop was what the staff referred to as the "telescope house," so named because of its unusual accordion shape. As I stepped out of the van, the damp, pungent smell of crab chum and shells hit me like a ton of bricks. Working past my discomfort, I helped Sylvia and Camila, the two Spanish-language translators, unload all the

FIGURE 0.2 Mobile clinic. Photo by the author.

equipment, files, and medications from the van. We quickly unpacked the large tent and folding furniture, including two long tables and a few chairs (see figure 0.2). Next, Sylvia knocked on the front door to ask if anyone wanted to see the provider. Eight women filed out wearing shorts, T-shirts, and flip-flops. I later learned that many of the women working in commercial crab processing on the Eastern Shore were from rural regions in eastern and north-central Mexico, such as Hidalgo and San Luis Potosí.

Migration has become a central strategy for rural development in these areas that have undergone substantial rural outmigration because of the devastation of small-scale agriculture brought about by the North American Free Trade Agreement and the Mexican neoconservative governmental regimes of 2000 to 2012.[8] In turn, the intensification of induced labor migration has deepened gendered and racialized employment patterns globally, such as those found within commercial seafood processing.[9] Economic conditions such as free trade, deregulation, and privatization coupled with progressively harsh anti-immigrant policies have led to a global trend toward hyper-flexible labor strategies.[10] Organizational practices such as nonstandard work arrangements and temporary, seasonal, and informal immigrant workforce have become the norm among businesses struggling to succeed in increasingly competitive markets.

I INTRODUCED MYSELF to Xiomara and Valeria, who were waiting in line to see Elizabeth. They represent foreign-born workers who account for a growing proportion (17.4 percent) of the U.S. civilian labor force, of which Hispanics/Latinos make up nearly half and Asians comprise 25 percent.[11] In her late thirties and single, Xiomara picked crab for the same company for thirteen years, from early spring to late fall. She had a father in Mexico and a brother and sister in the United States who were undocumented. Xiomara patiently explained that she left Mexico to work in crab processing because locally available jobs in orange and corn cultivation could not support basic survival needs: "You earn 400 to 500 pesos per week [US$20 to $25]. That is maybe enough to eat." As the sole economic providers for their families, a trend throughout rural Mexico noted by other scholars,[12] women like Xiomara face increased economic precarity, which led them to migrate for work. While official numbers show that foreign-born women's share of labor participation is slightly less than their U.S.-born counterparts (53.4 percent versus 56.6 percent), they, like foreign-born men, are highly segregated in a handful of low-wage, service-oriented occupations and more likely to experience poverty than the native-born population.[13]

Xiomara learned about crab processing jobs from family and friends. Her brother, who lives in Seattle, warned her that labor migration for women was particularly difficult because of the dangers posed by travel and work. He insisted that she contact a family friend for help: "So this young man helped me out. He checked it out, and he asked around, and that is why I came." Using a recruiter to secure a temporary work visa intended for foreign workers, Xiomara took the three-day journey to Maryland's Eastern Shore by bus from Monterey, Mexico. When she arrived, she was housed with eleven other Mexican female migrant workers in the telescope house. The women typically worked an average of eight to nine hours, sometimes more, depending on the daily crab supply. Xiomara showed us where they worked, directing us to the area where they had picked crabs a few hours earlier. It was a sizable sparse room that still felt wet and smelled of disinfectant. Inside, there were two long stainless steel tables. The walls and floors looked recently mopped and cleaned, and bilingual signs in Spanish and English instructing workers to wash their hands and wear boots hung prominently on the walls. Pointing to the stack of plastic containers and the sink area, Xiomara explained their work routine: "We pick up a plastic tub, and we rinse it with a water-bleach solution to disinfect it. We take out our tools, put on our apron, sit down, and fill the tubs. We separate the lump crabmeat from other meat and place it in a separate plastic cup. Every hour, the manager comes by and takes the crabmeat that you have produced and weighs it."

Xiomara returns every year because crab processing work ensures survival despite the challenges of living and working in the United States: "We are here because of the work! Because in Mexico, you do not earn anything! Imagine, we are paid about 100 pesos [less than US$5] per day. And that is all day and all evening. If you make money here and then go back home, you end up living a different life. But you suffer when you are here. Slowly, you suffer without your family and home. But you return." Valeria, who joined us after seeing Elizabeth, likewise affirmed: "It is because of work. That is why I came, too. If not for that, I would have stayed in Mexico. I am a single mother." Valeria was in her mid-forties and a mother to four children ranging from fourteen to twenty-three years old. She explained that she was lonely and sad because she missed her family. This was her first year working as a crab picker, and she did not know any of the other women living with her. She confided that she was worried. Her supervisor gave her only a few days to adjust to the pace of work to meet the daily quota of twenty-four pounds of picked crabmeat. If she did not meet this quota by the deadline, her employer could send her back to Mexico.

Spatial, Temporal, and Racial Configurations of Rural Immigrant Life

> I have experienced a cosmic cycle, with all its changes and evolutions for that which I have seen with my own eyes in this brief interval of time—things that no other mortal eye had seen before, glimpses of a world past, a world dead, a world so long dead that even in the lowest Cambrian stratum no trace of it remains. Fused with the melting inner crust, it has passed forever beyond the ken of man other than in that lost pocket of the Earth whither fate has borne me and where my doom is sealed.
>
> —EDGAR RICE BURROUGHS, *The Land That Time Forgot*

In describing the Eastern Shore as the land that time forgot, no one specifically referenced Edgar Rice Burroughs's 1924 novel of the same name. Burroughs's tale is a wartime sea adventure where the protagonist encounters a lost world, Caprona, where time has stopped. Menacing beasts, early evolutionary forms of man, and various strange life forms in the river inhabit Caprona. These beings engage in the process of reincarnation, where they gradually migrate northward, and their physical body and behavioral traits evolve both across and over time.

Caprona seems a far cry from rural Maryland, and Burroughs's novel bears little resemblance to this ethnographic study of the inherent relations between immigration, health, and rural precarity. Yet, I find it helpful to ask what it means to be a place or a community positioned outside of time and geography altogether, a land and a people forgotten, abandoned, and left behind. As social science and health scholars have indicated, movement across and between borders, disrupted rhythms of work and living, and retreating social safety nets tell us a great deal about the marginalization of immigrants and rural vulnerability.[14] Still, the invocation of the Eastern Shore as located *outside* time and space signals something in excess of these dynamics. Immigrants, in fact, have long contributed to the physical production of rural space through their racially differentiated labor; along with rural providers, they have invested in the meanings and making of rural vitality. Rather than reinforcing prevalent notions of immigrants as placeless and rural regions as abandoned, interlocutors' portrayal of the Eastern Shore as "the land that time forgot" indexes an intimate relationship between immigrant experiences and the organization of rural space.

In the United States and globally, immigration is coupled with territoriality, criminality, and the centrality of the nation-state. Scholarship on immigration and health, for instance, focuses on how broader transformations in labor and trade, along with the exclusionary aspects of immigration policies, increase noncitizen immigrants' vulnerability to disease, injury, and suffering.[15] Immigration experts and advocates have documented harmful labor practices and health policies that negatively affect immigrants' well-being.[16] Together, they have called for increased social and legal protections for immigrants, including those for the workplace, improved access to appropriate health and social services, and expanded cultural and structural competencies among key institutional actors such as health care providers.[17] This body of work, in effect, considers *legality* as the central organizing feature of immigrant life in the United States and *legal status* as the crucial mechanism through which immigrants experience health and health care. In fact, legal status and immigration status have come to mean the same thing. This predominant framing shapes research, policy, and public understandings of legal belonging as a primary determinant of immigrant health.

Yet, not all immigrant social life is knowable through the framework of legality. Defining immigration from the unitary vantage point of legality flattens immigrant knowledge, experience, and social identities. Legality naturalizes certain narratives of suffering and vulnerability. It works to hierarchically position individuals, communities, and nation-states, overlooking how social identities and relations of power can configure modes of living where immigrants negotiate spaces of subjugation and resistance. As such, legality can inadvertently reproduce discourses around immigration that equate it to inferiority and placelessness.

Further, a preoccupation with legality in the United States privileges narratives of specific immigration trajectories and immigrants, particularly non-Black Latinx immigrants from Mexico. As a result, social science and public health scholarship on immigrant health can reproduce the very vulnerability it seeks to describe and remediate. It renders "the immigrant" or "immigration" in exclusionary terms and relies on a conception of humanity as a singular identity, as bounded and absolute as a wounded, suffering, or vulnerable human.[18] Scholars often use structural vulnerability and social suffering frameworks to illustrate the embodiment of the social dynamics of exclusion among immigrants without interrogating how and whether such conceptual registers offer new insights into existential, economic, and political uncertainty. Such frameworks depend on the mobilization of the "other," characterized by experiences of victimhood related to legal status. This othering rests on constructing certain (non-Black) immigrants and (male) immigration trajectories as deserving of attention and care. Thus, immigrants manifest anew as "other" in discourses of liberal humanism that repeat the discursive separation they have already been marked by, though in new registers.[19]

Landscapes of Care moves away from these static approaches, foregrounding the spatial, temporal, and racial logics that shape immigrants' lives and are consequential for their well-being. It insists on the shared condition of immigrant and rural precarity to underscore care as both an object and a relation, its presence alongside scarcity, and how it operates within and beyond legal processes and organizational structures. Precarity related to rural living can deepen immigrants' experiences of social and economic marginalization and health inequities. A complex landscape—made up of policies that advance fiscal austerity and anti-immigration sentiment, a neoliberal era of health provision, racialized organizations that employ migrant laborers, and rural community contexts—shapes immigrant health. Likewise, rapid immigration severely affects rural health systems already struggling with a shortage of providers, limited health care access points, and high rates of uninsured and sick patients. Yet interlocutors' sense of place, time, and care unsettle discourses that reify immigrant and rural precarity as geographically and temporally constrained, resisting reductionary knowledge formation of immigration and rural health.

Precarity and the Predicament of Rural Immigrants

Rural and immigrant precarity are familiar yet overlooked manifestations of health and well-being in the United States and elsewhere. Precarity signifies an overall, persistent ontological condition of vulnerability, instability, and uncertainty. It is prompted by contemporary modes of racial capitalism, class relations, and multiple, intersecting historical and existential forces.[20] Judith Butler and others have described precarity as "that politically induced condition in which certain populations suffer from failing social and economic networks of support more than others . . . becoming differentially exposed to injury, violence, and death."[21] Conflict, displacement, and crumbling social safety nets in Latin America, the Caribbean, and the United States bring about a pervasive sense of uncertainty that makes precarity a common experience for immigrants on Maryland's Eastern Shore. Rural life in the United States, where disproportionate impacts of racial capitalism and exploitation render such inequalities particularly dire, also enhances experiences of precarity. People's description of the Eastern Shore as a place forgotten by time signals that life on the Eastern Shore is undetermined and ambivalent, marked by an everyday uncertainty that is simultaneously commonplace and extraordinary. As Anne Allison argues, "Uncertain about where/when/how one will make do in the present, the precarious lack handrails for anchoring the future as well. In this uncertainty of time, where everyday efforts don't align with a teleology of progressive betterment, living can be often just that. Not leading particularly anywhere, lives get lived nonetheless."[22]

There is a potential misstep in seeing precarity as existing everywhere and at all times. But this does not weaken its conceptual or practical value. Immigrant and rural precarity are not given conditions that exist outside any individual or collective life. On the contrary, they materialize through mundane material, emotional, and physical experiences such as racism, workplace injuries, and anxiety resulting from family separation. Precarity, therefore, is also a methodological orientation that "insists that an engagement with the lives of others must be attendant to the slippages, fraying, and importantly, the exposure of life itself."[23] Exploring the multiple facets of lived uncertainty and marginalization of immigrants and rural residents necessitates opening up to witnessing, listening, and accompanying the embodiment of others' vulnerability. Such considerations of experience bring into view the messy unruliness of the everyday. Rather than a standard configuration that outlines the predictability of patterns of work, home, and communal life, every day in the context of insecurity and violence, at times, forestalls coherent narratives altogether. Therefore, this study of precarity entails reconfiguring the ethnographic ground "as a provocation and a problematic that can lead us to think through modes of being attached to emergent forms that are still unfolding, always unfinished."[24]

Like other ethnographies of precarity,[25] *Landscapes of Care* clarifies historical and social forces shaping contemporary life structures by focusing on the emotions and feelings associated with people and places to convey precarity as an ontological condition that unfolds in the everyday. This book also extends existing scholarship on immigrant health by foregrounding how immigrants and rural providers negotiate displacement and belonging in racialized spaces to produce knowledge about immigration and rural health.[26] My thinking on precarity is deeply influenced by the intellectual and methodological labor of Black, Indigenous, and ethnic studies scholars who have underscored the importance of understanding precarity within the larger historical, political, and economic context in which vulnerability, neglect, and death are produced.[27] In rural settings, the state and multinational companies work together to oppress and exploit immigrant workers through labor coercion, induced migration, and racialized work regimes. Immigrant narratives, such as those expressed by Xiomara and Valeria, reveal multiple spatial logics and temporalities intrinsic to the uneven accumulation of global industrial capital: a constant but uncertain coming and going, traversing borders and social norms, and liminal existence. Likewise, rural regions, forsaken by capital and the state as they became increasingly poor and racially minoritized spaces, are plagued by declining social services, infrastructural investment, and fiscal development.[28] Yet, as the vignette detailing a day with Elizabeth demonstrates, immigrants and providers respond to such constraints through interdependency, affective labor, and the care of others. Precarity, therefore, reveals how the shared conditions of racial devaluation and socioeconomic abandonment among immigrants and rural providers generate forms of collective livingness—what Kevin Quashie describes as "the effects of struggle where struggle is not singularly defined as a condition of oppression."[29] Analyzing precarity necessitates a turn toward modes of worldmaking and forms of care, mutual aid, and solidarity work among those who have been targeted by state-sanctioned violence and surveillance in the purported "best interests" of their well-being.[30]

Further, studying the shared condition of immigrant and rural precarity exposes rural America's broader public and political imaginary and history. Rural America does not have a visible history outside the one authorized by political and moral myth-making. In the United States, the rural West figures prominently as exceptional and exemplary, reanimating key national political and ethical dramas that pit its ruggedness against the weak, selfish, elite, progressive northeast and West Coast.[31] Spatial imaginaries and racial representations of the American "heartland" obscure the significant diversity and dynamism that has long been part of rural life. These imagined and official renderings of rural America neglect the rural South and Midwest, where many Black and Latino people reside and work, including immigrants. They do not include the rural residents of Native reservations; they do not recognize the vast influence of prison and migrant economies throughout rural America.

Maryland does not fit into this picture of rural America because of its proximity to the nation's capital and its ranking as *the* wealthiest state in the country, with a median household income of $86,738 in 2019.[32] Yet, official and local administrative designations, such as those that originate from the Annotated Code of Maryland,[33] indicate that much of Maryland is "rural," including all Eastern Shore counties, based on factors such as geographic isolation, lack of transportation, and lack of health care access. On the one hand, such classifications reveal ongoing economic and social abandonment of rural regions orchestrated by the state and capital. On the other hand, these designations of the "rural" uphold popular ideas of the Eastern Shore and its residents as spatially distant, economically deficient, and socially different from urban spaces and residents. Official statistics between urban and rural Maryland further reinforce these ideas. This includes rural residents' lower per capita income (e.g., state average in 2018 was $63,354, with rural per capita income considered "lagging behind" at $54,687); higher rates of poverty (12.4 percent for rural Maryland compared with 9.0 percent in urban areas of the state) and unemployment (4.0 percent in rural Maryland versus 3.6 percent for metropolitan Maryland);[34] and a severe lack of health care access (e.g., no critical access hospitals, one rural health clinic, twenty-six FQHC sites, and seven short-term hospitals). These data also indicate that the Eastern Shore in particular has one of the highest poverty rates, the poorest health status, and the greatest need for health care access in the state.[35] Rural residents themselves articulate these differences through spatial and temporal logics. Those living in rural Maryland often felt "closer" to other rural communities in neighboring states than the "rest" of Maryland because of similar economic, geopolitical, and cultural histories.[36] The political and myth-making about "ruralness" entrenches these spatial and temporal differences by obscuring the racial diversity and economic abandonment of the Eastern Shore in particular and rural regions more broadly.

Reorienting the logic of the rural away from the realm of political and moral myth-making to one grounded in ethnographic details redirects our attention to understanding immigration and rural precarity as mutually constituted. While Elizabeth, Xiomara, and Valeria have very different stakes in the system, their shared precarity becomes visible in the realms of health and health care. Putting immigration and rural health into conversation with each other shifts our understanding of rural America from a pristine, untouched—the "real" America—to one that immigrants and rural residents experience as a state of constant precarity. Immigrants in rural America live at the margins, even though the public acknowledges their significance to rural economic vitality. Thinking about immigration and rural context together brings into view what the construct of "rural heartland" obscures— the embodiment and perceived pathologies of crisis and the stagnant futures, deteriorating presents, and collapsed pasts of people and places left behind. At the same time, it allows us to witness how individuals and communities constitute themselves and rural spaces through the care of others, strive for control and balance, and navigate in and through difficult circumstances, constantly anticipating and adjusting toward social worlds that are perpetually in motion but somehow experienced as without progression.[37] Immigration and rural precarity are central to each other.

Rural Landscape of Care

Spatial and temporal logics of health have long figured prominently in anthropological work.[38] Studies of clinical space, patient-provider interactions, and therapeutic landscapes and itineraries have focused on temporality and spatial patterns of care-seeking, pluralistic care systems, treatment networks, place-based health economies, and geospatial politics of risk and exclusion.[39] The underlying presumption in this work is that the material and physical space of health and health care is knowable, which has the unintended effect of privileging social hierarchies and marginalizing difference. *Landscapes of Care* advances anthropological scholarship on health by placing it in conversation with the work of Black feminist geographers to understand the spatial, temporal, and racialized organization of health care conditions in lived and imaginary space. In centering interlocutors' insistence on the inextricability of immigration and rural health, I move away from the conventional spatial logics of health care. Instead, I use "landscape" as a framing device and local practice to understand the precariousness of care in rural contexts.[40] The notion of "health care" denotes the continuum of public health and medical care that is physically bounded and often siloed, ahistorical, politically neutral, and tied to institutions. Spatially, many rural health systems tend to be composed of loosely integrated and ill-coordinated public hospitals, community health centers, local health departments, and free clinics. On the Eastern Shore, individual providers themselves offer the only semblance of a safety net or health infrastructure.[41] Essentially, safety-net patchworks and temporary, improvised care are the default in many rural regions throughout the United States.[42] Rather than envisioning health "systems"—through the standard tropes of organized, bounded, and singular entities—thinking in terms of a landscape emphasizes the relational assemblages, multiple exchanges, and violent mobilities where care unfolds.[43]

Landscape includes formalized pathways to health, but it also encompasses otherwise invisible sites of engagement and social relations of care that extend far beyond the reach of health care. Rather than insisting that immigrant health is limited to the discernible space of formal health care pathways, landscape privileges immigrant and rural knowledge and experiences of place, time, and social relations. In doing so, it discloses the violence of racial capitalist logics that inheres in our national health care and immigration policies and local practices of caregiving and care-seeking. Existing systems to treat immigrants and the working poor in rural America, at their core, are critically inadequate, racist, and exclusionary. Immigrants and rural providers manage and navigate this reality by engaging in complex social relations and mutual aid to care for themselves and each other. For instance, physical distance, availability of time, and social differences separate Elizabeth and the women for whom she provides care. Yet, against the backdrop of Eastern Shore's relative remoteness and its under-resourced and inequitable health system, immigrants and rural providers engage in various strategies to seek and offer care and improvise new forms of rural life, refusing what is commonly understood about the spatial and temporal constraints of their surroundings. This landscape of care is a vital feature of rural immigrant life. It lays bare the limitations of existing conceptualizations of health care and reimagines care as a deeply contested space, what Katherine McKittrick calls "the terrain of political struggle itself."[44]

In the United States, as lawmakers debate immigration laws, leaders from both political parties argue that federal funds for social and welfare benefits, especially health care, should not go to immigrants. A primary goal of the Affordable Care Act (ACA) was to reduce the number of uninsured Americans, which stood at approximately 50 million at the time, through the expansion of both private insurance and government-funded Medicaid.[45] Although the ACA drastically reduced the number of uninsured individuals, it falls far short of providing universal coverage.[46] The individual mandate and health insurance exchanges, critical features of the ACA, continue to uphold the importance of health consumerism and the private health insurance industry, reinscribing social inequalities between those able to afford health care and those who cannot. Other shortcomings of the ACA include inadequate coverage under both private and public plans (e.g., the most common selection by new enrollees for personal coverage was for "silver" plans, which cover only 70 percent of health care costs); higher cost-sharing requirements; privatization of Medicaid programs by some states; and accelerated consolidation of hospital systems and decreased funding for safety-net hospitals.[47] In addition, the ACA earmarked new funding for community health centers and increased reimbursements for primary care physicians, but many residents still face barriers to gaining access to providers (especially specialists and those who accept Medicaid).

The ACA offers new options to increase coverage for naturalized citizens and lawfully present immigrants. Yet many remain ineligible for these coverage options.[48] Undocumented immigrants are not entitled to coverage under the ACA. They are only eligible for emergency medical assistance, FQHC services, and specific public health programs. These are primarily limited and often interpreted differently in local contexts. Further, there is a time restriction for legal immigrants—those who have been in the country for less than five years have health insurance coverage through exchanges and premium and cost-sharing subsidies but are otherwise ineligible for Medicaid.[49] Popularly known as the "five-year bar," many individuals entering the United States on or after August 22, 1996, must wait five years after receiving a qualifying immigration status before becoming eligible for Medicaid or the Children's Health Insurance Program (CHIP)—two essential features of the American social welfare system.[50] Noncitizens who have not met the five-year bar and those not legally in the country may be eligible for emergency medical services through Medicaid, including labor and delivery services for pregnant women, if they meet all other eligibility requirements for Medicaid. This emergency program is not health insurance. Further, since 1999, immigration officers have abided by general guidance in determining whether an individual is likely to become a "public charge"— dependent on the government for support—in deciding to grant an applicant a green card or an extension of a visa. However, in 2019, the Donald Trump administration announced a new rule rendering poorer immigrants ineligible for permanent residency if they received public benefits such as Medicaid under the "public charge" rule, creating confusion and panic in many immigrant communities. Individuals afraid of the revised public charge guidance chose not to obtain needed benefits out of concern that receipt could jeopardize their legal status or their ability to stay in this country or put them at risk of being separated from their families.[51] While the public charge rule reverted to the former guidance in 2021, uncertainty and fear remain a challenge for many immigrants in applying for social welfare programs. The exclusionary and discriminatory aspects of the ACA, therefore, are purposeful and designed to prevent disproportionate access to public benefits by immigrants.

Even before the ACA passed, many on the Eastern Shore felt that the law would continue to uphold existing uneven and racialized geographies of health care access. Providers and administrators discussed the daily struggles of operating with already limited resources and a lack of health infrastructure while serving populations with high levels of mortality and morbidity. They noted that the region had experienced drastic rates of hospital closures over the years, diminishing Medicare compensation structures for providers, and an increase in health care alliances and networks. My interlocutors, especially providers, understood that under the ACA, new funding was set aside for rural health centers, and reimbursements for primary care physicians were supposed to increase. But they worried that shortages of physicians and nonphysician providers and specialists, high rates of uninsured, elderly, or poor residents, and limited public resources allocated to health care would continue to plague rural health systems, despite the promises of the ACA.[52]

Public discussion around health care and immigration unilaterally focuses on entitlement—the legal and policy provisions specifying the kinds of public services for which immigrants are eligible based on their legal status—or practical questions of access to formal health care systems. However, experiences of entitlement and access among immigrants occur through everyday bureaucratic, clinical, and social interactions, where local contexts, organizational processes, and social relations shape immigrants' experiences with care.[53] People often described existing care systems on the Eastern Shore as "Band-Aid" solutions or forms of "bastardized care" that are seen as a quick-fix or temporary remedy, underscoring the temporal and spatial logic of crisis itself. Inherent in this description is that Band-Aid care fails to address the long-term needs of those deemed most vulnerable.[54] Yet, Eastern Shore providers and immigrants engaged in various health and social care practices that were not limited to addressing immediate health needs. Band-Aid care was a response to immediate individual affliction *and* a means to act on the possibility of everyday living amid rural precarity, where spatial, temporal, and racialized dimensions of care unfold.[55] Such improvisation and other care strategies that characterize the landscape of care on Maryland's Eastern Shore are common throughout rural America and various under-resourced and unpredictable contexts worldwide.[56]

Overview of Chapters

The intimacy between immigration and rural health signals the continual reshaping of life and living amid precarity, and this story unfolds throughout each chapter of the book. Chapter 1 is an overview of the changing social and demographic picture of immigration in the United States. It illustrates how a focus on immigration patterns in more traditional, urban settings has come to shape our understanding of rural spaces as static and experiences of immigrant communities as singular. Ethnographic details of immigrant life in rural America reveal the shifting spatial and temporal dynamics of community identity, highlighting how rapid rural immigration brings complex entanglements between neglect and care into view.

Chapter 2 ethnographically details the rural economy and the immigrant labor force that sustains it. Immigrant labor generates vital resources and creates livelihoods within rural regions. Yet low-wage, low-skilled labor—characteristic of rural economies—intensifies existing labor segmentation dynamics and disadvantages immigrants working in the Eastern Shore's agricultural, poultry, and seafood industries. This chapter attends to the everyday violence of racial capitalism and its manifestation as a structured and ordinary experience within and outside labor regimes. It also centers on immigrants' embodiment of workplace injury, disability, and instability as new ways of understanding the body and the politics of care.

Chapters 3 and 4 focus on local contexts in which care is sought by immigrants. Chapter 3 describes the fragility of the formal rural health care system and how it intersects with immigration. The absence of funding and infrastructure and discriminatory policies present substantial challenges to health care delivery and care-seeking, affects immigrant vulnerability, and exacerbates health inequities. The experiences and perspectives of immigrants and rural providers underscore that spatial and racial logics articulate and manifest in the provision and delivery of care. Chapter 4 examines the everyday struggles of immigrants and providers within a system of Band-Aid care and how such care serves as a means to understand how to live otherwise under precarious circumstances, especially when such improvised care has increasingly become the standard of health and social care provision in many places around the world. Band-Aid care underscores immigration and health policy's social and cultural dimensions and its translation in localized and relational contexts.

Chapter 5 reflects on the themes discussed in previous chapters and on why issues of legality, although important, do not necessarily foreground the conceptualization and experiences of care in contexts of rural precarity. The social and political exclusion of noncitizen immigrants is grounded in a refusal to recognize them as complete social beings or ratified members of the moral community. Such declarations of illegitimacy authorize policies of "selective blindness" both to immigrants' health needs and to the landscape of care in which many live and work. Immigrants constantly contend with the broader logics of spatial and racial exclusion that are at the heart of health care and immigration reform while seeking care. Frontline providers engage in caregiving motivated by moral values and commitments around health care delivery and access and assumptions about immigrants' rights to certain kinds of political and social membership. Together, in this landscape, immigrants and providers unsettle and refashion dominant spatial and temporal logics of health and well-being through practices and imaginaries of collaboration and mutuality.

CHAPTER ONE

Journeys through the Heartland

Rural America as the "New" Receiving Destination

> Amid all the anti-immigrant fervor, nativists have overlooked a fundamental fact: In recent years, Mexican immigrants and their Mexican-American offspring have been rescuing the most iconic places in America—its small towns.
>
> —ALFREDO CORCHADO, "The Mexican Revival of Small-Town America"

Scorching heat. Unbearable humidity. Hollowed-out yellow school buses sitting in the middle of watermelon fields, like errant sunflowers or dandelion weeds. The stench of crab chum and chicken manure. Shoulder pain, skin blisters, and inflamed rashes. Eating kabrit en sauce (stew goat) with konpa music blaring in the background. Trump-Pence, Make America Great Again lawn signs. Well-weathered homes among loblolly pine forests. And the long stretches of time and place holding still and quiet. Memories of summer as scattered plots, unpredictable yet somehow certain.

—Author field notes from summer 2015, Maryland's Eastern Shore

ROSELINE, THIRTY-THREE YEARS OLD, has been living and working in the Eastern Shore region since emigrating from Haiti in 1995. She calls Seaford, Delaware, home. Seaford is a small town nestled on the Nanticoke River. This body of water flows close to sixty-four miles from the headwaters in Sussex County, Delaware, to its mouth at Tangier Sound in Dorchester County, Maryland, through one of the most pristine watersheds in the Chesapeake Bay region. Like many Haitian immigrants, Roseline travels routinely between Delaware and Maryland for work and to access services. On this day, she was in Salisbury, Maryland, seeking help from a small nonprofit that provides job training to immigrants in the region. She recently received her licensed practical nurse degree and was looking for work while completing her nursing credentials.

Roseline admits that she has not thought too much about the Eastern Shore or what keeps her in the area. Because she is caring for her husband, a small child, and aging parents, affordability and the quiet pace of life are significant considerations: "I got mature, got comfortable, and realized Delaware is good for raising kids. That is why I decided to stay. I think as my parents are aging, it is better to stay closer. I am an only child. I took that into consideration as well." Plus, there were more opportunities for immigrants in this region. Roseline describes these prospects in spatial and temporal terms: "Compared to other states, it is not as developed, so there is room to give birth to something."

Yet this scarcity inherent to rural regions—especially the absence of educational and employment prospects—also compresses time horizons and spatial mobility. Roseline explains: "Let's say somebody works at the post office. They may work there until they die, and you will never get an opening. So people stay where they are, and you have to compete with a lot of people because there are not many choices. I think a lot of immigrants come here because there is a lot of factory work. But for a college student or high school student who just graduated, if you don't want to work at a fast-food place, your choices are kind of limited." Rural regions spatially and temporally constrain newly arrived immigrants and those who have settled in the area: "So you find yourself working in the factory every day and not having a chance to do something different. For the younger generation, if they can move, they hurry up and move and get out of here. But a lot of older people coming here because they need work. So they keep coming. It is the same thing: working in factories, having children, and once the children grow up, those who can move, move; those who cannot support themselves stay around."

Roseline patiently explains the complex ways that temporal and spatial inequalities of rural living yield disparate life chances among immigrants. For those who come directly from Haiti, not being able to converse in English and a lack of transportation present significant barriers. Newly arrived immigrants often needed access to a car, transportation services, and English-language classes. "If you are a new immigrant, it is better for you to be in New York or Florida because the extra help is there. It is easy for you to learn something in order for you to work. But if you land in Delaware and you don't speak English," she says, "you are going to find yourself working at the factory, which makes it harder for you to get out of that because transportation is an issue. Not enough places for education is an issue. They give English courses at [the local school], but if you don't have anyone to give you a ride or you work at night or in the morning, they don't have enough classes to accommodate you. Or if you have children, you have to take care of them, and you find no time for education because you have to drive thirty or forty-five minutes to the place."

Roseline admits that there has been a steady rise in immigrants to the area during the thirty years she has lived here, despite the increasing challenges of rural life. This influx of immigrants has had complex effects on community relations, both positive and negative. Immigrants experience racial segregation and camaraderie in social institutions like schools and churches: "In high school, Spanish, Haitian, we come together because we all know that we are foreigners and because there is segregation among the Americans and us foreigners. But you also would see Haitian groups together, Hispanic groups together. Even though we talk among ourselves, we joke around when we are in class together. When there is a break, everybody goes to their own group. In my church, there is none of that. Everybody mingles. It is multicultural." However, increased immigration to the area has not resulted in a better sense of belonging among immigrants. Not mincing words about pervasive racism and xenophobia, Roseline attests, "There is judgment there. [Nonimmigrants] are very judgmental, even though they can recognize us."

Roseline's perspectives and experiences of living and working on the Eastern Shore underscore the ongoing spatial and temporal transformation of rural American life. Global economic integration, international migration, and technological diffusion reconfigure rural localities' social, economic, cultural, and political relations. Places considered "new receiving" locales or "emerging destinations" for immigrants are experiencing rapid changes in agriculture and land management, population racial diversity, community relations, and the politics of place. Despite these drastic changes, people often depict rural areas as "fly-over country," a pejorative term for regions of the United States that urban, wealthy, white-collar Americans see as only worthy of viewing by air when traveling. Moreover, rural areas have come to embody large swaths of the country positioned as economically, developmentally, culturally, and politically distinct in the national (urban and coastal) consciousness.[1]

Geographers, sociologists, and anthropologists have long theorized cities, suburbs, and rural areas as dynamic, relational categories rather than isolated geospatial systems. Yet the implicit assumption in some of this work is that transnational mobility and contemporary globalization are exclusively urban processes.[2] Scholars in rural geography and sociology have been increasingly critical of these analyses and instead encouraged studies focused on the interpretation of rural and urban space, the relationship between idealized representations of the rural (e.g., the "rural idyll") and lived realities, and the transformation of rural space in response to globalization, technology, and economic change.[3] There has also been some attention to diverse populations such as African Americans, Indigenous people, and immigrants living in rural regions. Today, however, the conventional archetype of rural America—reinforced by researchers, policymakers, and the public—is that it is overwhelmingly white and racially homogenous, geographically isolated, and stuck in time where past practices and customs are maintained.

In the following sections, I present information available through demographic surveys, census counts, and policy documents. I then move beyond these macro-level "bird's eye" accounts, centering the voices of people like Roseline and their communities and providing meso- and micro-level contexts about these population shifts and immigration patterns. Ethnographic details highlight how rapid immigration in predominately rural, politically conservative regions like the Eastern Shore has resulted in crucial debates over meanings of place, community identity, and belonging. Ethnographic data of rural contexts' social, political, and economic dynamics offer essential ways to broadly examine the effects of globalization and mobility. Foregrounding considerations of everyday rural community life helps to reorient academic scholarship and popular imaginaries about immigration and rural America.

Immigration in Rural America

For years, the United States has been undergoing significant demographic changes that reshape the makeup of cities, towns, and communities all across the country.[4] Evidence shows that immigrant settlement patterns across the United States are rapidly changing. Significant flows of foreign-born populations are shifting from more "traditional" areas to places without a long history of immigrant settlement (see figure 1.1). In 2000, close to two-thirds of immigrants lived in only seven states—California, New York, Texas, Florida, New Jersey, Illinois, and Massachusetts.[5] During the 1990s, immigrant populations living in those states declined significantly for the first time—from 75.8 percent in 1990 to 65.7 percent in 2019 (see table 1.1). At the same time, fourteen states, primarily in the Central and Southeast United States—including many states that had not previously been key destinations for immigrants, such as Alabama, Arkansas, Delaware, Georgia, Idaho, Indiana, Kentucky, Mississippi, Nevada, North Carolina, South Carolina, South Dakota, Tennessee, and Wyoming—saw foreign-born growth rates more than double the national average. These new receiving regions—or emerging gateways—experienced rapid growth in immigration. For example, in 2019, there were 4.4 million immigrants in new-destination states—nearly six times higher than in 1990 and fifteen times more than in 1970. As a result, one in every ten immigrants resided in a new-destination state in 2019, compared to one in twenty-five in 1990.

The global economic restructuring of trade, production, and finance has led to the growth of low-wage employment and driven immigration to these new receiving rural destinations.[6] The loss of manufacturing jobs weakened the economic base of manufacturing-dependent rural communities and hastened depopulation, including white flight.[7] These processes of abandonment have led rural areas to become poorer and more racially diverse, which has resulted in further decreases in social and economic investments by the state and multinational corporations. In order to mitigate these population and economic trends, rural communities, like urban regions, have courted low-wage employers who increasingly rely on immigrants to provide unskilled labor. As a result, in small towns and rural regions, devalued jobs that require no specific education level or specialized experience yet are

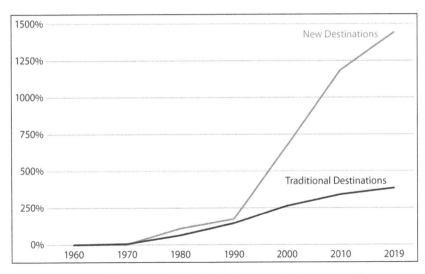

FIGURE 1.1 Cumulative growth in the foreign-born population, new- and traditional-destination states, 1960–2019.

TABLE 1.1 Number and share of foreign born in new- and traditional-destination states, 1960–2019

	New destinations*		Traditional destinations**	
	Number (1,000s)	Share of total foreign born	Number (1,000s)	Share of total foreign born
1960	286	2.9%	6,082	62.5%
1970	291	3.0%	6,476	67.3%
1980	601	4.3%	9,966	70.8%
1990	786	4.0%	14,990	75.8%
2000	2,201	7.1%	22,081	71.0%
2010	3,681	9.2%	26,833	67.2%
2019	4,412	9.9%	29,415	65.7%

Sources: Adapted from Terrazas, *Immigrants in New-Destination States*, fig. 1; see also Frey, "Three Americas." 2019 data from the 2019 American Community Survey; 2010 data from the 2010 Census; 2000 data from the 2000 Census; 1960 to 1990 data from Gibson and Lennon, "Historical Census Statistics on the Foreign-Born Population of the United States: 1850–1990."

Notes: * South Carolina, Alabama, Tennessee, Delaware, Arkansas, South Dakota, Nevada, Georgia, Kentucky, North Carolina, Wyoming, Idaho, Indiana, and Mississippi.

** California, New York, Florida, Texas, New Jersey, Illinois, and Massachusetts.

dangerous and require difficult physical labor are often the only available means of work where the average salary earned by workers is below or at minimum wage. The growth of unskilled, low-wage labor, however, is not an exclusively rural phenomenon; it has increasingly become a significant part of the overall U.S. labor market. According to the Bureau of Labor Statistics, unskilled and low-skilled labor will account for the maximum increase in jobs between 2014 and 2024.[8] In many ways, rural regions as racially devalued, surplus places are testing grounds for what Laura Pulido calls "new forms of neoliberal practice that will become increasingly common."[9]

These economic and policy shifts drive immigration trends along national/regional, racial, gendered, and class lines and are linked to the needs of the labor market, economic regulations, and visa regimes. As a result, the demographic and socioeconomic makeup of immigrants in rural regions like the Eastern Shore differs from traditional gateway destinations. For instance, immigrants living in rural areas tend to be working-age men who participate almost entirely in low-wage, unskilled labor. They also are more likely to be recent arrivals (since 2000 or later) who experience poverty, and they are less likely to be naturalized U.S. citizens or have health insurance.[10] Many are undocumented immigrants: the undocumented immigrant population in new-destination states grew by 80 percent between 2000 and 2010, from 905,000 to 1.6 million.[11] The immigrant population in the Washington, D.C., metropolitan area (which also includes Maryland, Virginia, and West Virginia in national surveys), for instance, surged by 457 percent from 1980 to 2019.[12] Immigrants in emerging gateways like Washington, D.C., are far more likely to live in the suburbs, small towns, and rural regions than in central cities. They also tend to be highly diverse, with relatively even proportions from Asia, Africa, Mexico, the Caribbean, and Latin America. However, they are more socioeconomically vulnerable and have lower rates of English proficiency and U.S. citizenship than those who have moved to traditional receiving areas.[13]

Demographers and other scholars studying population shifts also have traditionally approached variations in immigration patterns as urban phenomena.[14] Their work has documented how immigrants live and work in traditional receiving communities like New York, Los Angeles, and Miami and detailed how other urban locales such as Atlanta, Charlotte, and Minneapolis are experiencing rapid rises in their immigrant populations to become new immigrant gateway cities. Although there has been some work on the increasing movement of immigrants to suburban areas and small towns beyond the traditional urban settings,[15] studies have largely overlooked immigration to rural regions despite evidence that close to 2.5 million foreign-born persons live in rural America. This inattention is unfortunate because it leaves us with little understanding of immigrant experiences in the suburbs, small towns, and sparsely populated rural communities and how these places, which do not have a large concentration of established immigrant communities, adapt to newcomers.

Immigration to Rural Maryland

Maryland has experienced a rapid rise in immigration since 2000, making the state a new-receiving destination for immigrants primarily from Latin America and Asia.[16] One in seven Maryland residents was born in another country, while one in eight is a native-born American with one immigrant parent. The foreign-born population in Maryland rose by 191 percent from 1990 to 2019.[17] Twenty percent of the foreign-born were from Africa, 31 percent were born in Asia, and 39 percent were from Latin America and the Caribbean. Undocumented immigrants (approximately 275,000) comprised 29 percent of the immigrant population and 5 percent of the total state population in 2016. Demographers have argued that factors leading to this growth include proximity to the nation's capital and leading higher education institutions, a relatively diverse and robust economy, and progressive state and local policies.[18] However, despite Maryland's progressive policy climate for immigrants, gray (i.e., unpublished) literature indicates that approximately 13 percent of recent immigrants live in poverty and a large number are uninsured.[19] Public resources for immigrants are severely lacking, leaving state and local governments unable to keep up with the growing demands of largely uninsured noncitizen immigrant populations. As a result, some agencies have limited care to particular jurisdictions or resorted to a lottery system to manage the large influx of immigrants.[20]

Further, demographic data and the subsequent scholarship on immigration in Maryland centers on urban areas like Washington, D.C. Discussions about rapid immigration to Maryland's rural regions remain limited. Maryland's rural Eastern Shore, composed of nine counties east of the Chesapeake Bay, is a new receiving region. As of the 2020 Census, its population was 456,500, with just under 7.5 percent of Marylanders living in the area.[21] Maryland's Eastern Shore is part of the larger Delmarva Peninsula—a 170-mile stretch of mostly flat and sandy expanse that is part of the Atlantic Coastal Plain—which it shares with the entire state of Delaware and parts of Virginia's Eastern Shore. The region was relatively isolated from the rest

FIGURE 1.2 *Loading Stringbeans for Packinghouse near Cambridge: 1937* by Washington Area Spark is used under a CC BY-NC 2.0 license. This image was taken from a black-and-white negative by Arthur Rothstein and is part of the Farm Security Administration collection at the Library of Congress (LC-USF34- 025597-D [P&P]).

of the state as automobile transportation across the Chesapeake Bay was by ferryboat until 1952, when the first bridge opened for traffic. Residents and policymakers commonly invoke the Eastern Shore's rural identity as a product of implicit mythologies about authenticity and cultural heritage, often noting how the region's political conservatism and social values drastically differ from the rest of Maryland.[22] These descriptions conveniently omit the region's violent legacy of anti-Black racism produced and reinforced by its plantation-based economy and race-based system of coerced labor. The Eastern Shore has long depended on racialized migrant labor (see figure 1.2) and the history of racial capitalism stemming from slavery and Jim Crow continues to shape the challenges experienced by immigrants who work in the area's three key economic sectors: fishing along the coasts and particularly seafood (and blue crab) processing; farming, especially large-scale chicken farms; and tourism, mainly centered on the Atlantic coast resort of Ocean City.[23]

Recently, the Eastern Shore has undergone rapid growth in its immigrant population. The employment opportunities in seafood, livestock, and agricultural industries attract temporary and more permanent migrant workers from Latin America and Haiti. From 2010 to 2019, migration was also the primary source of population growth in this region.[24] The foreign-born population increased by approximately 90.4 percent from 2000 to 2019 across all nine counties on the Eastern Shore.[25] These permanently settled immigrants at times work and live alongside migrant farmworkers who continue to migrate to the region each year, along with their families, including children who enroll in federal education programs during the harvest months. A handful of local studies reflect these trends, indicating that the Latinx community is now establishing permanent roots on the Eastern Shore rather than staying temporarily as seasonal migrant workers harvesting vegetables such as tomatoes and melons for local growers on the Delmarva Peninsula.[26] My own observations substantiate that the Latinx population on the Eastern Shore is likely to be young, male, unmarried, foreign-born, and recently arrived. A growing number are families who migrate with their children. Many are undocumented. David, for instance, is an undocumented high school student. His parents work on the farm, and sometimes he tends to the chickens after school. He feels that there is more diversity among his classmates than when he first came to the Eastern Shore, especially from El Salvador, Guatemala, Mexico, and other Latin American countries. His intimate familiarity with their struggles related to precarious legal status, language barriers, poverty, and racial discrimination makes him want to help: "I see them sometimes crying because they do not understand, and I tell them to calm down because I experienced the same thing. When I can help, I do because others helped me when I first came, and I did not know anything. So whomever I can understand, I try to help."

There is also a well-established but hidden population of Haitians, Jamaicans, and other Black immigrants who have long migrated from Florida and the Caribbean for the harvest season. Vivian, a program director at a social services agency, discussed how local organizations are struggling to respond to an influx of Black immigrants, with mixed results: "I think that the Haitian group is probably the most vulnerable right now. I think partially because we have had twenty years of large Latino influx, we have that capacity in different service agencies now. Almost everywhere, someone speaks enough

Spanish to get to communicate fluently with somebody. We were the only place that spoke Spanish for years, so we could help address some of those issues. Now, in most other places, social services have language lines or Google Translate. Somebody speaks Haitian Kreyòl, and they come to us, and we try to help them as best as we can, but when people do not feel like there is anybody that they can go to that they can trust, then I think that is when they are the most vulnerable."

The Political Economy of Immigration to the Eastern Shore

While macro-level structural changes in law and policy have induced rapid immigration to rural regions, including the Eastern Shore, businesses such as farms, poultry plants, and seafood houses also have been key contributors to this transformation. The agricultural sector, for instance, is the largest commercial industry in Maryland.[27] Maryland has large swaths of fertile agricultural land along its coastal and central regions. The Chesapeake's hot summers and mild winters, which made Maryland ideal for growing tobacco, the state's earliest cash crop, now make the area well suited for dairy farming and specialty perishable crops like cucumbers, watermelon, tomatoes, peas, and squash. At the same time, there has been a steady shift over the past four decades to consolidate acreage and production to larger operations across almost all crop and livestock commodities.[28] Many farmers have switched from fruits and vegetables to grains, and tomato acreage has dropped significantly since the mid-1990s. In contrast, soybeans have become the most prominent crop by acreage planted in Maryland.[29] Others have lost their farms or have sold their lands to developers, resulting in the rapid transformation of traditionally farm-based communities into densely populated areas where residential, commercial, and other uses can conflict with the existing farm operations. Mark, a resident, details these changes: "The growers aren't growing. The growers are selling off their land to developers, and once it is not agricultural land anymore, it is gone. Look at Dorchester and Talbot Counties. Talbot is one of the most expensive counties to live in Maryland. It is right across the bridge, and people can commute to Annapolis and Baltimore. And a lot of that land used to be farmland orchards and stuff. I don't think there is even an orchard left in the lower three counties. Thirty years ago, there were orchards everywhere. So that is part of what is going on."

Long-term changes in the farming economy as a result of increased global competition, diminishing access to markets, and growing pressure to adapt to environmental change have led farmers to make drastic organizational changes that allow a single farmer or farm family to manage more acres or more livestock. The availability of labor is a key concern for farmers as farming is a labor-intensive occupation. Attracting local workers willing to work in agricultural production for low wages has long proved difficult for many farmers, leading to reliance on racialized migrant workers. Farmers, agricultural corporations, and other farming-related organizations regularly intervene in immigration policy to expand access to foreign labor.[30]

Like agriculture, the seafood industry has also lobbied for increased access to female temporary workers exclusively from Mexico. Crab processing has been a leading source of employment for migrant workers in Maryland for several decades. Blue crabs support one of Chesapeake Bay's valuable commercial and recreational fisheries. Revenues for blue crabs totaled over $45 million in 2019.[31] Although Louisiana currently boasts the most prominent global blue crab fishery, this industry has historically been centered on the Chesapeake Bay and Maryland.[32] The number of plants and workers fluctuates annually, depending on the availability of crab stock. Maryland currently has ten to fifteen crab processing plants, almost all small family operations, which employ under 500 workers.[33] Since 1986, crab processors in Maryland have used the U.S. Department of Labor's H-2B visa program to supply temporary, nonagricultural foreign workers willing to perform the grueling jobs at the low costs necessary to sustain their businesses, claiming that not enough Americans are willing to take on the work.[34] In the past few decades, seafood processors have increasingly relied on temporary foreign workers from Mexico to replace African American women who have traditionally worked as crab pickers.[35] As a result, most foreign workers in the crab industry are Mexican women admitted under the H-2B temporary visa program.[36]

Immigrants also work in food processing, especially poultry processing on the Eastern Shore. Maryland is home to Purdue Farms, the third-largest producer of poultry products in the United States. Chicken farming and poultry processing are essential parts of what is left of the state's agricultural and manufacturing industries. Poultry is a $3.4 billion industry on the Delmarva Peninsula, which anchors the top of a U-shaped poultry belt that runs from Delmarva south to the Shenandoah Valley through North Carolina and Georgia and north to Arkansas and Missouri.[37] The economic output of poultry processing in the region increased by 18.6 percent since 2014, producing 4.3 billion pounds of chicken. The industry employs about 20,500 employees and has about 1,300 chicken growers on contract. However, even with higher production, chicken houses have declined by 9 percent during the last two decades because smaller farms are unable to financially sustain increasingly larger and more technologically advanced operations. The meatpacking industry (including poultry processing) has long depended on racialized and immigrant labor. In the late nineteenth and early twentieth century, Eastern European workers, who at the time were racialized as nonwhites, made up the vast majority of the industry's labor; as plants moved from urban areas to rural regions in the mid-twentieth century, businesses sought new sources of labor, primarily poor African Americans. As African American workers began to unionize, industry leaders pursued foreign laborers who were more vulnerable and less able to organize to create competition and push African Americans out of the industry. Now, the sector mainly employs immigrant workers from Latin America and Haiti.[38]

Agricultural, poultry, and seafood processing organizations not only heavily influence state-level and federal immigration and labor policies, they also shape social life in rural Maryland. Iris, a long-time Eastern Shore social worker, discusses the growth of immigrant diversity over time in terms of country of origin, legal status, and labor trajectories, pointing to the impact that agricultural corporations have had on such trends. She notes that migrants are increasingly coming from within the United States rather than directly from abroad: "People are traveling up and down. They are originally from Mexico and Central America, but now these crew leaders are picking up people from Florida. The packers are coming here directly, and then the pickers are going from Florida to South Carolina to Maryland. There are definitely lots of immigrants. Men and women. Families. A lot of single men, but families, too. It is a lot of Mexican, a lot of different dialects. We have a lot more Guatemalans now than we had before and some Haitian and Central Americans. You will find that most of the packers are legal in some way. So, maybe they are here on a waiver. The pickers primarily are not legal unless you are talking about being here for a long time. There has been a means of legalization either when they opened it up or because employers have helped them up to this point because they have been good employees all of these years."

Moira has been working on the Eastern Shore for twelve years, helping migrants navigate legal challenges. Her observations suggest that the transition of sociodemographic patterns in immigration is often linked to the trend toward consolidation in crop commodities: "I think the people who do the tomatoes are more families. They are more into trying to find out how to manage living in the United States and progress. [They bring] the children and try to learn themselves. . . . People in the big group that we deal with pick watermelons, I think that they are more individuals, younger people, and men." She pauses to reflect: "I noticed a little more families in this first group [that picks tomatoes] and more individuals, young individuals in the watermelons. That is the impression that I have."

Further, local industries legitimate racial, gender, and class inequalities through routine processes and procedures, mediating federal and state-level laws and community relations. The protections afforded to H-2B workers are not as robust as those provided—at least on paper—to H-2A workers. Attempts to improve these protections in recent years have been consistently blocked by employers and Congress. Seafood processors on the Eastern Shore are legally required to pay $9.50 per hour to their workers, but most workers make a piece rate of $3.50 to $4.50 per pound of shell-free meat with minimum quotas to be met per hour after the initial training period.[39] According to survey data, the national average wage in 2019 for this occupation is $13.85 per hour, while the Maryland statewide average wage is $14.62 per hour.[40] Despite a 2015 Department of Labor and Department of Homeland Security ruling requiring employers to pay the local average wage, seafood houses pay H-2B workers—mainly poor Mexican women—significantly lower amounts than the statewide and average local salary. They are able do this because of H-2B legislative riders in the fiscal 2016 omnibus appropriations bill that included a provision expanding the use of private wage surveys.[41] Local seafood processors sell crabmeat for $40 to $60 per pound, making the labor cost of extracting crabmeat one-twelfth to one-tenth of the wholesale price.[42]

Additionally, employers make a profit from workers, deducting taxes and other legal withholdings from wages, along with rent and utilities, cash advances and loans, articles purchased from the employer such as rubber gloves, and long-distance telephone charges.[43] Women also pay all fees and expenses to local labor recruiters, take out loans with individuals and banks, contract with brokers to obtain H-2B visas, and travel to Maryland.[44] Elena recounted: "You find a contractor that tells you to go to a specific place because the owner has asked for you. You pay to be put on the list, the visa applications, passport, and transfer. Everything is out of pocket." Francisca provided additional details: "I paid 2,000 pesos to the consulate [and 6,000 pesos for travel] for a total of around 8,000 pesos [US$400]. The owner pays us back about $300."

Similarly, many Haitian interlocutors who either previously or currently worked in poultry processing described intense racial hierarchies within the workplace: white male administrators and African American "bosses" and line supervisors who oversaw and interacted with workers. Such occupational segregation reproduced racial stratification found across social structures, connecting racial assumptions delineating racial superiority and inferiority to material and social resources.[45] Many Haitians felt expendable as workers, able to be fired for any reason, including taking unauthorized bathroom breaks, taking time off to care for family members, or feeling ill. Daniel, who had worked in the plants for five years, explained the routine discriminatory treatment of Haitian workers in poultry processing plants: "They want us to work fast, and the boss or the leader put more pressure on Haitians to work fast. They need your brain. They need what you are able to do. It is like using you. Once you are not able to do the thing you used to do three days ago, then it is like get out of here. I will be working, working, working, and then my boss is watching me, seeing if I am going to make one mistake. She is just looking for one mistake, even if I am the best worker. And then I am gone."

Mirlande, likewise, recounted how her husband's boss at the poultry plant terminated his contract when he fell sick. Suffering from intense back pain, her husband was unable to sit, get up, or perform basic functions independently. Mirlande decided to take him to the emergency room, where they prescribed strong pain medication and told him to stay at home because the medication would interfere with driving and work functions. When she delivered the doctor's note to his supervisor, she was met with hostility and chastised for not calling in sick: "His boss said, 'Did he call?' and I said, 'He was in pain; he did not call.' He was just starting at her department; he did not have her number at the time. I said, 'That's the reason I am here, just to let you know.' She just walked away." Mirlande's husband stayed home for three days and went back to work as quickly as he could. His supervisor did not interact with him; instead, the supervisor went to the company's human resources department and had them terminate his contract immediately: "They called my husband like they were waiting to terminate him. And he was like, 'I was in the emergency room, and I sent a paper, a doctor's note.' They told him that they do not accept doctor's notes unless you were hospitalized. It is not that they give you a doctor's note and you stay home but are actually hospitalized."

The local organizations that drive the political economy of rural regions exert tremendous influence on national and local immigration, labor, and health policies and practices. Agricultural, poultry, and seafood operations have successfully petitioned for policies expanding access to foreign labor markets and undermined federal labor, housing, and antidiscrimination laws. These organizations severely limit immigrants' personal agency and collective ability to thrive, diminishing their access to resources and sense of belonging. They position immigrant workers as racialized others, rendering them disposable and illegible within conventional temporal terms. Occupational segregation within agriculture, poultry, and seafood organizations connect inherent racialized schemas regarding worthiness and aptitude to "workplace hierarchies, time-management rules, and even informal rituals of interaction between racial groups."[46] These organizations, therefore, are not race-neutral; rather, they engender and are produced by racial processes that shape public policy, community relations, and individual-level prejudice.

Community Contexts of Rapid Rural Immigration: Opportunities and Challenges

Experts have linked rapid urbanization stemming from rural–urban migration globally to various policy issues spanning demographic, economic, and environmental concerns.[47] Evidence indicates that moving to urban locales can improve individual and community well-being, with rural migrants experiencing increased access to better opportunities, employment, health, and education.[48] Yet rapid migration and subsequent urbanization can also pressure urban systems and their ability to ensure essential resources and safety nets for migrants, increasing their vulnerability to violence, disease, and death.[49] Undocumented women and unaccompanied children are particularly at risk for exploitation.[50]

Similarly, the last thirty years have brought dramatic changes in rural migration patterns in the United States. The nation is becoming more racially and ethnically diverse and experiencing an increase in immigration rates and the number of aging adults.[51] These changes, however, have been more overlooked in rural regions compared with urban and suburban ones, and there is less information on how such transformation unfolds in everyday practice and interactions, especially in racial attitudes and relations. Limited research indicates that the situation is complex. Generally, rural residents appreciate the economic boom provided by newcomers and believe that immigrants should reap economic and social benefits. On the Eastern Shore, sentiments like those expressed by Valerie, a social worker, were often shared: "They are here. They contribute to the economy and society, so why not make them a natural part of it. Many of them are paying taxes and may not ever get to retrieve any benefits from Social Security or social services that they are not eligible for."

Residents also welcome the cultural diversity introduced by new immigrant populations, especially exposure to different life experiences, value systems, and languages.[52] Clara, a long-time resident, confirms these sentiments. When Clara was a student, there were only a "handful of immigrant families" that she knew. But now, one generation later, about a third to a half of her children's classmates are from diverse immigrant families from Asia, Latin America, and the Caribbean: "It is much more cultural, which I think is great for the community. Way before my time, my parent's era, it was a very, very secluded area. The bridge was built in the 1940s, maybe 1950s, and it was very secluded, and there are a lot of old families here from the 1600s, and it was very private. So now I think it is definitely good for the community to see all of this."

Rapid population growth also tests rural communities' ability to provide housing, education, health care, and social services and often results in a heightened sense of racism and xenophobia toward immigrants.[53] Although rural residents admit that local industries strengthen the local economy, they blame these organizations and their immigrant neighbors for conditions brought about by structural abandonment by the state and businesses.[54] Immigrants materialize as solutions to rural decline, but in so doing, they are seen as being responsible for this weakening and, more broadly, the failures of development and modernization. As a result, many immigrants do not feel welcome as they enter small rural towns. Like Roseline and Daniel, immigrant interlocutors described their experiences of racialized division of labor, surveillance, temporal inequalities, and social and spatial isolation, which are examples of additional challenges to community-wide adaptation to rapid population change. Lara, who immigrated to the Eastern Shore a few years ago with her family, attests that this sentiment is pervasive among her nonimmigrant neighbors and the broader community: "Sometimes people do not like Hispanics for many reasons. More than anything, it is racism, and sometimes, they do not want immigrants. They do not want the Hispanics here because they say that we steal many things, but we are not stealing anything."

Rural residents' dependency on immigrant workers to sustain their economic and social well-being and the subsequent resentment it incurs underscore how immigrants are granted access to rural spaces but on the basis of continued exploitation under neoliberalism, where racism and white supremacy manifest in new dimensions. Maura, a local health provider, describes this context: "They consider themselves to be Southerners. They are very, very conservative. When it comes to the Hispanic population and immigrants in general, they hate them. I mean, we have the highest deportation rate in the state. And every one of them knows it, which is why when you ask me about [immigration] numbers, I say I can't really say because [immigrants] do stay very much below the radar here. The farmers here will say this to you. Candace is a classic example. She married into a huge farming family, and she is a health provider. I had her do a needs assessment for me on the Hispanic population three years ago. She said, 'But you don't understand. They are so much better taken care of on the farms, and we take such good care of them.' I am just like, 'Do you hear yourself speaking?' In their perceptions, they are humane to them, but these are the same people that would gladly go back to slavery tomorrow. They are just so culturally inept in their mindset."

Immigration and Rural Health

Rural health is a key domain where these structural, organizational, and individual articulations of rural and immigrant precarity unfold. Rural regions were abandoned by capital for decades, and as they became poorer and increasingly dependent on immigrant labor, they were also forsaken by the state.[55] A decline in services and resources discloses how a general abandonment by the state has deeply affected the health and well-being of those living and working in rural regions. The infrastructural decline of rural health comes at a high cost to rural communities. Mounting evidence indicates a significant rural–urban disparity in life expectancy in the United States, which has widened over time, especially for poor and racialized populations. For example, the likelihood of survival for African Americans and those living in poverty in rural areas is equivalent to that experienced by the urban rich and urban whites four decades earlier.[56] Moreover, experts expect this rural–urban disparity, driven mainly by urban longevity gains that have not been shared among rural residents, to continue to increase in the future.[57]

Across the United States, uneven distribution of resources, poverty, and lack of access to formal education disproportionately affect rural residents. Further, health care access challenges, increased exposure to occupational and environmental hazards, and worsening individual and community stress intensify poor health outcomes.[58] These structural disadvantages also affect people in poor white communities who live in such racially devalued spaces. For instance, there has been a spike in mortality rates among rural working-class whites. This rise in mortality stems from economic and psychosocial distress—what some researchers have described as "despair deaths," such as those resulting from suicide, liver disease, and opioid and other drug overdoses in response to rural precarity.[59] Analysis conducted by the U.S. Centers for Disease Control and Prevention found that suicide rates among those living in rural counties were significantly higher than those living in urban locales; moreover, the rates have been growing steadily since 1999.[60] Economic factors such as housing insecurity, poverty, and unemployment, which tend to affect those living in remote rural regions disproportionately, affect suicide rates and other negative health outcomes.[61]

Long-standing socioeconomic and environmental scarcity weaken already fragile rural health infrastructures. In turn, these spatial and temporal constraints engender poor health outcomes among rural residents and immigrants. Before lawmakers signed the Affordable Care Act (ACA) into law, data spanning forty years demonstrated that rural residents were more likely than urban residents to be uninsured and stay uninsured over more extended periods because of structural constraints and unfair policies.[62] Many uninsured people live in the U.S. South and West, where 22 percent and 21 percent of those under age 65, respectively, lacked health insurance in 2010. These are some of the same areas experiencing rapid rural immigration. Rural residents, even those with health insurance, face poor or limited coverage and high out-of-pocket health care costs related to insurance premiums, deductibles, and medical or pharmacy co-pays.[63] In addition, many rural health systems experience infrastructural abandonment by the state and corporations by way of critical shortages of health care professionals and facilities.[64] Market-driven changes in the 1990s toward managed care principles and an emerging emphasis on corporate and business philosophies significantly affected health care delivery everywhere. Still, rural residents felt these effects differently because there were fewer possibilities for cutting costs while increasing profits within rural markets.[65] In order to confront ongoing legislative, regulatory, and fiscal challenges, rural health systems increased the integration and assimilation of providers and institutions into systems and networks. Despite, or more aptly, *due to* these fiscal austerity measures, the enduring problem of resource distribution remains the hallmark of rural health care.[66] For instance, the COVID-19 pandemic brought much-needed attention to the long-standing crisis of rural hospital closures. Since 2005, 181 hospitals have closed, and the rate of rural hospital closures has continued to increase in the past decade.[67] As a result, rural residents travel great distances to seek health care services. A 2019 study found that while the closings of urban hospitals had no impact on surrounding communities, rural closings had devastating impacts on their populations, with mortality rates rising by 5.9 percent.[68]

As I discuss in detail in the following chapters, policymakers designed the ACA to provide much-needed relief to rural health systems. They earmarked new funding for community health centers and hospitals and increased reimbursement rates for primary care providers. However, many states with large rural populations, mainly in the rural South—Alabama, Florida, Georgia, Mississippi, North Carolina, South Carolina, Tennessee, and Texas—did not adopt Medicaid expansion. With a 90 percent federal matching rate, Medicaid expansion offers states the capacity to care for poor, uninsured residents, most of whom are Native, Black, and Latinx.[69] Under the ACA, health centers and their capacity for managing patients have grown.[70] Yet many people struggle to afford public insurance plans because of restrictive immigration and health policies.[71] Furthermore, insufficient funding, scarce insurance reimbursement, and reduced levels of workforce recruitment and retention remain critical challenges for rural health centers, including hospitals.

Rapid immigration compounds the unequal distribution of material resources that already constitute rural health systems. Social and infrastructural challenges within rural health disproportionately affect immigrants, who face even fewer opportunities to obtain routine care and treatment than native residents. Providers and immigrants chronicled in this book describe Maryland's Eastern Shore as plagued by limited health care resources, which creates barriers to health care access for rural residents and immigrants alike. Local providers felt conflicted because they could not provide adequate and meaningful care to immigrants and rural residents due to diminishing resources that have become the hallmark of rural health care. Immigrant participants also accessed and used health care services intermittently because of a lack of available or quality services.

Mobility, Migration, and Globalized Rural Spaces

Precarity brings into focus the persistence of the violent cycle between poor health and marginalized status for immigrants: Their health directly links to their social, economic, and political belonging, while poor health exacerbates their social, economic, and political marginalization. In the sphere of health, issues related to migration, immigration, and mobility are often inadequately understood because traditional methods of health inquiry (e.g., extensive surveys, randomized control trials) rely on random sampling methods and standardized definitions of study populations. This research usually involves populations with a lower likelihood of being lost to follow-up, which helps facilitate population-based estimates of health issues. Populations that cannot be easily bounded along such criteria (e.g., those who experience high mobility or are "hidden"), in contrast, are difficult to access, recruit, and retain in many traditional public health studies. Hence, the dynamics of disease prevention, health promotion, and, more broadly, the constitution of care and caregiving among highly mobile and hidden populations are often less understood and remain outside observational reach of traditional research studies.

Further, migration and mobility patterns are far more complex and heterogeneous than are commonly recognized in public health practice.[72] Many migrants experience cyclical, seasonal, or peripatetic mobility over time and for various factors based on economic opportunity, social ties, community relations, and forced displacement. In addition to these mobility issues, low-wage jobs without benefits, dangerous and debilitating working conditions, lack of health insurance, social isolation, racial discrimination, fear of deportation, and immigration policies restrict access to health services and prevent many immigrant populations from seeking assistance. These issues create severe barriers to multiple forms of care and negatively affect immigrants' well-being.

Additionally, the health infrastructure in rural regions is potentially the most fragile aspect of the rural health care continuum. Yet, relative to urban settings, there is a dearth of rural health and health care research in the United States. This has been theorized to contribute to a lack of rural-specific scientific evidence, a key factor in the complex system driving health inequities in rural and remote regions.[73] In fact, I was surprised at how my extensive training and experience in public health left me wholly unprepared to understand the multiple intricacies of rural health and the subsequent effects of rapid immigration on such landscapes. Rapid immigration to these regions can exhaust already limited and diminishing resources, leaving immigrants even more vulnerable. Community clinics, migrant health centers, and local community-based organizations can reach only a fraction of residents, especially immigrants. Most rural residents have no access or seek irregular health care services in emergency rooms or free clinics. These places "often are not prepared to provide the scope and quality of services so badly needed by the mobile poor (e.g., transportation, interpretation, financial assistance, preventive services, as well as clinical care)."[74] Few existing public health delivery models provide care that comprehensively addresses chronic and new challenges faced by rural health care systems and residents.

The significant impact of rapid immigration on rural communities such as Maryland's Eastern Shore makes the deliberate, steady dismantlement of rural health systems by capital and the state more visible. It also calls attention to the acts of care, cooperation, and solidarity that attempt to counter and resist ongoing rural and immigrant precarity.

The relative inattention to rural landscapes is rooted in the inability of public health and social science research to incorporate the violence of racial capitalism into its theoretical and analytical framings. Further, this neglect exposes inherent understandings and acceptance of urban spaces as epicenters of globalization and migration, where features such as "cultural admixture, economic dynamism, political and ideological transformations are often most visible."[75] Yet, specific characteristics of racial capitalism and globalization are evident within rural regions: global commodity chains, the production of new amenity landscapes, the commodification and extraction of natural resources, rapid migration, increased population diversity, and accelerated social and health inequities.[76] On the Eastern Shore, the complex convergences of globalization, economic value, and capitalist extraction combine with progressively harsh racialized anti-immigrant policies. These dynamics are reconstituted through policies, organizational processes, and ordinary articulations and local engagements about place, time, and racialized belonging. In schools, workplaces, and health clinics, structural processes become entangled with the mundane and everyday spatial, temporal, and racial politics of rurality, immigration, and health.

CHAPTER TWO

Ordinary Living

Everyday Injury, Disability, and Instability

The rural environment, especially where agriculture, mining, forestry, and fishing are important or dominant parts of the economy, presents extraordinary threats to health.

—THOMAS C. RICKETTS, "The Changing Nature of Rural Health Care"

Capital can only be capital when it is accumulating, and it can only accumulate by producing and moving through relations of severe inequality among human groups — capitalists with the means of production/workers without the means of subsistence, creditors/debtors, conquerors of land made property/the dispossessed and removed. These antinomies of accumulation require loss, disposability, and the unequal differentiation of human value, and racism enshrines the inequalities that capitalism requires.

—JODI MELAMED, "Racial Capitalism"

IT TOOK SOME TIME to convince Junior to speak with me. His loved ones were apprehensive about him conversing with a stranger—an anthropologist, no less—eager to record and observe personal details. Junior, in turn, was uneasy with discussing the intimacies of his life with me. He was also busy, working full-time at a manufacturing plant and taking care of his young family. Finding time to speak with an academic interested in Haitian life on the Eastern Shore was a distant priority. However, he relented after a few months, and I was thankful. At our initial meeting, it was clear that he still was not convinced our conversation was a good idea. He was polite but took some time to open up about what it had been like living on the Eastern Shore for the past ten years.

Junior and his parents came to Maryland to join an uncle who had been working as a farmworker for years. Junior was twenty years old at the time and intended to study. But instead, he deferred his dreams and quit community college to work and help his family make ends meet. Like many Haitians who come to the area, Junior's first job was on the assembly line of the local poultry processing plant. He found this experience so traumatic that it was hard for him to discuss it years later: "Still now, when I think about it, I hate the fact that I started working at the chicken plant. It was not a good experience. I did not like the people. I did not like the way they treat me. I did not like the way that the supervisor was treating me. Of course, I was not the only one, but that does not matter. I did not like the environment that I was working in."

I confess to Junior that my only understanding of poultry plants derives not from direct experience but from what I have gathered through descriptions in books and visuals from photographs and films. He laughs and tells me that I am lucky and paints a picture of what it was like to work at the plant, describing it in spatial and temporal terms: "There is an assembly line where I was working. They call it a grading line. I don't know why, but that is how they called it. You take the chicken by the leg, and then you hang it on a hook, and it keeps going." He describes how collaborative labor practices are central to plant operations and individual survival. A chorus of Black and Brown bodies move in unison, as one entity, to complete routine tasks: "If you miss a couple, a second person fills the rest, and then a third person tries to fill more, and then the fourth person has to fill everything that is left." I interrupt to ask if the hook used to hang chickens is sharp and immediately realize how foolish this question sounds since hooks to hang poultry by their feet must be pointed. However, Junior is too polite to call out my naivete, at least to my face. Cutting short my embarrassment, he answers: "They made it somehow that it will never hurt you. You have to be really careless to hurt yourself with it, the way that they made it."

When I ask him for additional details about his experiences of mistreatment, he explains patiently that the problem was not with the difficulties of the work itself; rather, it was directly related to the rigid racial hierarchies within the plant between Haitian workers and African American supervisors and the ideological and material framing of Haitian workers as disposable: "The problem I had with it was the fact that your boss is yelling at you, and you have to keep hanging at a very fast speed. And then when you slow down because you are human and you get tired, she will come riding at you on the bike and yell, 'What are you doing? Why did you stop? Why are you slowing down?' And you have to either pick up your speed or go to the office, have a bunch of 'blah blah blah.' Especially when you are Haitian, they do not expect you to stop." Managers treated Haitians differently because they were unable to talk back in English and did not understand their rights: "They always take advantage of the Haitians because they do not know the system. They do not know that they got the right to say, 'That is over my limit.' My first year, I did not have a lot of English, so everything they do, everything they said, I had to agree with them just because I did not have the language to explain myself and say, 'That is not fair.' So that is the year I suffered the most. The second year, I started picking up some English and then saying no and explaining why I think this is not fair. They did not like me because I could say 'No.'"

For Junior, these small but radical acts of refusal—learning essential English words and pushing back against constant harassment from his supervisors and coworkers—disrupted the racial hierarchy and the logic of disposability operating within the plant: "I think that the first time I said no is the first time things started to get better. I remember all of the guys in the line started treating me different because I can talk to them now. They no longer talk behind my back because I answer when they say something. So it does not mean I did not have friends, but most of the guys on the line did not treat me good at all. Because they felt like, as Americans, they were superior. They are Black American, and you are Haitian. So the white people were treating them low, and they are treating you low, as a circle-thing. So that is how it was."

Looking back, he realizes that working at the chicken plant was not a good idea. Yet, despite the daily indignities and exposure to physical harm, Junior spent four years at the plant. He remembers the day he quit: "One day I came and said, 'That is enough.' It is time for me to wake up and do something different—go to school and try to change my life." Even though he no longer works there, he feels tied to the plant, which represents the only form of work available to many Haitians in the area, including his mother. Consequences often proved dire, even for those who did not seek employment in poultry processing. Junior's dad, for instance, was never able to bring himself to work at the plant. When Junior's father first interviewed for a job at the plant, he became scared about the pace of work and the occupational risks involved. Without access to employment and earnings through a job at the poultry processing plant, his father did not have the means of making a living or contributing to his family's subsistence in America. Going back and forth to Haiti every six months became his father's only option for eking out a living. Unfortunately, such an arrangement proved as deadly as working at the plant. It eventually cost him his life when he died in the 2010 Haitian earthquake.

Rural Margins and the Crisis of the Everyday

There is a broad consensus that neoliberal practices are making work more precarious and that broad changes in global, national, and local economies are coercing people to migrate for work in low-wage labor markets.[1] The rapid rise of global industries and growing labor demand for cheap, precarious labor in North America has increased the number of workers employed under temporary visas and fixed-term contracts.[2] Anthropologists of labor have theorized the cultural and historical specificities of this type of precarious work and how it is embodied and lived by subjects.[3] This literature has richly illustrated how labor precarity engenders political, economic, and social exclusion, which leads to significant disadvantages for those involved. Workers are increasingly experiencing economic uncertainty, the loss of social provisions, threats of violence, marginalization and injustice, environmental destruction, and occupational injury and disability—where the possibility of life itself is in question.[4] Critical medical anthropologists have also conceptualized such disadvantages among precarious workers as it relates to immigrant and migrant health, primarily through the lens of structural vulnerability.[5] Much of this work focuses on Latinx undocumented migrant workers who are located within a matrix of disadvantage produced by structural violence.[6] The implicit assumption is that the health experiences of undocumented labor migrants and migrant bodies—both within and outside the workplace—are marked as extraordinary by the virtue of their legal status, unlike those of documented (nonimmigrant) workers.[7] Here, deportability, or even the threat of deportation, becomes the key mechanism for subordination, exploitation, and the lack of personhood in capitalist society.[8]

However, neoliberal dynamics and structural violence as a constituent of legality are only parts of the story. These conceptualizations of migrant labor, in fact, do not give enough weight to how the state and corporations actively authorize *racialized* geographies of risk and enact *racial* violence through injury, illness, and premature death. Junior's narrative, for instance, highlights how immigrant labor is integral to racial capitalism—the harnessing of racism by economic processes through mechanisms that order workers according to preexisting societal inequalities, create labor market segmentation, justify depressed wages and deplorable working conditions, and profit from the death and dying bodies of Black and Brown people. His accounts of racialized workplace hierarchies and inhumane treatment of Haitian workers signal how contemporary food production's reliance on racialized and unfree (coerced) labor, rooted in colonialism and slavery, is intrinsic to the uneven accumulation of industrial capital globally. Commercial agriculture, poultry, and seafood processing industries have long recruited racialized and immigrant workers from Mexico, Latin America, and the Caribbean to perform difficult and dangerous jobs (see figure 2.1). They have influenced U.S. federal labor policies and programs—along with national immigration laws—to expand global labor networks and ensure a vulnerable surplus of foreign workers. These dynamics have increased the number of undocumented workers and those without permanent status, deepened existing racialized dynamics of labor segmentation, and constrained immigrants to low-wage, low-skilled jobs in rural economies. Such forces profit not only from immigrant labor but also from extracting resources from rural environments, transferring the social and economic value of racialized bodies to the spaces they occupy.[9]

Racial capitalism produces social inequalities through routine functions, constituting interlocutors on Maryland's Eastern Shore as different kinds of participants in capitalist formations. The state is also a key actor in producing and sanctioning these differences through policies that govern labor

FIGURE 2.1 Billboard advertising poultry processing jobs. Photo by the author.

regulation and the mobility and surveillance of migrants. It engenders immigrant precarity through "border imperialism" as it determines various regimes of legal entry and incorporation of racialized migrants and sanctions their exploitation and exposure to premature death.[10] Immigrants experience the effects of racial capitalism as enduring, ordinary ways of life.

This chapter traces how immigrants working in the poultry, agricultural, and seafood industries in rural contexts live through and embody multiple, overlapping forms of immigrant and rural precarity in the realm of health and well-being. Racialized workers often described their living and working conditions by evoking slavery while employers commonly enforced discipline by controlling workers' spatial movements and free time to keep them in their place. Immigrants who engage in uncertain, unpredictable, and risky work live in an intense state of insecurity that emerges from and manifests in various dimensions of social life. Junior, for instance, struggles with economic precarity, racialized anti-immigration sentiment, geographic and social isolation, and painful working conditions. Yet he fashions life from the margins using narratives that underscore his racialization (e.g., being foreign and Black, being unable to speak English) as well as his right to belong (e.g., saying "no"). As his story indicates, immigrants engage in a politics of visibility, condemning racialized labor demands that create risk for injury and disability, despite the looming threat of financial insecurity, deportation, and physical harm. Such acts allow us to see injury and isolation as not limited to immigrants' bodies but extensions of state-sanctioned and racialized extralegal systems that seek to restrict and exploit immigrant life.[11] Attention to the ordinary ways in which immigrant and rural precarity is lived renders visible new possibilities of care and agency within immigrants' experiences of social suffering and structural vulnerability and their attempts at generating avenues for survival from that nexus.[12]

La Isla de las Mexicanas: Migrant Mexican Women in Maryland's Seafood Industry

Since the 1980s, the commercial seafood industry has used the expanded H-2B visa guest worker program to hire Mexican female migrant workers to further reduce crab production and processing costs.[13] Global processes (e.g., deregulation, privatization, and free trade) along with local conditions around the Chesapeake Bay (e.g., environmental degradation, urban development, and strict crabbing regulations) have created contexts in which business operations increasingly require cheaper labor, tax incentives, and less red tape. These dynamics have simultaneously fashioned circumstances of long-term uncertainty that directly affect Mexican women's labor market participation and work conditions.[14] Economic and social precarity in Mexico heavily shape their decisions to engage as temporary migrant labor in the United States. Gloria, a young single mother who scraped together a living selling tamales in Mexico, confided: "It is not that I like it, but I need this job. In Mexico, you earn very little, and here, I have secured a job. If I do well, the owner asks me to return next year. [I stay] because of the work. If not for that, I would have stayed in Mexico."

Yet, within localized contexts like the Eastern Shore, the expansion of temporary guest worker programs also severely restricted women's employment prospects and created conditions of extreme precarity, extending women's experiences of uncertainty beyond particular spatial and temporal dimensions.[15] In 2021, women constituted 35,127 of the 710,038 H-2A and H-2B visas or 5 percent of the temporary visa labor force.[16] Moreover, gender bias in employment recruitment and lack of government enforcement of anti-discrimination labor laws allow employers and recruiters to track women almost exclusively into the H-2B visa program. As a result, women receive lower wages, unequal income-earning opportunities, and fewer rights and protections than their male counterparts.[17] For instance, women who pick crab receive piece-rate pay, while men who cook and haul crab receive an hourly wage.[18] Further, women with H-2B visas lack many legal protections afforded to the mainly H-2A male agricultural workforce, such as receiving three-fourths of the total hours promised in the work contract, access to legal services, and other benefits, including workers' compensation or injury insurance coverage.[19]

Racial capitalist accumulation not only works to exploit Mexican women's labor and degrade the places where they live and work, but it also ruptures their spatial, temporal, and social relations. Capitalist expropriation and state regulation create conditions in which people are violently detached from each other, the spaces they occupy, and sense of time in ordinary ways. Women, in turn, experience community and belonging as ruptured social cohesion where collective life in rural regions becomes reduced "to the relations that sustain neoliberal democratic capitalism."[20] In describing their precarious experiences of working in commercial crab processing, women stressed the notion of "transformation" and the continual (re)adjustments made to fashion "ordinary" lives here, there, and in perpetual transit. Xiomara, who had been migrating back and forth for close to two decades, elaborated, describing her first migration journey: "I did not know anything at all. Every time you come here, it is like the first time. It is as if you are absolutely blind. You have never seen this, but you have."

Women recognize the past—their first journey—and retain an unfamiliarity with the present, even after years of recurrent migration. The Eastern Shore is both ordinarily familiar yet always a strange, routinized transitional moment. Loneliness and social isolation were everyday matters in this process of transformation on the Eastern Shore and beyond. Women expressed a deep sense of spatial and temporal estrangement from family and friends in Mexico and other female migrant workers and neighbors. Women live with other women, yet there is very little socialization or interaction among them. Their long work schedules, lack of established social connections with other women, and cramped housing conditions do little to foster close relationships or a clear sense of community. In addition, the constant worry of family in Mexico made it difficult to build social rapport even when it was a mutual concern among them. Xiomara explained: "Each of us keeps to herself, in our own world. We sleep, we get up, we eat, and [then it's] time to work. There's too much stress. I think too much. I worry about my family." Despite their shared experiences of routinized (and stressful) living and working conditions on the Eastern Shore and the constant anxiety about homes and families left behind, women like Xiomara described their distress as only affecting themselves in isolation.

The spatial and natural characteristics of the Eastern Shore also enhance the ordinariness of isolation felt by women, shaping their daily life and feelings of complete isolation from the "outside world," contributing to experiences and heightened awareness of being alone even in the presence of others. Women live on Hoopers Island, what locals sometimes refer to as *La Isla de las Mexicanas* (the Island of the Mexican Women)—three small, remote islands with about 500 residents connected by a causeway along the Eastern Shore located about a three-hour drive from the nation's capital. Even though women are technically free to come and go as they please, unlike many migrant workers working in commercial agriculture, they rarely leave because of the unfamiliar and harsh landscapes beyond their immediate surroundings. The burden of racism and anti-immigration sentiment on the Eastern Shore further heightened women's feelings of social isolation. Alicia described one outing to the local Walmart: "When you go shopping, you can feel the racism and bad feelings from people. They look at you strangely, make faces at you. It is pretty clear what they are doing. When you go to the stores and pay, they throw the change at you." As a result, women remained in their houses and on the remote islands. Victoria clarified, "We don't go anywhere. We don't leave the house. We work, come home, eat, and sleep and the days go by quickly."

"It's Like a Slavery Job, but You Get Paid for It": Industrial Poultry Processing and Haitians

Like Mexican women working as crab pickers, Haitians in the poultry industry migrated to the Eastern Shore because of severe economic precarity in Haiti or other parts of the United States. Darline told me: "Work is what brought me here because there isn't any in Florida. If there were work in Florida, then we would not have come here." She used a Haitian proverb to express the chronic uncertainty engendered by global and local economic forces that induce her labor migration along familiar colonial routes (Haiti to the United States) and constrain her to dangerous work and demeaning conditions in the poultry plants. "In Kreyòl, we say *Lè w pa gen manman, ou tete grann,*[21] which is something like, 'If you can't get breast milk from mom, you get it from grandma.' It means that when we don't have a solution to a problem, we must make do with what is available."

Like Mexican women, Haitians like Darline have a long history of immigrating to the United States. Colonial and neoliberal forces in Haiti have produced conditions of social, economic, and political instability, inducing its citizens to leave home. Haitians also have faced systemic racialized exclusion, portrayed as a group that posed significant threats to American public health, economic stability, and national security.[22] However, the catastrophic earthquake in 2010 in Haiti led to its inclusion as one of the countries eligible for Temporary Protected Status (TPS). In many ways, TPS did not stem from the exceptional event of the earthquake but rather from the durability of catastrophic structural conditions made visible by it. TPS gave Haitians already living in the United States, as well as those who entered under humanitarian parole, provisional permission to live and work here as conditions in Haiti improved, signaling a break in the repressive history of U.S. immigration policy toward Haitian migrants. At the same time, as the name implies, TPS and other policies were offered only as temporary measures of reprieve, with the understanding that the U.S. government will withdraw these provisions at an indeterminate but guaranteed time in the future. Thus, immigration policies illuminate the sovereign power of the U.S. government to make available and retract certain rights and suspend Haitians in a persistent condition of impermanence, between having rights and rightlessness.[23]

Precarious living for Haitians extends to their daily work experiences. The poultry plant symbolizes the racialization and spatialization of extreme marginality, perpetual insecurity, and the afterlife of slavery. Haitians associate their work to racialized legacies of the transatlantic slave trade and ongoing Western imperialism. Esther, in describing her experience, recounted vividly: "They take us for their robots, and we are human. We cannot do the same thing like a machine. It is really painful, physically. They consider us, Haitians, like their slaves because they need our blood, our bodies." Racialized workplace hierarchies, extraordinary harsh working conditions, and the precarious subjectivities they engender become routinized on the plant floor. In-between heavy sobs, Vanessa recounts her trauma of work: "The work is difficult, and you are working nonstop all day." She rapidly waved her hands up and down to illustrate how she would eviscerate chickens into parts using a sharp knife at superhuman speeds. "Like this, like this! It's in the same place, the same kind of work, same chicken, same pressure." Wilky adds how abuse toward Haitians was particularly commonplace: "We get humiliated because we are Haitians. They do not do that to the Americans, but they do whatever they want with us."

As Black immigrants who do not speak English and contend with uncertain legal status, Haitians are part of the growing surplus labor population, relegated to dangerous jobs that expose them to harm, injury, and premature death. They find themselves permanently positioned at the edge of "normal structures," perceived as indispensable as a condition and effect of their disposability within commercial poultry processing. Daniel explains this condition of feeling perpetually trapped and disciplined: "Working at a chicken plant, Haitian people call it like a slavery job, but you get paid for it. That is what it is. It is hard, and they do not really treat the people right. It is very controlling. I do not know how else to explain it." Such narratives linking plant work with slavery disclose how Haitians' bodies and their exposure to injury and death are deeply profitable—not only from the surplus created through the devaluation of Haitians' labor power in the production process but as a commodity itself.[24]

Like the crab workers, Haitians experience precarious conditions that extend beyond the spatial confines of the plant floor into daily life, precluding a sense of community and belonging. Extending Ruth Wilson Gilmore's description of racial capitalism as a tool of "antirelationality," Jodi Melamed describes this "social separateness"—the decoupling of relations between people and places—as an essential tool and consequence of capitalist accumulation.[25] Instead of finding strength in a common culture and history, Haitians felt connected by the experience of racism and abuse from other groups, "We try to be united. A lot of the other people do not like us. They do not like Haitians. Especially at work, they do not like us." For some, the related fear of jeopardizing their immigration status and losing their job kept them from congregating with other Haitians. As Madeline clarified: "In our Haitian community, we are reserved because we do not like being hurt. So we kind of stay on our own, try not to get involved in other stuff."

"People Age Here": Commercial Agriculture and Working the Fields

Similar to crab pickers and poultry processors, agricultural workers on the Eastern Shore—immigrants from Mexico, Latin America, and the Caribbean, primarily Haiti—often stated that they are only there to earn a living. In talking about Haitians coming to the Eastern Shore from South Florida or

Haiti every year to pick tomatoes, Fabienne and the women she lived and worked with made this assertion: "We come to work. It is not for pleasure. At least we get shelter." Like other immigrant workers, the women explained how they felt socially stuck and in limbo because of a lack of available work and a broad sense of economic precarity at "home" through spatial and temporal idioms. These uncertain conditions shaped their decision to engage in recurrent labor migration and continued to plague their migration trajectories on the Eastern Shore because of the difficult working conditions, social isolation, and prolonged separation from their families, especially their children. Yet they had no choice. "We do not want to come, we do not like it. But we will lose our job. We have to come."

In Maryland, agricultural workers toil mainly in nurseries and fruit and vegetable farms. The composition of farmworkers has shifted over time because of differing visa regimes. Carla, an immigration and labor outreach worker, noted: "There was a time that you saw only Mexicans, a few Puerto Ricans, Jamaicans, people from the Caribbean that came with special visas to work. When El Salvador started getting TPS, they started getting Salvadorians. They moved into communities, had better jobs, better pay, less movement. You see that with the Mexicans. The Jamaicans stayed after the amnesty in 1986 in the SAW program."[26] Labor migration for Fabienne and other women consists of following the crops along the Eastern migrant stream, from Florida to Maine; others move back and forth between Maryland's Eastern Shore to Florida. Interlocutors who worked in the fields picked mainly tomatoes, watermelon, squash, cucumbers, and strawberries (see figure 2.2). Agriculture is the largest commercial industry in Maryland, with cash grains (such as corn and wheat) valued at around $948 million annually. In addition, fresh market fruit and vegetables represent an earning potential of $94 million or more.[27] Upwards of fifty agricultural employers across the state of Maryland, including in six of the nine Eastern Shore counties, recruit around 700 employees through the H-2A temporary visa program each year.[28] Farmers must prove to the federal government that the foreign workers they plan to recruit through the H-2A program are needed because U.S. workers are unavailable. Often agricultural business owners do very little to recruit, train, adequately compensate, or protect U.S. workers, and the state overlooks how such "need" is rationalized. The farmer must technically provide the foreign workers, once hired, with transportation, safe housing, and fair wages for the duration of their seasonal employment. There is ample evidence that indicates that farms and the state collude to ensure that these provisions are deliberately not followed and routinely ignored.[29]

FIGURE 2.2 Watermelon harvest. Photo by Emilia M. Guevara.

Among farmworkers, like crab pickers and poultry processors, daily "structures" of work incorporate and reproduce precarity. Most farmworkers described having a work "visa," and some of them did come through the H-2A program. Even then, having papers to work legally did not offer protection from the constant threat of losing one's livelihood. "I am always worried about losing my job and about being too demanding," Manuel confessed, even though he had papers. Similarly, Yenni, a retired accountant from Venezuela, described her experiences of extreme isolation and uncertainty through normalized working conditions. She fled when the financial crisis hit her country, depleting her precious savings and losing her monthly pension to escalating inflation. She then came to Miami on a tourist visa only to find there was no work. Desperate, she decided to work in the fields. It seemed the only way to survive. Migrating along the East Coast of the United States, she works in tomato packing. Yenni described how spatial and temporal constraints structured her experiences: "There is the opportunity, but you give up a lot, too. People work hard here, and they do not rest. They work during the harvest season and then go to another region and do it all over again. They only know their children on the phone. It is awful, and not only for me. It is too much just to work and work. In the end, what would I have? What I would really have is nothing at all."

Like other immigrant workers, farmworkers shared narratives of uncertainty that extended far beyond the fields. In describing their living and working conditions, farmworkers discuss how spatial isolation and dilapidated housing were intentional mechanisms that kept them in their place, prevented social relations, and caused physical harm. Those working in commercial agriculture, for instance, lived in isolated migrant labor camps. Fabienne and her coworkers lived in quarters once used to house civilian conservation corps members who cleared tax ditches and worked on drainage projects in the area. Later, during World War II, over 1,000 German prisoners of war, who were contracted out to canning houses, sawmills, meatpacking plants, and farms throughout the Eastern Shore, lived there. Since then, the camp has held migrant workers and has received local and national attention for its squalid and inhumane living conditions. In a 1983 report, the state of Maryland's advisory committee to the U.S. Commission on Civil Rights provided a vivid description of the camp:[30]

[The] Camp . . . is one of the largest of the migrant camps in operation on the East Coast. . . . [It] is a sprawling complex of two dozen barracks-type buildings, separated by stretches of grass and dirt roads. Families live in single-room units without running water. Most units have refrigerators and small gas plates for cooking; sometimes doors, sometimes not. The single window is sometimes screened, sometimes not. Latrines offer stools without stalls, gang showers with no privacy, grime-crusted lavatories.

Just as prisons, Ghettos, and sin strips have their own notoriety, the complex of long, gray weather-beaten buildings along the highway . . . has achieved a special renown. Past the creek where people fill their jugs with drinking water, up the dusty road past the signs that warn visitors away, around the ditches filled with stagnant water and the gaping bins of garbage, this is the Westover farm labor camp.

The . . . camp, once a World War II holding pen for German prisoners, has acquired such notoriety that migrants from as far away as Texas refuse to stay there. It is the biggest and most infamous among dozens of rundown caps amid the fecund vegetable fields on the Eastern Shore of Maryland, Delaware, and Virginia. Maryland's Commission on

Migratory and Seasonal Farm Labor is so exercised about [the camp] that it wants Governor Harry Hughes to close the place.

The camp is still rustic but no longer resembles this description. In describing it, one health provider described it as the "Hilton" of migrant camps.[31] A central pavilion sits at the outskirts of the camp and the living quarters. The bathroom is one long building with two sides, one for men and one for women. Faded laminated health department posters line the walls. Residents were particularly excited that management had installed two tankless water heaters for the bathrooms. The kitchen and dining area, where the smell of baking and cooking constantly lingered, were in the middle of the campgrounds. A typical living area was sparse, the size of a small dorm, just big enough for two twin beds or a couple of bunk beds, a refrigerator, a small table, and a hot plate. Even though many appreciated the renovated conditions of the camp, farmworkers felt isolated because they lived in a highly remote setting, far removed from other people or structures. When asked about feeling safe, Fabienne and her coworkers resoundingly answered "no." Since they did not have a car, they were immobile. "We just stay here. We do not know anything else."

Housing conditions beyond labor camps varied. While Fabienne lived in the labor camp, Francisco and his wife lived in a dilapidated trailer, which he rented for $80 per week from his boss.[32] His annual salary was $11,000 a year, which meant that his rent was approximately a third of his income. Francisco thought this amount was absurd for what he considered *mugre* (dirt). The trailer's entry was difficult to access because of its waterlogged deck. Two bathrooms bookended two small rooms, a small kitchen, and a larger living room area where blankets covered the broken furniture. One bathroom had a collapsed floor, while the other stunk of sewage. Their employer, an influential lawmaker, refused to fix the damage. Francisco's wife attributed her deteriorating health (i.e., infected needle injection sites for insulin that didn't heal properly and psychosocial stress) to her home's dilapidated condition. In her eternal suffering, she was often praying to God to take her away from this misery.

Injury, Disability, and the Politics of Care

On the Eastern Shore, racialized work conditions discipline immigrants' time, activities, and access to space. Women who worked in crab processing, for instance, spent much of the day indoors picking crab or sleeping. They worked in daily shifts of eight to twelve hours to meet minimal quotas of picked crabmeat. Work hours were unstable, often predicated on the amount and quality of crab available daily, depending on the morning catch. Fabiola, who had left her young children in the care of relatives in Florida, described a typical workday picking crab: "We go to work early in the morning and come back at night. Sometimes, we come back in the afternoon if there is no more work. We hurry up and cook when we come home to get ready for the next day of work. We are used to this life because it is the same wherever we go." Similarly, Esther describes how psychologically debilitating and physically dangerous such spatial, temporal, and bodily disciplining can be at the poultry plant. These conditions are central to racial capital accumulation: "They do not allow you to do whatever you want when you need it. Like I need to go to the bathroom, and they do not want you to go when you need to go—because for them, leaving the line would not be productive. They give bathroom breaks, but when they give it to you, it is not when you need it. And you cannot say no. When you are ready, and you ask, you won't be able to go."

Racialized hierarchies and processes of disposability are also visible in the health and safety practices that routinely expose immigrant workers to illness and injury. The conceptualization of "dead labor" is apt in understanding how capitalism's exploitative living and working conditions profit from the premature death of immigrant workers.[33] Instead of complying with safety regulations, corporations have deliberately promoted the implicit acceptance of heightened risk to workers' health and safety through exploitative and harmful working conditions. The state is also complicit, doing very little to enforce workplace regulations to protect workers or ensure access to health care. Dry skin, cuts, scrapes, bruises, skin rashes, headaches, stomachaches, and broken bones were ordinary occurrences among immigrants because of the inherent violence that surrounds the food production process. Farmworkers, for instance, experienced prolonged exposure to pesticides and other chemicals, which induced them to illness and harm. They endured poor workplace protections and had very little access to health care. Pedro described how routine spraying of pesticides severely affected his health: "I did not have any training, and it got all over me. My eyes were really red. Then I had headaches, stomachaches, tearing, nose hurts, and throat hurts. Lots of symptoms. Even dizziness. Even drooling." Ricardo's narrative highlights how the disposability of farmworkers (and rural environments) as surplus people (and places) allows corporations and the state to undertake policies and practices that subordinate life to the dictates of capital—what

James Tyner calls an emergent "necrocapitalism."[34] According to Ricardo, "People work without shirts, they are really hot, and people spray pesticides on them. We were in a group, and they sprayed pesticides on us. We were almost drowning. Our lungs were burning, and we began to cough. If you get sick, the bosses say you are no good, and they fire you. You have to be strong there. You think to yourself, my God, what am I doing here."

Even workers like Yenni, who pack tomatoes and have the "safety" of not working in the field, still suffer from numerous work-related health concerns yet have difficulty finding treatment because it is too costly. For instance, Yenni agonizes over a recurrent eye irritation: "My eyes are watering on this side. Where the tomatoes pass next to me, there's bleach. The tomatoes are washed with bleach, and they pass right next to my face." She wants to purchase occupational safety glasses but can only afford reading glasses at the nearby Walmart. Yenni also takes medication for a thyroid condition, but the only available treatment is one she cannot afford: "I know that if I do not take it, I will get slow and sleepy, somewhat apathetic to things." Like her counterparts who work in the fields or various agricultural jobs, including packing fruit and vegetables, she experiences chronic pain in her legs from hours of standing. Her provider's advice is useless to Yenni because he tells her to walk daily even though she is in serious pain. She points to her ankle, which is swollen and red. She tries her best to remediate the situation using only what she has: "My son told me that it is an inflamed tendon. He told me to put a bottle of water in the freezer and to alternate between hot water and cold ice. I did it once, and it felt really good. I also took some ibuprofen. I thought it was the pill that helped but actually, now that I think about it, it is probably the alternating heat." Her son also told her that her shoes were too small and were probably exacerbating her pain. She exclaims: "My shoes are done for. I'm a size 39, but I'm wearing 7.5. So I need an 8. I hope that it takes the pain away if I get some new shoes. My son was not terribly happy with me. Those are the most pressing things right now. I mean, I can survive without them. It is not killing me, but it is a problem." Because she is unable to afford proper fitting shoes, Yenni uses an ankle cream as temporary relief. She insists that her bodily pain is a result of work conditions: "The pain started right when I got here, when I started to work. Maybe it is my circulation. I am always sitting down."

Women in crab processing plants also face exposure to common hazards like vapor generated by cleaning and steaming crabs, cuts from knives and crab shells, and constant contact with containers filled with salty water, bleach, and other chemicals. "There is an entrance where the crabs are cooked and kept. The vapor that escapes the crab when it's cooked gets inside and trapped. When we leave, we are stinky. Even if we wash our hands, we smell like crab. It is hot, and it smells like acid." Conditions within the crab processing plants often exacerbated existing chronic issues or precipitated them. Francisca described her situation: "I cannot wear gloves. They told me it was an allergy. In Mexico, I do not cough, but I started to cough when working here. I feel like I have a cold all the time." Marta explained that she, like many other women, has developed allergies to crab: "I get a breakout and lots of itching wherever the water hits the skin . . . could be the feet, arms, legs." Often, these allergies were temporary, and symptoms subsided when women left the Eastern Shore. However, severe infections stemming from everyday injuries related to cuts and contact with crabs also occurred. Like Ricardo, Vera tells a story that illustrates how the commodification of workers' bodies and subsequent profit from their deterioration and demise are central to the workings of capitalism: "[The boss] only cares about work. I cut myself once and was in the hospital. I did not know the crabs were infectious. I had a red line running up [my arm]. The manager looked at it and said it was fine. My sister told them that it was a serious infection and could get to my heart. She took me to the hospital. And from what I understand, the owner needs to pay for those kind of work-related injuries. My sister mentioned this to the supervisor, and she said that she wouldn't pay because I didn't tell them when it happened. I had to pay $1,100."

Additionally, immigrant workers suffered from numerous invisible injuries and disabilities. Astrid has worked at the chicken plant for only a short while and, like Junior, found it traumatic to talk about her job. She blamed her experience of preeclampsia, which resulted in her baby being born prematurely at twenty-seven weeks, to the extraordinary stress she experiences daily. Working almost nine hours a day from 4:00 P.M. until 1:00 A.M., five or six times a week, Astrid was forced to stand on her feet the entire time, even while pregnant. In addition, she experienced unbearable pain from "the velocity" of cutting up chicken. She cries every time she talks about this work: "It is forty-five rotations or sometimes more. There is not even time to grab them. There needs to be a cut without the bone, and someone else works on the wings and what they are taking out. So you leave it there, and someone else does it." Astrid felt threatened by the constant harassment from supervisors to work at a faster rate. "They are always screaming at you. They are always pressuring you to work faster. And you are obligated. They do not really have to pressure you like that because the line is going fast already. There is no way you can let that chicken go by without touching it. You have to do it. The conveyor belt itself is making you go fast. Sometimes you are tired." She stresses that these extreme conditions affect all workers negatively. Gina, her coworker and friend, has suffered from physical pain since working at the chicken plant. "The issue that I have, nobody can help me. Because when you go to the doctor, you try to explain it or how you feel, they send you for tests. And no results! So, you just live with it. They cannot tell how you feel in your body, how you feel inside. They cannot help you. They think you are crazy. And especially [male providers]. I know I don't speak English. I said, okay, maybe that is why they do not understand. I used the service interpreters and everything. I give up!"

Similarly, women who worked in crab processing reported experiencing recurring pain and myalgia from sitting for long hours picking crab in crouched positions. In describing her pain, Alejandra said, "Backache and my legs swell up because we are always sitting down. A year ago, I was given a pair of compression socks, but they wear out really fast. My chest hurts quite a bit. It was hard to breathe. When I make sudden moves with the knife, I am in pain." Mobile health providers explained that many migrant women in crab processing suffered severe back and neck issues that radiated pain down the arm because of repetitive motions and constant crouching over tables when picking crab. In addition, numbness, epicondylitis tendon injuries, nerve pain, and carpal tunnel were prevalent among women who performed delicate handwork for hours at a time. Further, providers noted that several women had developed vitamin D deficiencies because of long periods spent indoors and a limited diet, raising concerns about rickets, osteopenia, and osteoporosis. The nurse practitioner prescribed these women high dosages of prescription-level vitamin D supplements, even though she admitted that many would not continue this treatment regimen once they returned to Mexico. Providers could do very little to treat these invisible forms of injury and disability.

Immigrants openly discussed how the gendered and racialized ideologies that have become the grounds for their recruitment also heighten their risk of everyday injury and disability. Haitians, for instance, likened working in poultry processing to slavery, explicitly describing various experiences of dehumanization. "They see Haitians as lower" was a typical articulation that called attention to their placement on the threshold of humanity. Mexican women in crab processing likewise indicated that employers and labor recruiters claimed that women exhibited more significant levels of speed and agility and were more patient and productive than men (see figure 2.3). "Our boss says that [men] don't have the patience like a woman to pick the

FIGURE 2.3 Women picking crab. Photo by Emilia M. Guevara.

crabmeat." Women themselves internalized these ideologies, explaining that men did not have the "patience" to pick crab because it required "delicate," "careful," and "hard" work, describing crab picking as exclusively "women's work." Many discussed supervisors' perceptions of the appropriateness of immigrant workers through racialized notions of work ethic. As one worker said, "[My supervisor] told me that Americans aren't going to wake up at 4:00 A.M. to do the work. She told me that we are hard workers, that no one else is going to come to do the work!"

Despite the daily risk of injury and disability, workers had little access to care and treatment because of the lack of health facilities or sites and because even the meager care that was available was too expensive. Seafood or agricultural workers relied on mobile clinics or local federally qualified health centers (FQHCs). They paid a flat $15 for an entire season of primary preventive services, including essential prescriptions. However, the FQHC, like its mobile health unit, was not equipped to handle specialty or urgent care, and the premium that women paid did not cover specialty care or treatment.

Workers who needed urgent or emergency care or specialized treatment had to access them through the regional hospital located about 120 miles away. Those who did need to access these services incurred massive debt. Yolanda described her situation: "I had an ectopic pregnancy and serious pain. I was mopping the floor, and I started to bleed. I went to the hospital. They did surgery after the ultrasound. It was very expensive. They sent several bills. It was $22,000. I will be done [paying] in seven years."

On the other hand, farmworkers often used a bus or found transportation to get them to the local FQHC. Many did not use services because it would mean loss of wages from missing work or required getting permission from supervisors; the high cost of services was another deciding factor. Viola, for instance, has diabetes and high blood pressure. She has insurance from Florida but could not use it here and has to pay out of pocket. Viola insists that providers have told her that even though her insurance plan is part of "Obamacare," she has to purchase a different insurance plan while she is here. She was frustrated because the cost of services is higher than in Florida. "The bill was supposed to be $95. I agreed to that, even though when I go to Florida for the same thing, I only pay $40. But when I got the bill, it was $200. They lied to me." Another woman indicates that the local FQHC told her, through a translator, that "if you do not pay right away when you go to the clinic when they send you the bill, it is going to be more than that. I had a Pap [smear]. It was $60, and they told me if I do not pay right away, it will be $400."

Poultry workers often saw providers within the plant or those approved through the company's insurance plan. In many ways, having a clinic on-site provided more coercive care. For example, Zora remembers suffering from pain and swelling in her hands. "I worked on the line for two months, and I started having problems with my hands," she said. "My hands and wrists were getting swollen, and I had to go to the nurse every morning. I would wrap my wrists." She explains that this is relatively common and that many poultry workers often suffer from hand and should injuries: "Standing in one spot all day, not rotating, many of them end up having many problems with their hands and feet. Their fingers are swollen. Sometimes they go to the nurse, who gives them ice or . . . a couple of aspirin and sends them back to the line. Not really examine, you know, the *real* problem."

As I discuss in more detail in chapter 3, many counties encompassing the Eastern Shore are federally designated health shortage areas, yet only two FQHCs, organizations that receive special federal health care reimbursements to assist underserved populations, serve the nine counties. In addition,

Maryland has expanded Medicaid and created state-based exchanges to provide subsidized health insurance for low-income residents under the Affordable Care Act (ACA). However, rural residents face severe financial and systemic barriers in receiving adequate care and treatment, and Maryland has enacted health care access restrictions for immigrants. Insurance coverage and health care accessibility for H-2A and H-2B workers depend on these immigration and health care laws.[35] Employers can choose to offer health care benefits for H-2A and H-2B workers but are not required to do so under immigration law. The ACA does not require employers to provide health insurance to workers, including H-2A and H-2B visa holders. H-2A and H-2B visa holders can purchase ACA-compliant health insurance within sixty days of their arrival or other temporary short-term medical insurance. However, these insurance policies often only cover "new" injuries, conditions, or accidents. Many interlocutors did not have insurance through their employers; their only option was to purchase the basic insurance plan from the local FQHC or pay out of pocket.

Both the broader conditions and the routine nature of work and life led immigrant workers to perceive their physical health, much like their social lives, to be constantly in flux, in a continual process of transformation and transition. Wideline, a Haitian poultry worker, explained how the violence experienced through racial capitalism—rather than the body—determined physical and emotional well-being, "I know that when I am in pain, it is related to my work. Not my health. My blood pressure comes from work but not from my body." Beatriz, who picked crabs, elaborated on the growing vagueness between health and illness under capitalism by drawing attention to the enduring nature of risk, injury, and disability as well as its temporal limitations. "Right now we are well," she said, "but you could get sick just like that. I am always worried. We will all eventually develop something or another."

Racialized labor conditions in rural contexts heightened immigrants' risk of injury and disability, made the provision and delivery of care complex, and intensified experiences of precarity. Work-related injuries, disability, and illnesses borne by immigrant workers embody social violence enacted through discriminatory labor conditions and racial capitalism where the wasting away of workers' bodies, as a fundamental manifestation of capital accumulation and profit, signifies the blurring of the traditional boundaries of life and death. Further, workers' narratives and actions sought to destabilize normative spatial and temporal logics of enduring embodiments and workplace injury and disability not as individual, isolated experiences but as collective state-sanctioned suffering. Accounts of bodies and health as contingent, mutable, and fluid resisted dominant ideologies of illness, disability, and ability as fixed and chronic categories.[36] Immigrants' analysis of work and life focused on the continuously shifting boundaries between material and experiential states of being.[37] Ernie Lightman and colleagues suggest that "such bodies-at-odds create discomfort because they possess the ability to live sometimes as healthy, sometimes ill, sometimes able, and sometimes disabled."[38] Immigrant workers' reimagining of embodiment, in many ways, opens up critical spaces of representation that incorporate precarious living as ordinary lifeworlds and as a part of the phenomenological experience of self.

Racialized Labor and Ordinary Lives

During the global COVID-19 pandemic and accompanying lockdowns, characterizations of "essential" workers became part of our lexicon to describe people required to continue in-person work under lockdown conditions, including those employed in global food production sectors.[39] The pandemic exposed the disproportionate numbers of racialized workers in the agriculture, poultry, and seafood production and processing sectors. It also intensified the effects of long-standing structural racism, forcing people to work in dangerous workplace conditions without adequate safeguards to protect them from a highly transmissible virus. Laboring and living in crowded conditions without personal protective equipment and adequate ventilation and unable to self-quarantine at home, many food production workers and processors experienced high levels of illness and death. While there has been a wealth of research on work required to maintain the supply of fresh produce and meat demanded by American consumers and the capitalist food supply regime through which that is organized, the COVID-19 pandemic, in many ways, rendered visible to large segments of society the precarious working and living conditions experienced by food workers and immigrants in particular. The paradox of "essential" workers became commonplace in public rhetoric—the compensation, benefits, and status of those whose work we depend on the most hardly reflect how critical they are to the functioning of civil society. These discussions of essential-yet-disposable workers, however, often obscured the valorization of immigrant workers for profit by the state, capital, and society itself and the ways that their labor and injured bodies function as forms of commodity and property. They also neglected how policies enacted in the wake of the pandemic to protect public health and essential workers become secondary to preserving and cultivating the economy.

Ample evidence suggests that a constellation of conditions, including the growth in high-value products and goods for foreign export and domestic consumption and the subsequent expansion of the U.S. guest worker program as well as declining employment opportunities and low wages for workers in Latin America and the Caribbean, induce labor migration to and within the United States. These structural forces spatially and temporally reconfigure new labor networks and migration flows that mirror existing gendered, racial, and neocolonial frameworks, engendering precarity among immigrant workers.[40] Despite the financial, social, and health costs involved, workers perceived temporary, flexible labor in the United States to be financially more lucrative than engaging in wage labor at "home" (e.g., in one place) because their earnings often afford them social and material rewards that otherwise may be elusive. Yet their narratives of forced migration trajectories, exploitative racial capitalism, ruptured sociality, and workplace injury also indicate that they deeply understood the uncertainties of such migration strategies. Suspended in a continual holding pattern, in a state of perpetual transformation and living uncertainty, immigrants felt simultaneously outside and inside, both "home" and "away," even as they tried to live with the continual transition as a more or less fixed or unchanging mode of being. Many conveyed desires to end recurrent labor migration and temporary labor, wanting to stay in place with their families or, at times, risking overstaying their visas and remaining in the United States without papers. Still, they expressed even these longings in noncommittal terms as improbable futures.

Workers engaged with the cultural and material production of extraordinary conditions of unstructured and unknown futures brought forth by temporary labor and visa regimes through a series of everyday actions and relations. They navigated a precarious existence that foregrounds intimate entanglements of subjectivity and bodily injury in the face of significant social and institutional barriers, including gendered, racial, and ableist social expectations, harmful work and living conditions, risk of early return or job loss for not meeting employer expectations, social isolation, and fractured socialities. Immigrants also used various structures and connections with the United States, Latin America, and the Caribbean to access and remain within the U.S. labor market. Moreover, they lived with and refused the violence of immigrant expendability and gendered and racialized disablement, reconfiguring the possibilities for ordinary living through the continual renegotiation of space, time, and belonging. On the one hand, workers embodied and conformed to a capitalist ideal of the able-bodied and productive immigrant worker integrating illness and injury into the self to safeguard their economic and social mobility. On the other hand, amid the risk of deportability and financial insecurity, they criticized racialized labor demands that created risk for injury and disability, actively seeking care for visible and invisible wounds and embodying the fluidity of disability. In negotiating these spaces of denial and resistance, they refused the nation-state as a source of protection against the reach of racial capitalism, underscoring the dire consequences affecting people and places left in its wake.

CHAPTER THREE

Place, Personhood, and Precarity

Rural Dynamics of Health Care

PRESIDENT BARACK OBAMA: There are also those who claim that our reform effort will insure illegal immigrants. This, too, is false — the reforms I'm proposing would not apply to those who are here illegally.

REP. JOE WILSON (R-SC): You lie!

PRESIDENT OBAMA: It's not true.

— BEN SMITH, "A Voice from the Floor on Illegal Immigrants: 'You Lie'" (reporting on President Obama's address to a joint session of Congress, September 2009)

MARYLAND'S EASTERN SHORE faces considerable challenges in responding to drastic increases in immigration given its relative geographic isolation and often limited resources. The impact of rapid immigration has been severe on a health system already struggling with provider shortages, high rates of uninsured and sick patients, and limited public resources.[1] Many Eastern Shore counties are federally designated health professional shortage areas (HPSAs), which are spatial markers of health care provider shortages in primary care, dental health, or mental health for geographic, population, or facility-based reasons. Worcester County, for instance, had 100 percent of its population residing in a primary care HPSA. Kent County had 100 percent of its population living in a dental care HPSA. Caroline, Cecil, Kent, Somerset, Wicomico, and Worcester Counties had 100 percent of their population living in a mental health HPSA. In addition, all counties on the Eastern Shore have a more significant percentage of their people living in a primary care, dental care, or mental health care HPSA than the statewide percentage. Eastern Shore counties are also considered federally designated locations or have population groups that lack primary care resources. They are designated medically underserved areas and medically underserved populations (MUAs/MUPs) based on four criteria: a high infant mortality rate, a high percentage of the population living in poverty, a high percent of the population that is over age 65, and low primary care provider ratios. Caroline, Kent, Somerset, and Worcester Counties have 100 percent of residents in MUA designations. Dorchester and Wicomico Counties have the most significant populations covered by MUP designations.

These spatial designations—which indicate devaluation and deficiency among places and people—allow each jurisdiction to be eligible for federal programs and other benefits, including federal workforce development programs and enhanced Medicare reimbursement. Federally qualified health centers (FQHCs) are a key outgrowth of such designations. FQHCs are community-based health care or safety-net institutions located in or near a federally designated MUA to serve MUA residents and others in an MUP. Unlike private clinics or hospitals, FQHCs serve low-income individuals, the uninsured, and the underinsured who would otherwise not have access to health care services. They provide services to all individuals, regardless of their ability to pay, offering a sliding-scale fee to eligible individuals based on income and family size. Their cost of care is among the lowest; they decrease the need for costly hospital-based and specialty care and are designed to save billions of dollars for taxpayers. FQHC operations are supervised by a consumer board of directors governing structure and the Health Resources and Services Administration (HRSA), a division of the U.S. Department of Health and Human Services. FQHCs receive federal funding under Section 330 of the Public Health Service Act. In addition, they are eligible for enhanced Medicare and Medicaid reimbursement, receive medical malpractice coverage through the Federal Tort Claims Act, and purchase prescription and nonprescription medications at reduced cost through the 340B Drug Pricing Program. Experts and policymakers have long argued that expanding and strengthening FQHCs would further reduce health disparities, increase access to high-quality and regular care, and boost local economies.

Two FQHCs serve the nine counties of the Eastern Shore despite multiple designations of service and population need in the region.[2] In effect, these federal designations and the presence of FQHCs have not alleviated challenges related to poor health status or access to care. Instead, these federal programs and initiatives continue to maintain spatial and racial inequities in health care access. Although HPSA, MUA, and MUP designations provide key measures to classify underserved populations and prioritize places and people lacking access to adequate primary and preventive health care, research indicates that these designation systems fall far short of their intended effects.[3] Areas with primary care shortages are difficult to identify correctly, and federal resources to benefit underserved people, especially immigrants and the rural poor, have hardly been adequate. Rapid shifts in information or inaccuracies that emerge from combining data points from different designation systems severely limit the ways federal public health entities identify the extent of "need" in underserved areas.[4] Even when these systems accurately identify underserved areas, they cannot provide tailored information to decide which programs best suit the area's particular needs.[5] As a result, programs may design interventions for a specific area that may not directly benefit the specific subpopulation with insufficient access to care. An example is the Medicare Incentive Payment program, which provides bonus payments to all physicians treating Medicare patients in geographic HPSAs, even though a different group than Medicare patients—such as migrant farmworkers—may be those underserved.[6] Moreover, there is little assurance that small clinics and FQHCs on the Eastern Shore allocate federal funds for those most in need.

In 2010, the Affordable Care Act (ACA), the first major health care reform in forty-five years, instituted guidelines that allow those who purchase coverage to receive a minimum of preventive health services through an "individual mandate" that requires many Americans to buy health insurance. However, the benefits offered by the ACA vary based on whether or not each state has initiated Medicaid expansion and introduced requirements.[7] To date, forty states (including Washington, D.C.) have expanded Medicaid. Several studies have reported the substantial positive impact of the Medicaid expansion on overall revenue margins for medical institutions, especially in rural regions, mainly through a reduction in uncompensated care and an increase in Medicaid revenue.[8] In addition, Medicaid expansion has led to the rise in the number of health centers and their ability to deliver care to a more significant number of patients.[9] Yet many people accessing medical care continue to face a substantial burden because they struggle with higher cost-sharing levels through deductibles and coinsurance and rising overall out-of-pocket costs. In addition, many immigrants and rural residents do not qualify for participation due to income or anti-immigration restrictions.[10] Further, despite federal help, a lack of funding, inadequate reimbursement rates, and weak workforce recruitment and retention incentives continue to be critical challenges for rural health systems.

These challenges synergistically interact to limit immigrants' access to care on Maryland's Eastern Shore.[11] Many immigrants are unsure of where and how to receive services. They are fearful of high costs and discriminatory exchanges with health care providers and institutions. Further, many individuals I worked with were entirely dependent on employers for access to health care and social services or were uninsured. As a result, regular, affordable care was not possible. Only emergencies (if at all) spurred engagement with providers or health care institutions, often at a high financial and emotional cost.

In the following sections, I explore these challenges of navigating health care from the perspectives of immigrants and providers using details of individual experiences and provider perspectives on rural health care provision and delivery. The narratives of providers and immigrants highlight how an inadequate health care infrastructure, lack of insurance and high cost of services, and racially discriminatory policies present significant challenges such as long wait times, lack of continuity of care, cultural and language barriers, and unaffordable costs even when accessing care through local safety nets. These narratives also disclose how the state and capital collude to accumulate profit from sick and injured bodies and abandoned places. These challenges stress the convergence of immigration and rural health and how this coupling affects immigrants on the Eastern Shore. Health care—how it is articulated and manifests—is inseparable from the spatial and temporal context in which it is embedded and experienced. Immigrants' daily encounters with health care delivery and access demonstrate how the context of immigration opens up new ways of rendering visible rural precarity and the exclusionary, extractive, and profit-driven nature of health care, while rural landscapes of care also offer possibilities of belonging for immigrants.

Challenges in Navigating Health Care Provision and Delivery

On a beautiful clear morning in August 2014, I ordered coffee at a local café overlooking the Wicomico River—a twenty-four-mile-long tributary of the Chesapeake Bay on Maryland's Eastern Shore that drains low marshlands and farming country. The river has been a major shipping route on the Delmarva Peninsula over the last few centuries and has now become a popular spot for canoeing, kayaking, water sports, fishing, and crabbing among locals and visitors. I was there to meet with Jon—a provider at one of the FQHCs on the Eastern Shore. Jon arrives in a good mood, excited to tell me about his work for the local FQHC as a mid-level health provider. Dressed casually in khakis and a light blue polo, he was boyishly handsome with dark brown hair, wire-rimmed glasses, and a wide smile. Jon had been in his position for over eight years. He moved to the Eastern Shore from Washington, D.C., where he received his training, because he wanted to work in primary care and adult medicine. "I felt like that was what I was trained to do. This feels like what my original training was about." As an immigrant himself, he appreciated that charity care was the FQHC's mission to address migrant workers' health; it meant that they were attentive to the specific needs of migrants. He gave me examples: The FQHC provided transportation and English translation services for its clients, its location was close to the migrant labor camps, and appointments and identification documents were not required. "The migrant and immigrant component is still very much there," he said.

Jon repeatedly expressed his dedication to working with migrant and immigrant clients. "They are so appreciative of the care, and most take care of themselves." He told me that many of his clients came from Florida, South Carolina, and Texas from June until October to work in the tomato picking and packing industries. They used to come with their families and enroll their kids in school for the autumn months, but now it is mostly men and women in their twenties to thirties (and sometimes older) who are coming from other U.S. states or directly from Mexico, Honduras, Guatemala, Panama, and Haiti. Men work in the tomato fields enduring long hours hunched over to pluck the fleshy fruit before lifting it on their shoulders onto a waiting truck; a proficient picker will fill a thirty-two-pound bucket every two and a half minutes, earning perhaps 65 cents for each one.[12] Women are often found in the packinghouses, which are typically open structures and do not have air-conditioning. Older adults are left to clean the plants. Those who work in supervisory positions may be documented, but the vast majority of those working do not have legal documentation. His clients do not disclose their documentation status, and Jon does not ask for verification. "I think when you do not have papers, the tomato packing plant is seen as a safe place to work. No one ever raids the tomato packing plants."

Despite his commitment to the mission and vision of the FQHC model, Jon expressed concern and frustration with the drastic changes he had witnessed over the past few years. He felt strongly that his employer had deviated from their core values, shifting from a patient-centered to a profit-driven model. The results had been devastating for providers and migrant clients alike. Increased patient volume became a requirement; providers who did not meet these goals were severely admonished: "Mid-level providers like me are expected to see so many patients per year. We have to see 5,000. But most health centers like ours see, like, 2,500 to 2,800 patients per year, almost half the number I have to see." Services like emergency care, which used to be centrally located and provided within the clinic, were now referred out, rendering such care spatially dispersed and inaccessible. "We can do them," Jon said, "but the management feels like we will spend too much time attending to those things than seeing more patients." To add insult to injury, even as services were reduced, administrators' compensation increased to levels higher than at comparable FQHCs. Jon expressed his anger and exasperation: "Our directors are making around $500,000, which is much more than other nearby health centers. These are private practice rates, and so it is all about making a profit. They are not building any new buildings or subsidizing care, so where is the money going? It is going to management." Jon and some of his colleagues have been outspoken against these changes, but the threat of retaliation prevented them from moving further: "It is a fine line because we can get fired and replaced and who loses in the end? The patients. So we do not want that. We want to stay to care for our patients, but we have to meet these expectations."

FIGURE 3.1 Clinic waiting room. Photo by Emilia M. Guevara.

Community health centers including FQHCs, where most rural providers work, are the main source of comprehensive primary care for those considered medically underserved in the United States (see figure 3.1). Jon's
experiences underscore how rural health care systems, in particular, face
complex difficulties in employing budget-driven measures that began in
the 1990s and continue today.[13] Rising overhead costs and lagging fee-for-
service reimbursement, along with heavy administrative burdens to achieve
necessary certifications and follow required processes for optimal reimbursement, underscore the increasing corporatization of rural health care
systems. Under the ACA, there has been noted growth in the number and
capacity of health centers due to increased patient revenue from Medicaid
expansion, private health insurance, and federal investment.[14] However,
even with such progress in coverage, many of those who use health cen-

ters remain uninsured and underinsured because of increased cost-sharing associated with insurance plans, so they have not experienced marked differences in the level of access since the passage of the ACA.

Jon's experience also reinforces how local providers feel constrained in supporting their immigrant clients when they are already operating with few resources in this rural landscape of care. A key issue related to the health of immigrants on the Eastern Shore is the scarcity of formalized care infrastructures and increasing abandonment by the state. But the lack of institutional care is an issue for all Eastern Shore residents, not just immigrants. Like Jon, many providers stressed the continuous "struggle" to provide patient care to immigrants and nonimmigrants alike because of the severe lack of funding and resources for services and workforce development. Cindy, a county-level health administrator, explained how providers have creatively strategized to deliver migrant health services in the absence of funding. For instance, migrant health services were within the county health department's communicable diseases program. Then it was moved to the health promotion department for a couple of years after a significant loss in funding. Cindy said, "It was a program where we would go out to the camp every day, and I pretty much did nurse case management out there. It was a lot. It was typical case management, so we cared for them if someone came home from the hospital after having open-heart surgery. If we had an end-stage AIDS patient out there, we took care of them. That was phenomenal. I would do that every day of life if I could. And then we lost funding. They cut us significantly, so now we get a $15,000 grant from the state of Maryland, and we beg for that every year."

Many Eastern Shore counties receive over 50 percent of their local health department funds from the state to work with private hospitals, medical societies, voluntary organizations, and others in their communities. As a result, they cannot raise revenue themselves (since per capita income and real estate tax revenues are low).[15] Like Jon and Cindy, many providers involved directly in immigrants' health care and those who provide ancillary social services to immigrants emphasized that it was challenging to support immigrant clients whose needs were more than what they had the capacity to manage. Tina, a local social services administrator, expressed what I often heard. "I think the hardest one is when they do have the intrinsic motivation to do something different, and I have to say I can't support you and your family for the twenty-fours months that it is going to take you to do this. The funding just is not there. We cannot fully support a family while they go to school. They have to be able to work part-time and do different things. I think that is the hardest part that we deal with. We all work really hard. There is a reason they are in our program. So that is really difficult [and] disheartening for the staff and our clients." Providers indicated that these structural challenges created contexts that prevented them from having extensive knowledge of the conditions that affected immigrant clients because immigrants were not regularly accessing care due to lack of insurance, prohibitive costs, and fear of authorities. Laura, a nurse supervisor, felt that she did not know her adult population because they were not getting care: "I am quite sure there is a lot of diabetes, lots of things that we do not know about. Nutrition is always up there. They tell me they do not have enough money for food. We either give them a bag of food or a gift card to go to Walmart to buy some food. Other than being hurt on the job, a lot of them have tuberculosis."

Moreover, providers described racialized sentiment and anti-immigration policy as significant obstacles to providing quality care for the growing immigrant population. Sandra, a social services administrator, felt that providers were not allowed to express opinions that could be considered political. "I think that the system is broken, completely broken, whether or not it has been about incentives for people to migrate into the system." She felt most of her clients were not properly documented and were fearful to stand up for their rights because of their precarious legal status: "What is this doing toward society economically when you have a disenfranchised group competing with local labor? It is a mess all around. I definitely wish that we could figure out a way to fix it. We now have second generations where the parents are still not properly documented. We just announced maybe two or three weeks ago that we were able to serve DACA.[16] Before we were even able to serve the DACA youth, we had to convince the Department of Labor to finally agree with us when we said that you could not discriminate if somebody has employment work authorization just because of how they got it. So we were glad that they were able to see that."

Providers discussed how discriminatory policies and practices inherent within U.S. health care placed individuals at risk, limiting their access to lifesaving treatment because of prohibitive costs and visa regimes. Jon, in a frustrated tone, expressed how continuity of care did not exist in migrant health. He often saw his patients once a year, if he was lucky. A related challenge was making referrals for specialty care within the context of the current system. "We refer people out, and when they need specialty care, we try to work with specialists to give them charity care or help them make the payments in smaller amounts or for a reduced fee," Jon said. "We always try our hardest to do those things, but that is not what [the FQHC] was designed for, and it takes a lot of time to coordinate this. We often do not have the capacity to follow up with the referrals. For instance, a woman needed a hip replacement, and we got her a private doctor to do it, and she had an appointment, but I never followed up to see if she had it done or whether she went back to Mexico to do it because she did not have the money." Like other providers, Jon expressed how he was forced to routinely make medical decisions based on affordability rather than need for his migrant patients: "Some of the day-to-day challenges that I have is to figure out how to diagnose people but also make decisions about affordability—is it necessary to order this test? I do think that the affordability thing comes into play more when I am thinking about a migrant or undocumented patient."

According to providers and administrators like Cindy, Tina, and Jon, the lack of funding for health and social services and health care infrastructure development negatively affects health services and delivery for everyone in rural areas, not just immigrants. Norma, a nurse practitioner who has received several grants from the state health department, was frustrated with the disconnect with funding priorities and the local context. "Right now, they just wrote another $300,000 or $600,000 grant on smoking cessation. And yet, we are the fattest county in the state, and we have so many other problems. Why are we focusing on cigarettes? I believe that it is important, but considering that there is the state fund for tobacco-free programs, why are we going after the same issues, because it is an issue that they are comfortable with." Norma ran her own small rural health clinic and was able to continue to provide select primary care services for migrants. Many others who worked for FQHCs or other facilities felt overburdened and unable to provide quality health care to those who needed primary and specialty care. Dawn, a nurse practitioner who worked with migrants for an FQHC, recounted how she was providing care to only a handful of individuals every several weeks, a drastic shift from the number of patients she usually was asked to see. She lamented in an exasperated tone much like Jon how increasing budget cuts, elimination of provider positions, and a heavy caseload for remaining staff had become a reality for many working in rural health. Her narrative points to the complete corporatization of health care, even among so-called safety nets, where the focus is on fiscal austerity, efficiency, and positive profit margins rather than care: "We have migrant health funding, but it does not do what it is supposed to do because it all goes into federally qualified health clinics. The problem is that they become their own machine, and to meet all the requirements and restrictions, they become top-heavy with administration and very bottom poor with services."

A Struggling, Abandoned System

Immigrants also discussed the uncertainties and struggles of navigating care on the Eastern Shore. Adela, for instance, has lived in Maryland for fifteen years with her family, including her husband and two young daughters. Life in Mexico for her family was difficult at best. They could not find work, and it was tough to survive. Migrating to the Eastern Shore in the hopes of a better future became the only option. Yet Adela's life in Maryland has been equally challenging. For instance, she was able to find work cleaning homes. However, the work is irregular and highly dependent on how she feels that day. Adela lives with chronic pain and suffers from constant headaches and pain in her arms and knees. When the outside temperature rises, her head throbs. She does not know what brings on the pain, and the uncertainty frightens her.

Adela often wonders if the pain is the lingering effect of a debilitating stroke and massive hemorrhage that she suffered in 2003. She was in the hospital for two weeks and lost the ability to speak and express herself. These memories are vivid for Adela; she recalls the terror and confusion she felt in not knowing what was happening to her body. "My tongue turned upside-down. When I walked around, I felt like I was floating. My brain was in shock because I was blank. My brother told me to write what I wanted to say, but my brain would not help me. I just scribbled on some paper, but I do not know why. I knew what I wanted to say, but my brain was not helping me pronounce the letters in my mouth to be able to write." Despite her distress, her doctors did not explain what was happening to her.

Not feeling cared for, and being stuck in the hospital, unable to communicate, became unbearable for Adela. "I could speak very little, pronounce very little, like a little baby. I was dizzy and felt very tired. I felt like I was going around in circles. I felt faint. I could not be my own person because my body would not help me. I could not get up." Her doctors wanted her to stay another week, but Adela refused because she was lonely, sad, and did not like hospitals. Each passing day at the hospital caused her anxiety. Adela tried to ask how she could prevent another stroke, yet her providers did not provide her any information about care on discharge. "I do not know how to take care of myself." After leaving the hospital, she was determined to avoid stress and sunlight in order to stay healthy for her family. Being uninsured also contributed to Adela's anxiety over being hospitalized. Her work hours were inconsistent, and her husband's income was barely enough to cover their basic needs. At the time of her hospitalization, she was not working and her husband earned $300 weekly. "We had to pay the light bill and the girls and everything. I was so stressed out. How was I to pay all of that? I had the will to pay. But with what? We do not have enough. So this was a difficult time for all of us." Adela worried that she would face jail time or litigation if she could not pay. She found help from a small, local religious organization that encouraged her to work with the hospital to find an appropriate repayment plan. "Little by little, we do it," she said. "It does not matter if you owe your entire life. What matters is that you are OK, and they keep taking care of you."

Other immigrant interlocutors, likewise, recounted significant barriers in accessing and using services. They frequently mentioned anti-immigration policies that prevented them from qualifying for public assistance or insurance as a barrier that resulted in a lack of affordable services. But they also understood that health care, even with legalized forms of support, had become prohibitive because of the high cost of services. Adela, for instance, reiterated that she only sought services when necessary because of the exorbitant cost of care and lack of insurance. Others reported spending hundreds or thousands of dollars for routine and emergency visits. For example, a young woman in her thirties, Miriam, who was documented, recounted how unaffordable the cost of care is. "I spend $250 to walk in the door for an outpatient visit," she said. "Sometimes, if I am really sick, I will go to the hospital, but the hospital is really expensive. Like, you breathe the air, and you have to pay. If you get a shot there, it is like $2,000. It is too much. That is why people won't go to the hospital even if they are really sick. They refuse to go, even if it is serious, because of the cost."

Adela's struggles with affordable and accessible care continued long after her discharge. Her primary physician at the local FQHC—who she described as "Hispanic" and fluent in Spanish—asked her to follow up with a radiologist, but she could not afford to go because each visit cost $500 out-of-pocket. "They wanted to make sure that I did not have a heart attack because my mother had one. They did not want the same thing to happen to me. But I do not have money, so what am I going to do? He said that that is the way it was." She asked for her medical records to determine whether she needed to see a radiologist. The clinic never sent them. Her primary provider has since left, and her new physician does not speak Spanish, making it difficult to communicate about her chronic pain. She told him how the pain prevents her from being able to even bathe, hoping that he might refer her to a "bone doctor" (orthopedic surgeon). But her doctor refused because the office visit and treatment would be too expensive for her to afford. "He told me to come back in two to three weeks, and I would get an injection. I did not know what they were going to do." When she returned, another, different physician, who also did not speak Spanish, administered the injections without explaining their effects.

Many emphasized that FQHCs, safety-net care, and migrant health programs designed to help the poor were extractive because they structurally discriminated against the uninsured. A lack of infrastructure, the high cost of health care services, and the large number of uninsured patients living in the area limited timely access to quality care. Jorge, a young man in his twenties, recounted like Adela how difficult it was to get care because of long wait times: "Sometimes you wait for an appointment, and they ignore you because there are a lot of people who do not have insurance. Lots of people who do not have money or the undocumented that cannot obtain insurance go there. So, sometimes you wait a long time." Max, a father of four who worked at the tomato canning plant, emphasized that "people here use the emergency room for medical care because they can't afford to go regularly." Thomas, likewise, noted that many Haitians like him felt that health systems existed only to make money from ill and dying people because they focused solely on profit rather than care. He recounted a close friend's harrowing experiences at a nearby hospital: "One of my friends, sick, went to the hospital. She is tired and [she] sleep, sleep, sleep. After couple hours, when she wake up, she say she feel OK. No pain, nothing. Wait for the doctor, but after sleep, no pain and [she] go home. After couple weeks, they send a bill to her. But the doctor did not see her. Listen up, that is bad," Thomas said. "If you are Medicaid, that is fine. If you do not have Medicaid, they do not care about it. You can die if you do not have Medicaid because when you have Medicaid, they can get money. They see exactly where they get money. Only then they take care of you."

Others like Henri expressed that prohibitive costs and inaccessibility were more of a barrier to obtaining care than fear of deportation among undocumented people. "I think the fear [of detainment and deportation] is not the barrier for us; 75 percent is not related to immigration-related papers." Close to 5 percent of the state's residents, or approximately 275,000 people, are undocumented immigrants.[17] Many have described Maryland as "inclusive" in enacted legislation or public acts supporting undocumented immigrants.[18] For instance, Maryland provides undocumented immigrants the ability to obtain noncompliant driver's licenses or identification cards. It also does not have an enacted statewide policy regarding how agencies collaborate with the Immigration and Customs Enforcement (ICE) agency. Instead, local jurisdictions decide whether to cooperate with federal authorities on civil immigration enforcement.[19] Although the Cecil County Sheriff's Office officially participates in the 287 (g) program, allowing local law enforcement agencies to engage in federal immigration enforcement activities, none of the other Eastern Shore counties have publicly cooperated with ICE.

Poor quality and timely care, lack of access, high cost of services, and routine discrimination wore people down and wasted their time, even those with resources. Cristina, a single mother, described the sheer exhaustion and uncertainty in navigating the landscape of care as an immigrant who was easily able to access services: "I have been all over, and what I don't like is that when I bring my son in, I tell them that he has whatever symptoms, and they maybe do a cursory look at him, give him some pills, and that is it. I feel they do not do a detailed, comprehensive checkup. It is usually just half-done," Cristina said. "If you want more, you have to go all over the place. They do not have Spanish speakers in every clinic, and you are sent elsewhere. Sometimes, they won't see you. They do not want to help. I had a problem with my molar, and I went to an FQHC dentist, and then they sent me to another place where they asked me for identification, Social Security, and my insurance. If I didn't have any of those things, what would I have done? So, they are asking me for all of these things or insurance; then they might not see you. That is what I understood."

Further, Adela, like many, found it difficult to understand interactions with providers without a translator. Although the FQHC has Spanish-speaking translators on-site, they are in short supply. Adela experiences long wait times at the clinic, and by the time she is seen by a provider, the translators have left for the day. "The interpreters leave at 5:00 P.M. I was supposed to have my appointment at 4:15 P.M., but they finally got to me in the evening. I thought they forgot about it. The doctor was surprised to see me and asked if I had been there the whole time because they closed at 7:00 P.M. I told her that I had been waiting since 4:00 P.M." Sometimes, when she can, Adela schedules care appointments in the afternoon so that she is able to bring her daughter after school to help with translation. Translation services for immigrants had drastically improved in the last decade, and the demand for language interpreters continued to outpace availability, leaving many people like Adela without adequate support. Demaris, an older woman who had been using the local FQHC for several years, confirmed what I heard

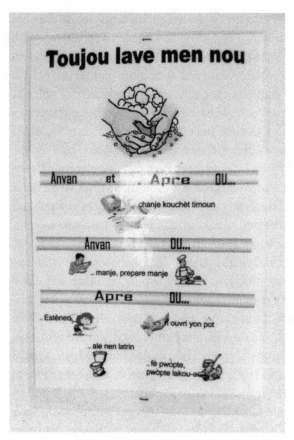

FIGURE 3.2 Handwashing instructions in Haitian Kreyòl.
Photo by the author.

often: "[The clinic] only has one Spanish translator. That translator has to work between dental as well as medical." Toni revealed that translation services were nonexistent at one of the few hospitals in the area: "Despite being a state-funded community hospital, they are not at all friendly toward the immigrant population. I do not even know that they have a Spanish-language translator staff."

Still, interpretation for non-Spanish-speaking immigrant groups, such as those who speak Haitian Kreyòl, was rarely available or nonexistent (see figure 3.2). A Haitian Kreyòl-speaking interlocutor said in frustration, "You know the main issue is that the Haitian community does not even have a Kreyòl translator. They have nothing. They do not have any information." Many complained of interpreters who deliberately mistranslated information because they looked down on poor immigrants. A family member, for instance, described a clinical encounter between her aunt and a translator: "I am listening to the translator and the provider, and there was so much lost I was just shocked. I could not believe what he did not translate. There were all kinds of things being said that he just threw out the door."

Care in Unlikely Places

Even with persistent challenges in accessing and receiving adequate care, immigrant interlocutors remarked that they received better support and care from a handful of providers on the Eastern Shore than in other places. Some revealed that if they had stayed in other states or countries, they would not have received the same type of care or survived. Adela, for instance, was adamant that her circumstances in navigating and accessing care on the Eastern Shore were better than in Mexico, asserting: "If I had been in Mexico, they would have let me die. Here, good or bad, they give you a payment plan." Carmen, who migrates with her family from Florida to the Eastern Shore every season, noted that the care she receives on the Eastern Shore is far better than any of the other states she passes through, including Florida, Georgia, and North Carolina. Her wait times have drastically improved from four or five hours to less than three hours. "Here, I can get in and out pretty quickly, and some doctors are trying their best to be helpful. I noticed those details. Because if my child is sick, they always try to help. When it comes to my kids, I like the way they deal with them. More than anything, it is the health services that help a lot. For the kids and me, if I go to the hospital, they help me very quickly," she said. "Or if I go to the clinic, they help me. I have not gone yet this year, but the care has been really good in previous years. I am setting up dental and medical care appointments right now."

Likewise, Lud, who lived at the migrant camp owned by a national tomato company, explained that he routinely migrates to the Eastern Shore from Florida during the summer months. Lud described in detail how he planned his medical visits according to labor migration patterns and delayed his visits until he arrived in Maryland. He describes how clinic vans pick up migrants directly from labor camps and drop them off after appointments, which he insists is a luxury compared to other states. Lud has been migrating from Florida to Maryland for thirteen years, and he confirms what providers like Jon and Norma have reiterated—health services have disappeared or been constricted over time. He mentions that they have not had a health fair yet, even though they typically have three or four throughout the tomato picking season. The mobile clinic also stopped running the last couple of years, and nurses, who used to go daily, only go to the labor camp a couple of times a week.

Despite the reductions in services, Lud is emphatic that care on the Eastern Shore is better. To make his point, he angrily recounts his experiences with racialized health care in Immokalee, Florida. He reveals that the last time he sought care in Immokalee was three years ago. He arrived at the clinic at 7:00 A.M. and was still waiting to see the provider at 2:30 P.M. Lud has asthma and was upset because he missed work to come to the clinic. After waiting all day in pain, he decided to go home. A clinic supervisor called him at home and asked if he wanted to come back: "I said, 'No, I am not coming back. Remember, anything happens to me, you guys in charge.' I spend seven, eight hours and sit right here. I got asthma, and nobody care about that. [The supervisor] said, please can you come back. I said, no, I am not coming back. I already spent my time, and I do not have that much. So, since then, I decide I do not go over there no more. The system is not working, and it is discrimination because I'm Black." He insists that on the Eastern Shore, providers like Jon treat him more reasonably: "They just treat everyone the same at the clinic when you go. So I think that is a fair shot. It is different when you go to Immokalee." Lud reveals that he values his care in Eastern Shore so much that he stopped getting care in Immokalee. When I ask him how he can keep up with his treatments for asthma, he reveals that he gets enough refills to last him until the following year. "I go just when I am leaving and tell them I am leaving and need a refill and they write extra prescriptions to last me a year," Lud said. "They are doing everything they are supposed to do over here to keep me alive and healthy."

The Rural Landscape of Care

Focusing on the inherent relations between immigration and the precarity of rural health reorients long-standing categories of care and belonging. For example, health scholars have discussed chronic shortages of providers and services in rural areas.[20] Yet they often overlook how such spatial, temporal, and racial aspects of a lack of formal health care may disproportionately affect immigrants, who may face even fewer opportunities to obtain routine care and treatment than native residents. Likewise, a robust scholarship in anthropology has pointed to the dire disparate health outcomes and the social suffering of immigrants without foregrounding spatial, temporal, and racialized contexts in which such experiences and effects unfold.[21] On the Eastern Shore, the domains of immigration and rural health are not conceptually distinct.

Instead, they couple in spatial, temporal, and racially salient ways to shape daily life. Federal and state-level designations categorize the landscape of care on Maryland's Eastern Shore as spatially deficient and in need of enhanced benefits and support for population health. But providers' and immigrants' narratives indicate that despite specialized federal resources, diminishing health infrastructures, high health expenditure, and discriminatory policies prevented immigrants and rural residents from obtaining health insurance, saddled them with high health care costs, and augmented health care inequities. This violent cycle unfolding in rural health conceals the exploitation of immigrant bodies and rural spaces for profit and the ways that people and places function as forms of capital. MUA/MUP designations, along with FQHCs and the ACA, portray populations and entire areas as "underserved" and "vulnerable," attributing the problem of poor health and a lack of health infrastructure to the inherent deficiency of immigrants and rural spaces rather than to the external extraction of value from communities and environments by the state and multinational companies.

Rural residents tend to be more often uninsured and more likely to report that health care costs limit their medical care than those living in metropolitan areas.[22] However, these factors affect immigrant populations more severely.[23] There is ample literature — primarily focused on Latinx immigrants — substantiating undocumented immigrants' unwillingness and inability to access care because of fear of deportation and anti-immigration policies.[24] On the Eastern Shore, however, immigrant interlocutors further underscored that weakening infrastructures, diminishing resources, and rising health costs — the spatial and temporal logics that fashion rural care landscapes — were more critical to understanding their experiences. They also described how racial discrimination and poor treatment further complicate access to care for populations that speak Spanish and Haitian Kreyòl. Language barriers, for instance, severely hinder access to health care, impede quality of care, and negatively affect the health outcomes of those with limited English proficiency.[25] Even though gaps in language services exist in health care settings despite a federal policy requiring equal access for those with limited English proficiency,[26] this issue is particularly challenging in rural health settings, which have far fewer resources for such services.

Although the ACA promised to make health insurance accessible for millions of people, including 350,000 uninsured Marylanders, it has not changed the discriminatory exclusions that target recently arrived legal immigrants and those who are undocumented.[27] In Maryland, legal immigrants who have been in the country for less than five years have access to health insurance coverage through insurance exchanges and premium and cost-sharing subsidies. But they are otherwise ineligible for Medicaid. Undocumented immigrants in Maryland, who comprise 17 percent of the state's uninsured population, are not eligible for any coverage under the ACA.[28] As a result, immigrants, especially undocumented, continue to face barriers. They are further dependent on local safety-net providers, despite ACA's full implementation in Maryland.

Exclusive focus on immigrant experiences of health care or crumbling rural health systems overlooks the rural context in which immigrants live and the care relations that exist within them. There has been growing attention to systemic racism in health care, yet much of it focuses on access to quality medical care or poor patient–provider relationships. But as providers and immigrants point out, the significant burden of bureaucracy and high costs plaguing U.S. health care that grinds away at people on a daily basis often in ordinary ways, especially immigrants and the rural poor, is also part of how systemic racism works in health care. FQHCs and safety-net care ensure that everyone has access to health care, but they have to navigate complex pathways to manage health conditions and their general well-being. Providers felt burdened by providing meaningful care to a growing population of immigrants within the context of long-standing resource distribution problems that characterized rural health care. Immigrant interlocutors accessed and used health care services intermittently or only in a dire emergency, strategically seeking out providers and sites responsive to their needs. Institutions and regulations structure the landscape of care on the Eastern Shore, yet providers and immigrants have fashioned it as a space of engagement to reimagine care, aid, and sociality otherwise.

CHAPTER FOUR

Band-Aid Care
Small Fixes and Gaping Wounds

A critic looking at these tightly focused, targeted interventions might dismiss them as Band-Aid solutions. But that phrase should not be considered a term of disparagement. The Band-Aid is an inexpensive, convenient, and remarkably versatile solution to an astonishing array of problems. In their history, Band-Aids have probably allowed millions of people to keep working or playing tennis or cooking or walking when they would otherwise have had to stop. The Band-Aid solution is actually the best kind of solution because it involves solving a problem with the minimum amount of effort and time and cost.

—MALCOLM GLADWELL, *The Tipping Point: How Little Things Can Make a Big Difference*

Is a Band-Aid the right tool for the task? Is it enough? Or might it mask a deeper problem while providing false security? . . . At what point, and under what conditions, might a Band-Aid transmute from a modest improvement into a deceptive response? When does the inflection shift, from doing "a little good" to "little good"?

—PETER REDFIELD, "On Band-Aids and Magic Bullets"

ON A HOT AND HUMID AFTERNOON in early August, I sat down with David, a local physician and community clinic director. David was one of the few in the area who worked with temporary migrant workers and more permanently established immigrant families. It was challenging to get a hold of him during the summer months because it was peak harvest season when many migrant workers travel to the Eastern Shore to work in the region's agricultural, poultry, and seafood industries. David's small community clinic was often full of activity on the days that I had visited. It felt strange to be there when it was quiet and still.

David was highly animated when we began to talk. I sensed he wanted to tell me something right away. Before I even had a chance to ask a question, he recounted an incident that had been ongoing for several weeks, something that he was working on right before I arrived. He explained: "The nicest man came in one day. He was not feeling well. He complained of being tired, but he was very thin, active, and healthy appearing." David decided to run some tests on the man and the results were surprising: "He is just spilling sugar in his urine, and I thought to myself, 'Lord, he's forty-two.' So I asked him, 'Have you ever been told that you have diabetes?'" When the man responded that no one had given him that diagnosis but that his father had diabetes, David decided to do additional tests. "I did the tests as best I could. I get indigent rates from the lab company for certain tests, and I often eat the cost myself and don't even charge the patients. In his case, I told him he had diabetes and had to be on insulin. I have an excellent relationship with the insulin reps, so I told them, 'I have an undocumented gentleman. He can't go through patient assistance.'"

David paused for a moment before continuing, surveying my face to see if I understood his patient's predicament: "There are patient assistance programs through the pharmaceutical company if you are poor, but if you're undocumented, you are *nothing*. So I got the reps to give me the medicine for him." He went on, "He ended up in someone else's care. They called me and said, 'Why are you doing this to this man? He can't afford this medicine. He does not pay for it.' They said I could not continue to do this for him. I said,

'Why not? Nothing is stopping me from continuing to do this for him.' So I have an agreement that when he runs low, he comes by."

When I inquired about what "they" wanted David to do, he responded matter-of-factly: "Put him on regular insulin, which he would have to do every four hours. I have him on a pen that costs about $400 that he can do once a day, and he is doing well. He can't test his sugar before he eats or a sliding scale of insulin because he is in the field!" Then, shaking his head in disbelief, David uttered, "Insulin has to be refrigerated. What are you supposed to do? Have a little fanny pack of ice with him as he goes through the chicken houses that are 110 degrees? So you have to be creative about the environment [in which] they exist. It is difficult at best, but it is difficult for everybody." Referring back to those who chastised him, David declared: "But the hardest problem for them to deal with is that I give him free care, and the point is that they have to purchase medication or services." Then, he paused for what seemed like a long moment, looking past me out the window, and said quietly: "No matter what I do, I feel like I am just putting Band-Aids on things that need stitches."

This chapter examines the everyday work and struggles enacted by immigrants and providers within what David calls "Band-Aid" care through the analysis of recent transformations related to health care and immigration reform, long-standing issues of precarity among rural health systems, and theories of the political and moral economy of health. Spatial, temporal, and racial configurations of unequal access, moral and material exchanges, cultures of relatedness, and the politics of exclusion characterize everyday experiences of health and health care provision in places like Maryland's Eastern Shore. Rather than signifying formal health care systems, these dynamics constitute the landscape of care in rural regions, where moral and material circulations of caregiving and care-seeking mediate and are intensified by the logics of exclusion and inequality. David and other providers on the Eastern Shore applied the metaphor of a Band-Aid to signal temporary, provisional measures they undertake to care for people who require more sustained attention and long-term treatment yet are left out of health care. They used the concept to illustrate the critical inadequacy of existing systems to treat immigrants and the working poor in rural America. Yet the care enacted on the Eastern Shore is far more extensive than the insufficient, modest form of care associated with Band-Aids. The notion underscores the lived ways that people create mutuality and care in the face of precarious economic conditions and a hostile political climate (see figure 4.1). Such modes of improvised care increasingly have become the standard of health and social care

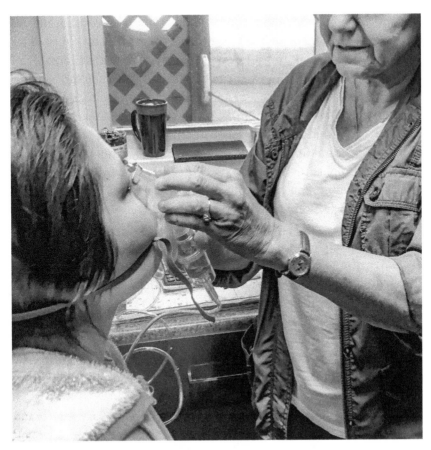

FIGURE 4.1 Medical provider using a nebulizer during a mobile health clinic visit. Photo by Emilia M. Guevara.

provision in many places, including the United States. In his analysis of minor technological fixes to significant, complex issues, Peter Redfield contends, "In their small and flawed utility, little devices can at least open larger questions that otherwise might remain foreclosed."[1] I extend Redfield's argument and maintain that attending to Band-Aid care requires simultaneously examining the impersonal and self-interested logic of formal health care access and a deeper analytical engagement with the landscape of care's interpersonal, relational, and reciprocal nature.

Band-Aid Care in the Field

The challenge of rural health care was a frequent topic of conversation on the Eastern Shore. Immigrants and providers told me that it was impossible to decouple immigration from issues of rural health care provision and delivery. Increased immigration intensified health care precarity in rural regions, and rural precarity made it difficult for immigrants to obtain care and access public resources. People often described these existing care systems for immigrants on the Eastern Shore as Band-Aid solutions or forms of "bastardized care." Over the years, I realized that providers and their immigrant clients enacted Band-Aid care through informal care transactions of medical and nonmedical forms of care such as bartering, rationing, hoarding, willful noncompliance, and goodwill. These transactions were everyday instances in which immigrants and providers negotiated health and other kinds of supportive care within an economically constrained and racially charged environment. Although rural health systems were not a central part of my research interests, what particularly struck me were interlocutors' interpretations of these informal transactions as vital to the understanding of spatial and temporal modes of rural health provision and delivery. I became increasingly interested in why issues of immigration and legal status, although important, did not necessarily foreground the conceptualization and experiences of Band-Aid care in my field site. Instead, I wanted to understand how immigrants and providers came to view such care as a temporary state of permanence in rural health and why informal transactions signified such care landscapes.

Band-Aid describes the care seen as a quick-fix or temporary remedy and underscores the temporal logic of crisis itself. Inherent in this description is that such care fails to address the broader, longer-term needs of those deemed most vulnerable.[2] However, David and others engaged in various types of health and social care practices that were not limited to addressing the immediate health needs of immigrants. Band-Aid care maintained and made life possible on the Eastern Shore. Christine, a social services provider and nurse, told me: "Anybody who is a provider knows that when somebody comes in, you can see their leg is practically ready to explode. But they are busy telling you their car broke down because that is the most important thing they need. So long ago, we learned to say, 'What is the most important thing that's happening at this minute? Let's deal with that.' We honor what they think is a priority to stabilize their situation. We do what we call 'stabilize the family,' interacting with landlords, utility companies, car mechanics, automobile insurance dealers, courts, and public defenders." Care, as Christine explains, is both a response to immediate individual affliction and a means to act on the possibility of everyday living.

The precise use of Band-Aid care in anthropological literature is hard to come by. Nevertheless, anthropologists have documented the notion of such care in various resource-poor settings or whenever people have had to navigate complex and tenuous circumstances related to providing and receiving care. Scholarship on therapeutic itineraries, for instance, has illustrated how care seekers traverse dizzying circuits of ill-coordinated state and non-state institutions, care providers, and treatment options in places struggling with shifting political, economic, and health structures.[3] For instance, in their work on parents' health-seeking practices for their children in rural and urban Guinea, Melissa Leach and colleagues argue that people's pursuit of health care in an emergent African therapeutic landscape can no longer be limited to common spatial and temporal distinctions between the traditional and the modern and public versus private.[4] Instead, they illustrate that in places struggling with weak political and economic structures and an unregulated rise in health providers and treatment options, residents often make critical decisions about care-seeking based on diverse forms of expertise. These include choices based on their own experiences of caring for children, multiple framings of health issues and treatment options, and emergent forms of social solidarity. There is no unified health system but many contexts which influence Guinean parents' care-seeking experiences. Therapeutic landscapes, in this regard, represent material and symbolic forms of care-seeking and care provision mobilized by social networks that are understood and (re)fashioned through everyday experience and practice. This scholarship richly documents how such therapeutic itineraries have increasingly become the norm in the Middle East and Africa, even as they pose considerable challenges for those who seek care.[5]

Similarly, scholarship on U.S. health care safety nets has also documented the experiences of the poor and uninsured within a loosely organized collection of publicly subsidized hospitals, local health departments, clinics, and individual providers. These safety nets offer free or low-cost care, illustrating how this care is continually at risk of disappearing because of market pressure, public spending reductions, and patient demand increases.[6] This literature has focused on health care safety nets as outgrowths of various neoliberal policies and programs and the multiple roles undertaken by providers in the process of helping clients navigate complex public welfare systems.[7] In many ways, this scholarship on U.S. safety nets focuses on noncitizens and others who lack mobility and entitlements to health care, such as immigrants and the working poor—those the literature on therapeutic itineraries sometimes overlooks. Specifically, scholars have documented how the embodiment of the complex dynamics of exclusion—economic exploitation, political marginalization, social discrimination—leads to immigrants' physical and emotional suffering, including the internalization of individual and collective unworthiness. These exclusionary forces also propel popular constructions of immigrants as an "undeserving" and "illegitimate" social group, further restricting their access to and use of health care services and exacerbating stress and poor health. This scholarship powerfully illustrates how the enactment of the right to health for immigrants occurs through moral claims and personal values and commitments rather than formal legal interpretations rooted in universality and equality.

The notion of the Band-Aid also builds on the ethnographic accounts of mutuality and cooperation in uncertain and improvised care settings.[8] Rina Praspaliauskiene's concept of "enveloped care"—informal monetary and nonmonetary exchanges between patients, families, and providers—encapsulates how ambiguous forms of exchange engender mutuality as a routine practice of health and care.[9] Likewise, Julie Livingston's work on the only cancer ward in Botswana identifies adaptive or informal strategies that providers, patients, and families use while under challenging circumstances, illustrating how improvisation is a fundamental aspect of health care provision and delivery in highly under-resourced and unpredictable contexts.[10] The spatial and temporal dynamics of improvisation were a central feature of providers' work and life on the Eastern Shore. Providers often used the concept of "creativity" to signal these types of informal and unofficial engagements. Laura, a nurse practitioner, for instance, recounted the story of a migrant client in Texas who was diagnosed with having a mass in her breast; she then migrated to the Eastern Shore without a follow-up for an ultrasound. She came to see Laura with only the referral for the ultrasound procedure: "I do not have the original mammogram. I do not have anything to follow up with, and I have got to figure out how to get her over to the hospital, which has very limited hours for mammography, without impacting her work environment. She also has no insurance. And so you get very creative."

Health workers were not alone in this type of improvisation. Immigrants also improvised. Isabelle told me that when she first came to the United States, she was undocumented and cleaned houses to make ends meet: "I worked for very good women who let me clean for them. The people who I assisted were doctors' wives, lawyers' wives. It was not like come here, work for me like a housemaid. They would say, 'Isabelle, come and bring the bill.'

One family paid for my insulin at Walmart for eight months. Another paid my schooling fees for two years. So this is how I would get by." Through her professional and personal network, Isabelle also developed a close friendship with Maribel, an immigration consultant at a migrant farmworker organization. Maribel used her expertise in immigration to help Isabelle apply for permanent resident status: "I have always had people, really good people around me [like Mari]. My neighbor drives me to appointments, and my son helps me find the medications online. I am lucky." Although Isabelle's case is somewhat uncommon, it illustrates how many immigrants actively navigated complex care systems in unintended and informal ways. Practices such as dispensing and receiving high-cost treatments for free or for a low cost, or in exchange for other resources or services, are part of a complex moral economy of care that is increasingly common among those living and working in Maryland's Eastern Shore. For both providers and immigrants, improvisation highlighted the particular and ongoing decisions and practices in providing "good enough" care beyond formal therapeutic interventions and sites.[11]

Informal Care Transactions

Informal transactions constitute the everyday work of Band-Aid care on the Eastern Shore. Providers and immigrants engaged in informal transactions as a means to negotiate care within a landscape comprised of rural precarity and against the backdrop of growing political uncertainties related to immigration and health care reform. Such transactions worked to produce new alignments of social relations and alternate values of place and personhood. They also engender a particular kind of relationship between informal and moral economies.

Bartering

I had heard of numerous accounts of bartering practices—the exchange of goods or services without using money—from those seeking care. Diego, for instance, told me that his provider often offered to "write off" the cost of his care because he was undocumented and uninsured. But Diego was explicit about paying whatever amount of cash or goods he had on him: "Hispanics have a lot of pride. I don't want to do it for free, so we have a system already set up where my doctor will charge me like $20 or whatever I have that day." Others were also able to negotiate down certain costs of care with various providers, sometimes on their own or with the help of other providers.

Some providers were equally open about engaging in bartering practices. Mary, a nurse practitioner who worked in a small, impoverished community, constantly worried about the affordability of primary medical care for her patients and bartered care for goods and services with new immigrants and long-time residents alike: "When I say that they can pay me with whatever their product is, I actually mean it, and they have finally understood that." When I asked for specific examples, she explained: "Ana is the best tamale maker in the world, and she would come with her kids. My rule has always been if I take care of your children who are insured, I take care of the family for free, whether they are insured or not. It's about family medicine. I need them to buy their medicine, and so I'll say to them, 'Please don't pay me. Please buy your medicine.'" Mary walked over to the refrigerator, opened it, and showed me some of the tamales Ana had given her that she had stashed away. Bartering practices also aligned with temporal and spatial ebbs and flows of local subsistence patterns. For instance, Mary described how she handled the seasonal shifts that threatened to disrupt the exchange: "I do this with my watermen. They pay me with crabs. At this time, I get crabs, and in the winter, I get oysters. From January through April, they do not have harvests, so I do not accept anything. They then say they have me on crab consignment." Mary pointed to some boxes next to the tamales: "Actually, I have three pounds of crab in my refrigerator right now from payment today."

Similarly, Ana, who I knew to be undocumented and therefore did not have any means of accessing medical or other forms of care from the state, was reasonably comfortable bringing her children to Mary's clinic to receive routine preventive care. Ana's children were born in the United States and as citizens had public insurance, qualifying through the state's insurance program for low-income families. Mary's moral reading of "family medicine," to provide care for all family members regardless of their ability to pay or their insurance status, as well as her stance that Ana and other undocumented immigrants should have the right to receive health care, motivates her to offer care. Ana and others are heavily dependent and rely entirely on select providers like Mary for care, and they are obliged to comply with moral directives to engage in follow-up care and purchase treatment regimens in exchange for vital care.

Rationing

Rationing is the limiting of goods or services that are in high demand and short supply. Often, people discuss how governments or institutions undertake rationing as a way of mitigating the impact of scarcity and dealing with economic challenges. Here, immigrants and providers practiced forms of rationing to ensure that they had care or were able to offer care to others. For instance, emerging literature has documented the negative impacts of policing on immigrants' care-seeking strategies.[12] However, many on the Eastern Shore avoided (or rationed) care until they faced medical emergencies because of high costs, not policing. Alba told me firmly: "If I get sick, I hold out as long as I can until I absolutely have to go to the doctor." When I asked her to why, she continued: "I do like the doctor, but sometimes you spend so much money. I do not go because I save the money for other things."

Others used a combination of formal therapeutic options and alternative forms of care. Monica, for instance, purchased health insurance through the Affordable Care Act (ACA), but the plan she was able to afford provided only minimal coverage for services. Her diabetes medications were still too expensive for her to afford, even with insurance. She was adamant that she could manage her diabetes by rationing her prescribed medication and swallowing live *gorgojos chinos*, or Chinese weevils, shipped in from Mexico. She believed the substances released by the insect in her stomach could control her diabetes. Juan Carlos, an undocumented farmworker who lived in a labor camp, was diagnosed with kidney stones. He was charged thousands of dollars for an MRI (a medical imaging technique that generates images of the body's anatomy) at a local hospital. He was too afraid to go back for additional treatment. His recourse was to buy herbs from Mexico to treat his kidney stones: "It has a funny name, and we call it Oaxacan tea. But you take it, and that water disintegrates the stones. So I asked around, and there is a man who sells these things here. He was going to get some things from Mexico, and he asked if I wanted some. I said yes, please send them. So he sent me the herbs." He continued: "I've been taking it here, and I feel fine."

Likewise, a key tactic used by Rhonda and other providers I encountered was to modify normative modes of treatment when working in nonclinical spaces such as migrant camps or housing, often prescribing generic or cheaper medication. Rhonda, a nurse, detailed how temporal and spatial disruptions to care and treatment are the norm within this landscape. Available work requires migrants to be highly mobile in order to coordinate their life with the harvest season. U.S. health care systems are not equipped to handle people who experience a high degree of mobility, and health care delivery and treatment are premised on immobile, fixed populations. Rhonda explained: "They do not get continuity of care. They do not get follow-up on what has been started. High blood pressure is outrageous. They can stroke out at any time. I can't treat as aggressively as I would with high blood pressure and diabetes because if they stop some of these meds, they will stroke out. So I have to say, 'OK, we will start this. Did you need more? Follow up with your doctor when you get back home because this will not be enough,' and I focus on the $4 medicine. Or $10 for three months." While sophisticated medicines and treatment options for chronic conditions such as diabetes and high blood pressure certainly exist in the United States, these options remain elusive for many in this landscape of care because of the high cost of treatment. Rather than what some might consider "inappropriate prescribing" resulting from wrong medical decisions, Rhonda practiced therapeutic rationing where she prescribed affordable regimens given her intimate knowledge of high drug costs and migrant clients' lack of prescription drug insurance coverage. Rhonda paused to gather her words: "Because if we put them on some fancy medication that I got as a sample, they could not afford it. You have got to be realistic."

Hoarding

Sara, a physician, told me about the strategies she employs to deal with her large caseload, which included hundreds of migrant men and women working throughout the Eastern Shore. Sara performs a system of "triage" to prioritize those based on illness, injury, severity, prognosis, and resource availability. She admits that given her heavy caseload and the long distances she has to travel, she can only focus on people in extreme medical distress during her visits to remotes areas. The topic of triage and treatment, especially the scarcity of prescription medications, was a key component of conversations between Sara and the rest of her care team. Many migrant workers, however, did not receive care even when Sara's mobile clinic was in operation. Because the mobile clinic operated approximately once a week, sometimes women waited in line and still did not get seen because the mobile clinic ran out of time. Women were not often seen for weeks because the mobile clinic did not have enough time to visit. Migrant workers frequently lined up for hours to request medications—ranging from ointments for rashes to high blood pressure treatments—even though Sara and her staff could not provide a thorough examination and assessment during their visit. Sara had devised a way to get around this constant source of tension about the lack of time and resources. She stockpiled extra medication as a way of providing care to those she could not see directly. She ordered medications in bulk given her caseload, and often, local pharmacies provided duplicate prescriptions by mistake. Sometimes medications were never picked up or delivered to the person in question because of the limited time or availability of care. However, because she was working with a severe shortage of staff and resources, instead of reporting these mistakes or throwing the medications away, Sara would carefully save these prescriptions for use by other clients in the future, what she called "a rainy day." Sara accumulated these medications and then dispensed them to clients she could not triage or who could not come into the clinic to be seen or did not have money to get prescriptions. These were ways Sara circumvented the precariousness of health care provision and delivery, especially for immigrants.

Similarly, many documented and undocumented Latinx and Haitian farmworkers on the Eastern Shore, most of whom migrated north from Florida during the summer months, explained that they often waited to receive care in Maryland through the state-sponsored subsidized migrant program. At the local federally qualified health center (FQHC), immigrants found ways to amass enough medication until their return the following season. William, for instance, has diabetes. Since he began to work for a local contractor three years ago, he has spent the summers in Maryland. Like so many others, he was hesitant to seek health care in Florida because of racism and rations his medication obtained from Eastern Shore providers: "It is better. I would rather go to the clinic right here every day than go once a year there. I like the way they treat people over here. When I am about to go back to Florida, I tell them I am leaving and need a refill. They give me medication that lasts me for six months, maybe a year. I space them out, so I have enough until I come back."

Willful Noncompliance

Both providers and immigrants demonstrated various modes of willful noncompliance with bureaucratic mandates. Such practices ranged from looking the other way to deliberately refusing to comply with rules and regulations related to formal health care provision mandates. Cassie, a nurse, for instance, frequently kept immigrant clients on a low-cost migrant health plan even though they no longer qualified. These clients were former farmworkers who decided not to return to farmwork. Recently, a local poultry processing plant with over $6 billion annual sales recruited two of her longtime clients, both Haitian immigrants. They were thrilled to find full-time jobs at the plant so they could stay in the area almost permanently. However, the plant did not offer insurance for the first three months of employment, a practice that contradicts continuity of care, a key component promoted by the ACA.[13] Articulating the immediacy of her clients' suffering, Cassie stated: "They are diabetics. They could not afford their insulin. They were so desperate for their insulin. They came back to me, and I ordered their insulin and their diabetic meds because they could not make it otherwise. They were trying to get through their ninety days at the poultry plant. That was their only chance at any life."

Anne, a local clinic director, also reluctantly revealed that she often ends up giving "free" care to those without the ability to pay by not reporting the interaction, disrupting a critical step in the order of standard health care delivery. "So, I often eat the cost myself and don't even charge the patients," Anne said. "It is just easier for me to document nothing big. Sometimes this population comes to me at the end of the day, once they are done in the fields. So it is five o'clock at night, and they walk in the door at night and say, 'I have a bladder infection or vaginal discharge,' and it will be an undocumented female, and I say, 'Come on back, let's get it over with and just do it.' It is so much easier."

Ernesto, a local charity care provider, discusses how he deliberately avoids verifying legal documentation when helping his clients access social resources. "They all have false social securities," he said. "If I am filling out an application, I say to them, 'Do me a favor when you get home; this is the social that you have.' Not that I think I would run into trouble because I am sure everything else I am filling out is fine, so I do not worry about that. And if I call an agency, they will say to me, 'I need their social,' and I will say, 'I can give you their birthdate.' 'Alright. But you don't have their social?' 'No, I don't.' I try not to say they do not have a social."

Nina, an immigrant herself, similarly circumvents authenticating legal documents. "I had a case where this person needed help. He took out his green card. I can't say yes, but I was 95 percent sure that it was fake," she said. "I did not ask for anything or ask any questions, so I did not have to know. I played dumb. I made the photocopy, and I gave it back. And he is a client of ours. My colleagues do not have a green card to begin with, because they are all citizens. All the green cards look the same to them. I have a green card, so I know what it is like."

Rovert and Esther, a Haitian couple, obtained legal status through the Temporary Protected Status (TPS) program. They chose not to purchase health insurance because it is unaffordable. The ACA requires taxpayers to have full insurance coverage, claim an exemption, or pay an individual mandate penalty tax, and many like Rovert and Esther elect to pay a monetary fine for remaining uninsured instead of purchasing health insurance.[14]

Rovert explained: "I do not have the money for insurance. I just can't afford it. Now they are charging me and taking from my IRS money because I do not have insurance. It is Obama's law. If you do not have insurance, they take that money from you." They tried to enroll in the ACA but made too much to qualify for free care. Yet their options for insurance remained financially prohibitive. I asked them what they will do. Esther pronounced that she would continue to overlook the legal mandate: "I will wait for another government. They have got to change that."

Goodwill

Providers also used the goodwill of personal networks and contacts to support immigrants, while others worked with immigrants outside the scope of their formal work duties and hours. Rosa, a social services provider who herself was an immigrant and had lived on the Eastern Shore for decades, described how she has taken clients, on off-work hours, to the post office to get passport pictures or to fill out forms. When friends give her clothing, she distributes it to her most needy clients. For Christmas, when local agencies give out presents for poor children, she directs her clients to put their children's names on the list so they can get backpacks for school or other presents. Maria, a social worker, cared for her immigrant client, Valeria, for several weeks as she recovered from major surgery so she would receive postoperative care in her home and have help caring for her children. Others like Dana, a social service provider at a small community center, helped operate an emergency food pantry and a thrift center, conducted health screenings and counseling, and provided immigration and housing assistance (see figure 4.2).

When Maryland began issuing "second-tier" driver's licenses that allowed undocumented immigrants to drive, register cars, and obtain insurance, many pro-immigration advocates heralded the move as highly progressive. Yet, getting driver's licenses was challenging for many immigrants, involved enormous bureaucracy, and was costly. For example, the most significant worry for Dana's undocumented clients was the need to show proof of residency using a lease or utility bill to obtain these licenses. "It is a problem because they have so many people sharing housing; then if the lease is in one person's name, it eliminates everyone else," Dana said. To circumvent unexpected barriers that would prevent clients from obtaining this valuable resource—identification—Dana worked outside the spatial confines of her professional networks. She engaged closely with a trusted group of personal

FIGURE 4.2 Charity thrift store. Photo by Emilia M. Guevara.

contacts who were landlords willing to continuously amend leases to reflect new tenants for the sole purpose of allowing individuals to obtain licenses. As she explained, "I have clients with landlords that know them, trust them, and know that they pay their rent all the way on time. Once one person settles, the landlord will rewrite the name, so that year they do not extend it or make it fake, but they just add the person to the lease and take the one who has the driver's license off the lease."

Goodwill was also reciprocal. Carmen and her husband Gabriel were naturalized citizens. They had known Mariana, an immigration advocate who helped them become naturalized citizens, for over two decades and had developed a deep friendship over this period. Carmen and Gabriel lived in the Eastern Shore from April to October, working as temporary farm laborers, and then returned to Zacatecas, Mexico, for the remaining months. Mariana visited them frequently in Mexico. When Mariana's husband had died a decade earlier, Carmen was one of the first people to get in touch with her to provide emotional support to her and her son during a difficult time. Carmen and Gabriel also helped Mariana care for her son regularly while on the Eastern Shore.

Exchanges and Economies

Pluralistic forms of exchange, both material (e.g., monetary) and moral (e.g., obligation, reciprocity), ground these informal negotiations around Band-Aid care, signaling intimate connections between care-seeking and provision and broader transformations in governance and social and economic relations. For example, in tracing the effects of the introduction of antiretroviral treatments on the HIV/AIDS epidemic in Francophone West Africa, Vinh-Kim Nguyen states, "Therapy always involves a form of exchange and is embedded in 'regimes of value.' An exchange may be monetary, as in the purchase of medicines, or it may constitute 'moral economies' as individuals call on networks of obligation and reciprocity to negotiate access to therapeutic resources, thus drawing attention to the constraints that shape therapeutic itineraries."[15] Informal transactions on the Eastern Shore likewise highlight the circulations of exchange, value, and social relations. However, within formalized health care delivery in the United States, marked by health consumerism and profit, the importance of the private health insurance industry, and exclusionary provisions related to poverty, racism, and citizenship, these transactions are illicit, even illegitimate, and ultimately forbidden.[16]

Providers and immigrants who engaged in dynamic and fluid caregiving and care-seeking transactions were surveilled, criticized, and marginalized for their participation. In addition to David, whose story introduced this chapter, others were often warned or punished by their supervisors and others. According to Jennifer, a social worker, "There was an undocumented man, and I would talk to him in Spanish because you never know. I was able to get his paperwork worked out. I was not supposed to do that, but I was not giving him legal advice or anything. He just needed help." She continued with another example: "There was another client who had a case with us related to work, and he needed to return to Florida. He had no money. I bought him a ticket, and I put it on a credit card. They admonished me because I should not have done that—it was not my job. But what to do?" When asked if she would continue to do this despite the possibility of negative consequences, she replied that she would do it again but not tell anyone. "How could you leave someone in the street like that? If someone needed help, I am supposed to say no? I can't."

Others have written about ethical dilemmas providers face in the rationing of care in this therapeutic economy, particularly on whether their participation implicitly continues to maintain support for existing politics of exclusion.[17] Rural providers, in many ways, routinely struggle with the realization that their temporary measures to ensure health services have become the norm, as part of the rural health infrastructure. Moreover, in caring for the uninsured and undocumented, providers permit relegating care to the realm of humanitarian aid instead of the state.[18] The durability of Band-Aid care and providers' discomfort about the growing permanency of their services in many ways illustrates the synchronization of the work of the humanitarian sector to the rationale of state-sponsored health care. The resulting ongoing and coextensive relationship between the two expands neoliberal governance practices, reaffirming the state's humanitarian values while avoiding obligations to ensure entitlements. David confirms how this affects providers: "The biggest hurdle I deal with, whether it be migrant or the settled population, is that many do not have insurance. I can do what I can to provide, to help them out and provide free care, but when they need specialty services, there is *nothing*. Then, when you add in [undocumented status] and you just start stacking all these issues, the hurdles become higher than the average person."

Many interlocutors felt that the ACA sustained inequitable neoliberal policies because it left the current corporatized, for-profit model intact and failed to regulate insurance claims. In addition, no price adjustments of any kind were permitted when determining pharmaceutical prices in Medicare. The benefits offered by the ACA also vary based on state requirements and whether or not Medicare expansion has been initiated, with no clear guidelines for other health services like alternative medicine, vision, dental, or mental health care services.[19] Other effects of the ACA include inadequate coverage under both private and public plans, higher cost-sharing requirements, privatization of Medicaid programs by some states, accelerated consolidation of hospital systems, and decreased funding for safety-net hospitals.[20] Furthermore, the ACA substantially increases the number of individuals who have health insurance.[21] But 13 million legal immigrants and 11 million undocumented immigrants are not covered since the ACA left intact earlier restrictions for immigrants (e.g., the Personal Responsibility and Work Opportunity Reconciliation Act and the Illegal Immigration Reform and Immigrant Responsibility Act). Congress designed the ACA to be firmly restrictive to thwart immigrants' access to public benefits, prohibiting undocumented immigrants from receiving any benefits and imposing a time restriction for legal immigrants from accessing Medicaid benefits.

Such enactments to provide care in the absence of a rights-based notion of health and health care access on the Eastern Shore increasingly occur through claims articulated around the moral economy of health care—shaped by social and cultural forces and personal values and commitments.[22] Anne and other providers often spoke about a moral responsibility to serve and provide, especially those with minimal means. "You don't ever do this because you want to make money. You do it because you have a passion for it," said Anne. "I often go months without a paycheck. I am okay. I live a decent life. It is perspective. I have got nothing to complain about." Similarly, David, the clinic director, confided: "I have been in settings where people feel very entitled because they are wealthy. Folks who do not have much are often more appreciative and are also more giving than those who have a lot as far as their time or anything they might have. I have always liked working with the underdog." Although such moral imperatives disclose forms of hierarchies and uneven power relations, providers' engagement in Band-Aid care was also a way to act on their commitment to notions of universality, fairness, and equality. As I have documented in previous chapters, providers were steadfast in their belief that immigrants should have entitlements that allowed them to obtain care without constraints, regardless of their legal or economic status. As David told me, "I think that our patients would do better all the way around if they could become legal. I think that is a huge barrier. It's a huge fear." Providers working in this landscape were attuned to the temporal and spatial logics of the precariousness of care. But this moral recognition is constitutive of and mediated by understandings of a fundamental right to health, deeply connected to forms of legal and social belonging.

Place, Personhood, and Precarity

Randall, a physician who traveled to remote and sparsely populated areas of the Eastern Shore to provide care to migrant workers, was down to seeing only a handful of individuals every several weeks. According to Randall, increasing budget cuts, eliminating provider positions, and a heavy caseload for remaining staff became a reality for many rural health workers. He explained that when he started working with immigrants on the Eastern Shore, three to four providers were working full-time in addition to a mobile clinic. His employer suddenly cut the staff positions and the mobile clinic: "It became cost-prohibitive. At least that is what I was told. And then another person just left. And then another person left, and they did not replace her. They said they were advertising, but they could not find anybody. And for three years, it was just me. We know that one provider is not going to be able to touch base with as many people." He recounted working sixty to seventy hours without being paid overtime and routinely having his hours cut. Over the years, Randall's work conditions deteriorated. As a result, the number of patients he can see has drastically dwindled: "I have had to focus on a few camps to give them decent care, and hopefully the rest can get into clinics." He detailed the spatial and temporal logics that structured migrant health delivery: "I used to go out and draw blood in the camp. When you are trying to see fourteen people in fifty minutes, they come with a bag where the label is faded, and it has got your name on it from last year, and they have four things that are really a problem. At the same time, I am trying to process blood, and it is ninety degrees. You need it to get spun down within an hour or so, or else the sample is not good. It clots. I used to do all of that. But then we decided that one person could not do that because I was spending like two hours on getting it processed, and it was time that I had to spend without seeing patients. So I decided I could not do that."

In particular, Randall's experience underscores the continued devaluation and abandonment of rural health care systems by the state and financial institutions, forcing the implementation of cost-saving and profit-motivated measures that began in the 1990s.[23] Operating with already limited resources while serving populations with high levels of mortality and morbidity, rural health systems experienced drastic reductions in hospitals, lower Medicare reimbursement payments for rural providers, and a rise in the consolidation of health care delivery through the formation of care alliances and networks.[24] FQHCs, like the one that Randall worked for, are the main source of comprehensive primary care for those considered medically underserved in the United States. Under the ACA, there has been noted growth in the number and capacity of health centers due to increased patient revenue from Medicaid expansion and private health insurance and federal investment.[25] However, even with such progress in coverage, many of those who use health centers remain uninsured and underinsured because of increased cost-sharing associated with insurance plans and the inability to recruit and retain personnel.[26]

When asked about the continued needs of rural communities such as those on the Eastern Shore, one provider explained the dire situation of rural health delivery in the wake of health care reform: "A dentist? What is that? We do not have an eye doctor in this entire county, and we have one pediatrician. We have *nothing*." These spatial and temporal depictions signifying precarity, deficiency, and scarcity were common among those living on the Eastern Shore. Immigrants described the Eastern Shore as a liminal space—a "land that time forgot," noting its sparse population and rural, isolated landscape. This description suggests the temporal and spatial distinctness of place as isolated, backward, and undeveloped and shapes immigrants' daily lives and feelings of complete isolation from the "outside world." Everyday living in this context for providers and immigrants assumes distinctive racialized temporal and spatial attributes. These features are characterized by seasonality concerning the availability of work and food supply, economic devaluation, political abandonment, racist and xenophobic attitudes, and the general invisibility of rural economic and social life.

Depictions of both place and people as *nothing* signal "how racism operates as an ideological process" (e.g., David's comment in the opening vignette about how formal health care equates undocumented immigrants to nothing). It indicates the devaluation and subsequent abandonment of racialized immigrants *and* rural spaces by government agencies and economic institutions. It also portends precarity as a shared condition in which immigrants and rural regions contend with social, economic, and health insecurities. The Eastern Shore (and rural spaces overall) is deemed disposable because it is primarily a poor and increasingly minoritized space. In her seminal work on the intentional poisoning of the people of Flint, Michigan, Laura Pulido writes, "White people living in a Black space find that their whiteness is of only limited utility in escaping the devaluation associated with poor Black people and places."[27] David, the clinic director, profiled at the beginning of this chapter, speaks directly to how racism is spatial and how white rural residents who live on the Eastern Shore, many of whom are poor, also contend with exclusionary care systems and lack of safety nets when he states, "It is difficult at best, but it is difficult for everybody."

Although precarity implicates some more than others through an unjust and racialized distribution of vulnerability to harm, violence, and death, it is also relational, generating circuits of social connections and belonging through the care of others.[28] Precarity diverges from neoliberal notions of an individualized self and suggests a profound dependence on others and a responsibility to each other in consideration of that precarity. Judith Butler depicts precarity as "living socially, the fact that one's life is always in some sense in the hands of the other. It implies exposure both to those we know and to those we do not know; a dependency on people we know, or barely know, or know not at all." Butler argues for a coalition politics that mitigates against such conditions of vulnerability.[29] The care provided and the recognition of this interdependence as opening up possibilities for a livable life is a political act in itself, one that exceeds the boundaries of legality.

The neoliberal logic that shapes American health care engenders precarity. But precarity is also a generative force for conditions of sociality and interdependence. Band-Aid care and the everyday transactions that characterize it signify and underscore that precarious working and living conditions are not exceptional but rather ordinary facets of life. Band-Aid care also reconsiders American health care as a set of assertions related to our interconnectedness. Immigrants and providers simultaneously forgo and take up particular kinds of care in ways that reaffirm precarity as a configuration of mutual cooperation and concern. Although providers and immigrants have very different stakes in the system, care more broadly (and health care specifically) shapes their common and shared insecurity because the idiom of health on the Eastern Shore signals uncertainty. Health care is a familiar manifestation critical to rural and immigrant precarity and the demoralized sense of self and space that precarity engenders. In the indeterminacy of everyday life on the Eastern Shore—against the backdrop of health care reform, an ongoing immigration crisis, diminishing welfare safety nets, and deepening infrastructures of racial exclusion—precarity entails suffering and anxiety. But it also brings about resourceful ways to react to precarity through the provision and quest for care. Band-Aid care, in many ways, serves as a way for providers and immigrants to enact an *insurgent politics of care* that is suggestive of social relationality and cooperation and where moral and legal dimensions of health care access are continually in flux.

Because it is both far-reaching and communal, care also conditions identities, especially people's sense of being and belonging. In this landscape of care, interdependence, rather than being experienced as a dilemma or hindrance, becomes "the principal mechanism for personhood."[30] Despite experiencing various conditions of precarity themselves, rural providers engage in improvised caregiving. They are often denounced, reprimanded, and marginalized for this labor. Yet, such work confers a sense of obligation and legitimacy by way of moral positioning as caregivers to the neediest of individuals. Immigrants are not simply subjected to obligations to engage in medical care, and their means of navigating these complex landscapes of care are neither passive nor conditional. Most immigrants expressed being supported by providers and incurring material and moral rewards through informal and formal care transactions. They, like their providers, incorporate themselves into a social and moral system in which they generate both ruptured and fluid life rhythms. Such experiences of sociality and interdependence engender opportunities (however fraught) for living—to be something, rather than *nothing*—despite their precarious legal, social, and economic status. Such exchange relations between providers and immigrants in this landscape of care, although still enmeshed in social hierarchies and inequality, are experienced and lived as worthwhile, moral, just, and necessary under the neoliberal logics of exclusion and inequality.

Radical Remedies

Neoliberal reform's impact on rural health systems and rural populations has been severe. Rural health systems consist of scattered formal health institutions that lack integration and coordination. They also encompass individual providers who constitute the only semblance of a safety net. It is a spatial and temporal logic of safety-net patchworks, Band-Aid care, and improvisation that has become the default in many rural regions throughout the United States. Add an increasingly tenuous economic and policy environment to this landscape of care, and it becomes understandable why many of those living on Maryland's Eastern Shore feel that the ACA or state interventions do very little to shift everyday living conditions. This landscape, like an archipelago, is a time-space assemblage that is detached but still connects in its logic as an exemplary and ordinary site of exclusion and linkages between people and places.[31]

This precarity that characterizes rural health systems is intensified for immigrants who must constantly contend with the broader logic of racialized exclusion, exploitation, and extraction at the heart of corporatized health care and immigration reform while seeking care. Frontline providers who care for immigrants are left to improvise forms of caregiving under heavy surveillance and scrutiny. Providers and immigrants engage in informal transactions such as rationing, bartering, hoarding, willful noncompliance, and goodwill as a way to negotiate and navigate this landscape.

These circulations of moral and material exchanges between providers, immigrants, and others strengthen and dynamize social relations and meanings of place fashioned and remade in the context of caregiving and care-seeking. Providers frame informal transactions as a way to provide Band-Aid care that is motivated by moral values and commitments around health care delivery and access, as well as assumptions about immigrants' rights to certain kinds of political and social membership. Although challenges and hurdles by way of social injury exist at every turn for immigrants in such contexts, they are by no means wholly encumbered and left only subjugated by such transactions and the broader landscape of care. They gain entry and access to vital resources through various social entanglements and particular forms of care practices. They also gain recognition as vulnerable others in need of and entitled to fundamental rights for living, such as the right to health care. In a landscape defined and shaped by neoliberal logics of exclusion and inequality, Band-Aid care and informal transactions serve as a way of experiencing precarity. This landscape of care allows for the exchange of vital resources and operates as a mechanism for restoring social personhood and place value through relations of interdependence.

Informal transactions specifically, and Band-Aid care more broadly, blur clear boundaries between formal and informal and between shadow and the more visible, free-market health economy.[32] Yet they are reactions to the restrictive federal and state-level immigration and health care policies that create uneven, racialized geographies of access to public resources for immigrants, including health care, and marginalize frontline providers who work mainly with immigrant populations. Moreover, immigrants' ineligibility for various health care benefits renders them unable to access primary and specialized forms of care, forcing providers who care for them to engage in multiple modes of improvisation. Band-Aid care, however, has an emancipatory effect. It allows providers and immigrants the potential to refuse racialized and capitalist rhythms of American health care by conferring a sense of sociality and interdependence, reinscribing value to rural spaces, and shifting the possibilities of living precarity.

CHAPTER FIVE

On Hope and Indeterminacy

It is in collectivities that we find reservoirs of hope
and optimism.

—ANGELA Y. DAVIS, *Freedom Is a Constant Struggle*

People are very conscientious about the conditions in which we
work. Sometimes, I am red like a tomato. The next thing I notice
is somebody else who needs water more than me. They are human
beings. You treat people with respect, and that's all you want.
Whatever is provided, to have the opportunity to know about it,
and give you a chance to use what is available. To be part of the
community. All the things that we do, my intention is to show you
this year, and next year I don't have to because you are showing
someone else. Because that is what happens. You use whatever is
available. I am not doing anything special. I know that this exists
here. I will share it with you. And if you need it, great, and if you
don't, maybe someone else needs it. Now, some people need a
little more help than others. Yes. Some people give you more gray
hair than others. Yes. And you just don't give up because eventually,
good things are going to happen. The experiences people have . . .
some people come to you very broken, and you even try to help
them out is a struggle because they are not used to being helped.
They take a little longer. If you have people like that, just find
as much as you can about the problem and discreetly help
them. I think that there are a lot of people who are like that.
People that study sociology, like me, use anthropology to do
things because you can. You don't think about why because you
have the opportunity to do it.

—ANGELA, legal outreach worker

IN MAY 2017, a local media outlet ran a story explaining "why a Mexican flag flies high in a Trump county" (see figure 5.1). The piece featured Maryland crab processors who declared that their livelihoods and small rural communities depended on female Mexican guest workers.[1] It focused on Hoopers Island. These islands, locally known as *La Isla de las Mexicanas* (the Island of the Mexican Women), were named for the female migrant laborers who work in the industrial crab processing plants during the spring and summer months. The story made headlines because much of the public attention on the growing gridlock within then-president Donald Trump's political administration—between their pledge to modernize the nation's temporary worker visa program to ease long-standing labor shortages in predominately rural, politically conservative regions and their rigid stance toward decreasing immigrant admissions and reshaping the selection of foreign-born workers—focused mainly on the agricultural industry and male migrant workers in the U.S. West and South. As a result, many were shocked to learn of female migrants working in Maryland's renowned blue crab industry.

The feature opened with a color photograph depicting an unlikely couple—an older white man in jeans and a weathered T-shirt and a Mexican woman wearing a hair net, apron, and rubber gloves. They were smiling at each other while standing behind a steel table full of crab innards and meat. The narrative described him as the owner of a local family-owned crab processing plant and the woman as a migrant worker who picked crab for his company. It stressed how Mexican migrant women, like the woman pictured, have become the "lifeline" of an "iconic" crab processing industry over the past two decades. Employers, like the man in this story, underscored the lack of available American workers and, consequently, the importance of migrant labor in sustaining small, family-owned businesses in this predominately white, blue-collar, and politically conservative community. The feature then explained how the crab processing industry and migrant women depend heavily on H-2B visas. This U.S. government program allows employers to bring foreign workers to fill temporary nonagricultural jobs.

The story described the woman as a widowed mother of four from Hidalgo, Mexico, who migrates annually to work in the same crab processing

FIGURE 5.1 American and Mexican flags displayed in front of a commercial crab processing plant. Photo by the author.

plant for twenty-one years. The article depicts the woman as someone who has transformed from a complete novice to a renowned "master picker" whose hands are a "blur of activity as she tears off claws and shells, picks the juicy white meat, and sorts it into small plastic tubs." The story mentions that her employer has appropriately compensated her by paying money and giving her a job in exchange for labor migration and occupational injury risks. Her physical wounds, "two decades of cuts from stubborn claws and slippery knives," are not only translated as material benefits to Mexico by way of school fees, mortgage payments, and small business financing but also as sacrifices for the good of America's small businesses and rural communities. This discourse of compensation, gratitude, and sacrifice that frames the story provides a moral cover for how global economic policies and local labor regimes engender injuries, disability, and premature death experienced by female migrant temporary workers. This article exemplifies how the American economy has increasingly depended on migrant workers, primarily from Mexico, Latin America, and the Caribbean. Using temporary guest worker programs, food production industries such as commercial crab processing have recruited foreign workers to perform complex and dangerous jobs since the 1980s. Such labor policies and visa programs have expanded global labor networks and the economic mobility of foreign workers. Concomitantly, these processes have deepened existing gendered, racial, and class dynamics of labor segmentation found within commercial businesses, disadvantaging migrant and racialized workers within the U.S. labor market, especially those who live and work within rural America.

Despite rapid increases in immigrant populations in rural regions with crumbling health systems, we know very little about these communities, their experiences of care, and their ability to access and use health services. In tracing the shifting relations between immigration, health, and rural precarity, using Maryland's Eastern Shore as a case study, this book illustrates that precarity specific to rural life engenders and is shaped by the racialized dynamics of social exclusion experienced by noncitizen immigrants. Immigration and rural precarity are embodied as physical suffering and emotional anxiety, which are mediated by social relationality and mutual cooperation. These findings help us understand how the unprecedented rise in immigration to rural regions and the challenges tied to the unique nature of life in rural areas affect everyday life and community relations. Specifically, they highlight the spatial, temporal, and racial logics of immigration and health and the long-standing issues of precarity among rural systems that have fashioned the landscape of care on Maryland's Eastern Shore and many other places around the world struggling with the indeterminacy of global migration and health governance. The health needs of immigrants and their family members, provider attitudes, the underlying health system, increasingly restrictive and rapidly shifting policy contexts, and institutional and social values influence this landscape of care.

Community and Care

In this book, I bring together the context of immigration and rural health, which we often see as disparate domains. Immigration is a process and a field of study, but it is also a way of experiencing and being in the world. In the United States (and arguably throughout the world), our understanding of immigration is inherently tied to territorial epistemology—the nation-state and its history, policies, rules, identity, and values. Issues of immigrant inclusion and exclusion are prominent narratives within national debates and scholarly articles. More recently, the enforcement of immigration laws has become a hotly debated topic within academia and policy and activist circles. For instance, experts and researchers have pointed to how heightened immigration enforcement has negatively affected people's health and well-being. In particular, they have highlighted how immigration status influences health outcomes and access to health care and urged public health officials to pay greater attention to immigration policy.

What goes unnoticed, unsaid, and unchallenged in these discourses is that legality has become the foundation of how we come to know immigration. When legality becomes the exclusive governing analytic in the scholarship about immigration, it hides more than it discloses. Precisely, legality as a prevailing frame often reflects a worldview rooted in the boundedness and fixed, knowable nature of borders and the people they contain or leave out. These geopolitical and relational boundaries themselves become natural and apolitical over time. As a frame of analysis, legality leaves out other processes, relations, spaces, and economies that shape immigrant embodiment. As this book shows, immigrant lives and living represent something in excess of legality.

Landscapes of Care builds on the generous work of feminist borderlands projects and Black geographies that have richly advanced our understanding of borders, explicitly naming and analyzing the omnipresent conditions of border imperialism and calling attention to the relationships borders have with intensifying neoliberal practices of empire.[2] As activist Harsha Walia argues, connecting borders to the processes of colonialism, racism, and displacement opens up space to think beyond national borders as inert territorial extensions.[3] Border imperialism links the politics of borders to global systems of power and repression rooted in colonization and slavery. Understanding borders, therefore, necessitates an analysis of the function of borders and how they govern, discipline, and oppress Indigenous and racialized people navigating colonial territories.[4] It also requires attention to the diverse ideologies and practices related to racialization, gender hierarchies, class oppression, and ableism that engender immigration. Social violence together with health inequities, premature death, and social fragmentation are essential functions of capitalist accumulation; such violence is also spatially determined. However, marginalized people, even within such spaces of contradiction, violence, and exploitation, formulate ideas of resistance and sociality while living aware of their non-belonging, difference, and alienation.

On the Eastern Shore, legality is critical to understanding the connections between immigration and rural health. But it is not the only determining factor that conditions immigrants' experiences and perspectives with care. Narratives throughout the book highlight how axes of difference along racial, ethnic, class, gender, and disability articulate with, through, and outside of immigration status and concepts of legality in the realm of health and well-being. Rather than interpret immigrant health as simply a condition or reflection of current immigration policies and politics, the preceding chapters interrogate the complexities of immigration and the long-standing fragility of rural health as an intentional project of white settler states, neoliberalism, and globalized racial capitalism.

Narratives of immigrant or legal status as a social determinant of health are integral to portraying a singular or universal vision of immigration and the immigrant. Positioning legal status as a factor that influences all other social relationships forsakes processes (e.g., racialization) and groups (e.g., Black immigrants) that fail to fit into the logic of its framework.[5] Examining the impact of legal status, specifically how legal status affects immigrants' ability to access health-protective resources, without considering racial production not only informs how immigration is conceptualized but also shapes political and social interventions.[6] In such analysis, the proposed "interventions" consist of "more humane" measures enacted by the state and institutions, with little reflection of their foundational tenets in white supremacy, settler colonialism, and racial capitalism and their proclivity to sacrifice people and places in the name of profit. Further, the focus on legality and particular immigrant groups, rather than the convergence of racial ideology with profit, leads to better outcomes for some while failing to consider capital and the state's continuous need to construct difference elsewhere. These are not simply discursive or theoretical erasures; they have real-world consequences.

For instance, Lud, who migrated from Florida every year to pick and pack tomatoes, recounted the time when a local health group carried out a breast cancer screening for "migrant" women. When they arrived at the camp, they proceeded to screen only Latina women and refused to allow Haitian women to participate. When questioned by Lud and others, health care workers stated that Haitians did not meet the inclusion criteria for the screening, insinuating that they did not fit the category of "migrant" women because they were Black. Lud and several Haitian migrant workers became upset and told the health workers to leave. Similar issues, such as the lack of Haitian Kreyòl language translators, disclose how predominant immigration and rural health discourses, rooted in anti-Blackness, dehumanize and erase the existence of Haitians and other Black immigrants on the Eastern Shore and the United States more broadly.

These moralizing agendas focused primarily on legality also obfuscate immigrants' experiences and social relations on the ground. For example, on the Eastern Shore, various immigrant groups work and live side by side. Those from Latin America, the Caribbean, West Africa, and Asia struggle to make a life in rural Maryland, and they have different immigration trajectories and experiences. The narratives and perspectives of interlocutors featured in this book highlight how there is no single story of immigration and how legality is only one of several ways immigrants come to understand their experiences. Many Haitian immigrants, for instance, were incisive in their analysis of anti-Black racialization and capitalist extraction, demonstrating how dying bodies and decaying spaces become profitable as they transfer their value into the commodities they produce. They also spoke openly about how care gets unevenly distributed through hierarchies of race, language, and national origin. Haitians compared their positioning not just against whites but also African Americans and other immigrants. Migrant Mexican women working in crab processing astutely discussed the gendered hierarchies in the H-2B temporary visa program and crab processing while also subverting discourses around injury and disability and their connections to notions of immigrant legality.

In viewing immigration predominately through the lens of legality and its inherent coupling with the nation-state, one can fail to notice other histories and processes that influence immigrant life. In engaging in this project, I felt forced to confront my unawareness of the context of rural health and its complex spatial and temporal relations to immigration. Like many scholars of immigration, I wanted to document immigrant experiences with health in a particular place. But, as my interlocutors quickly pointed out, I failed to recognize that I could not analyze immigration or health separate from the broader context of precarity in which they are lived and experienced. Such conjectures are not simply about the dynamics of immigration and health within a specific region or binding individuals and groups in place or to particular notions of "health." Instead, they highlight how rural spaces, health terrains, and processes of immigration are continually shifting and altering each other. This approach to immigration accommodates the ruptures, ambiguities, and detours that engender spatialities of health and immigrant life, oppression, struggle, and radical and discreet forms of resistance.

Shifting the analytic lens from legality to the spatial, temporal, and racial contours of rural health allows for a reading of immigrant life that is not overdetermined by violence and suffering. It also permits an understanding of rural health that is not reducible to absence and deficiency. Official, scholarly, and public discourses often render scarcity as the defining feature of rural health, portraying this insufficiency as self-evident, expected, and enduring (so much so that there is very little scholarly attention to the subject). Yet rural health, reimagined as a landscape of care, also becomes an indeterminate space—a dynamic geography constantly in motion—and a field of social arrangements deeply influenced by the conditions of slavery, colonialism, imperialism, and global capitalist accumulation.[7] Bringing rural health into conversation with immigration situates immigrants, rural providers, and their geopolitical concerns of immigrant health not on the margins or outside of time but within spaces and temporalities where living and becoming unfold in unpredictable ways.

Focusing on strategies employed by immigrants and providers navigating the landscape of care allows us to center on various manifestations of immigrant knowledge and experience and how the embodiment of suffering and vulnerability shifts and evolves across time and space. Attention to the spatial, temporal, and racial logics of rapid immigration to rural regions also discloses the tremendous variation present in immigration trajectories and immigrant communities. The convergence of rural and immigrant precarity ruptures predominant framings of immigration and immigrants as extraordinary, spatially bounded, and knowable only in relationship to the nation-state. This shared condition of uncertainty and disposability also generates radical forms of sociality, mutual aid, care, and rural vitality.

The daily encounters of immigrants and providers within rural health care delivery and access point to how the production of space is bound to the construction of difference and disparity. Policies and structures that continue to dismantle and fragment rural health infrastructures and prevent access to formal care, along with daily forms of racial discrimination and anti-immigration sentiment, present significant challenges for immigrants. Yet, such issues cannot be viewed only as "immigrant" problems or matters resolved through legal recognition and integration. Daily living in Maryland's Eastern Shore demonstrates how geographies of exclusion configure and maintain everyday mechanisms of modernity and belonging. Foregrounding rural health reorients us to the connections between space, place, and power, particularly to the disproportionate impacts that neoliberal policies, fueled by the fatal entanglements of white supremacy and racial capitalism, have had on people and places.

The context of immigration, as this book demonstrates, allows for new ways of thinking through rural precarity and how rural landscapes of care have the potential to generate spaces for belonging among immigrants. For instance, mapping the contours of experience of immigrants working in the agricultural, seafood, and poultry industries in rural contexts through

FIGURE 5.2 Local community organization sign. Photo by the author.

narratives of precarity as an enduring, ordinary way of life centers "the situated knowledge of these communities and their contributions to both real and imagined human geographies [as] significant political acts and expressions."[8] Immigrants' embodiment of pain, injury, and disability as a condition of belonging (as exemplified in the news story mentioned at the beginning of this chapter and others throughout the book) highlights the precariousness of some at the expense of others. It also lays bare the impossibility of portraying immigrants as injured or cared for because they are always already recognized as nonbeing. Even though precarity stems from the inherent vulnerability that characterizes both immigrant life and rural living, it is not a presumed, totalizing condition. Immigrant stories and actions reveal an acute awareness of injury, violence, and even elimination and the ability to critically question the conditions under which it becomes possible to understand a life as precarious. As Judith Butler and others note, such spaces hold potential of looking beyond encounters with precariousness and precarity to imagine life and living otherwise (see figure 5.2).

This space of "livingness" or "aliveness" surfaces in what we often tend to conceptualize as the realm of health, health care, and health systems. Yet it takes on different and shifting forms. Providers' and immigrants' stories indicate how they engage in a dynamic landscape of care. This type of care exceeds health and the body and consists of visible and intangible measures to care for individuals, families, entire communities, and places. The notion of landscape better captures the spatially organized forms of care and mutuality on the Eastern Shore. It highlights the alternative spatial and temporal frameworks that signify place and the communities living and working there. The landscape of care on the Eastern Shore is a terrain of struggle for belonging and placemaking. Immigrants and rural providers have long understood care as a site of cooperation, fellowship, and recognition rather than an extractive, discriminatory, and commodified system.[9] This landscape of care refuses dominant modes of claiming immigration and rural health and imagines place and belonging otherwise.

The Eastern Shore is a region that grapples with anti-immigration sentiment and economic exploitative and harsh conditions of social and geographic isolation. Such violence is not outside of individual experiences, which are felt and embodied. Yet, despite their fraught relationship to places and their legacies as well as movement and migration, immigrants live and survive within and outside physical, social, and spiritual boundaries that mark some people and places as less than others. Immigrants perceive the Eastern Shore as home (however temporary or permanent), despite being considered perpetual foreigners. The landscape of care is alternate geography that lingers beside and is entangled with prevailing immigration and rural health ideologies. This landscape is not just spatial. It articulates a desire for a place rooted in social cooperation and social justice. In the most unwelcoming and desolate places where immigrants encounter discrimination and exploitation, the landscape of care demands the possibilities for immigrant survival—of living, being, and forging sites of care and resistance.

Moreover, the landscape of care excavates how rural health and immigration are connected. It highlights how immigrants and rural providers strive to disrupt the capitalist ideals of health care, place, and personhood. By foregrounding how diverse immigrant communities are central to the making of rural spaces and how rural health is vital to a broader struggle for recognition and equality, the landscape of care on the Eastern Shore is a place of shared geographic and political possibilities.

Acknowledgments

My interest in immigrant health in rural regions was fostered by work I had done as a public health practitioner working on disease outbreak investigations for the federal government. During visits to remote places, I was stunned by what I did not know and what I had never thought about. There was little conversation among leading public health officials about the complex issues related to immigration and the shuttering of public health services in rural regions. I was frustrated with the limitations of what I could publish from this work, given the politics of government public health. The critical and fast-paced nature of public health work also did not allow for time for long-term engagement. I longed to understand and support those providing and receiving care in these settings.

In shifting to academia, I was extraordinarily lucky to be able to spend more time (when I was not teaching) with providers and immigrants in rural Maryland. As I began to publish my work as journal articles, I received requests to translate my findings for the public. I also saw the need to talk more openly about the racial logics affecting those with whom I worked. Most importantly, I wanted to honor those who taught me a great deal about the inherent connections between rural health and immigration. This book is a result of these longings, and it began to take shape a lifetime ago. It has taken a while to find my voice in a field that I never felt a part of and where discomfort around association still exists. Further, finishing the book amid the COVID-19 pandemic, national racial reckoning, solo parenting, and eventually an international move to Ethiopia and the subsequent civil war there has been something that I have yet to process or articulate. Writing two books simultaneously, this and another on HIV has been challenging, to say the least, and something that I would not recommend to anyone.

Yet, writing has been a solace, a balm, and a resting place to ground me during this time of enormous grief and uncertainty. I wrote on airplanes and in cars (as a passenger!) and in hotels. I wrote at hockey, baseball, and tennis tournaments, across five different countries, during an international evacuation, and while caring for elderly parents and children engaged in virtual schooling. Sometimes I wrote simply because I was overwhelmed with everything else. Perhaps so much writing is not healthy and I need to find other outlets, but engagement with this book saved me from the hellscape of these past two years. Writing is a solitary endeavor, but the ideas and experiences that inform writing are always in accompaniment with community. I am deeply indebted to many people and institutions for their support and resources in bringing this book to life. Their investment in this project has been supportive and generous.

I begin with my colleagues at the Centers for Disease Control and Prevention (CDC), especially Karen Kroeger and others at the Division of STD Prevention and the Office of Health Equity at the National Center for HIV, Viral Hepatitis, STD, and TB Prevention. They allowed me the time and resources to conduct disease outbreak assessments in rural settings and learn about health contexts and the politics of care in such spaces. In addition, my experience working in rural regions of North Carolina and Louisiana opened my eyes to the realities of rural health for the first time.

Colleagues and various colleges, offices, and programs at the University of Maryland have provided unwavering support for this project and book since 2014. The College of Behavioral and Social Sciences Dean's Research Initiative and the Department of Anthropology provided generous funding from 2014 to 2016. In addition, Greg Ball, Carl Lejuez, Jeff Lucas, and Paul Shackel ensured that I had the necessary resources and the time needed to write and publish this book. This book could not have been completed without sabbaticals and writing time made possible through generous financial support from the Graduate School's Research and Scholarship Award, the Office of Faculty Affairs, the College of Behavioral and Social Sciences, and the Department of Anthropology. Finally, thanks to the generous support of the TOME@UMD program, led by the University Libraries in partnership with the Office of the Senior Vice President and Provost and the College of Arts and Humanities, this book has been made open access. Toward an Open Monograph Ecosystem (TOME) is a national initiative to advance open-access publishing (OA) of monographs in the humanities and social sciences. Even though a range of public spheres should facilitate public access to research—a fundamental feature of global human equality—access to knowledge continues to be prohibited in fields like anthropology and public health. OA expands the possibilities for knowledge on immigrant health to be used in unexpected and innovative ways beyond mainstream professional research. OA will further allow the book to reach two key audiences—immigrants and readers in rural settings—both groups otherwise restricted by the high price of traditional U.S. academic publications. In this way, OA ensures the book is available to the very communities who made it possible.

This book also would not have been possible without the generosity of colleagues near and far. I am particularly grateful for the encouragement received from Jenny Acosta, Vincanne Adams, Adia Benton, Megan Carney, Lauren Carruth, Heide Castañeda, Mounia El-Kotni, Sulma Guzmán, Jennifer Hammer, Seth Holmes, Kiran Jayaram, Nora Kentworthy, Katherine Lambert-Pennington, Jennifer Liu, Sean Mallin, Lenore Manderson, Marlaina Martin, Herns Marcelin, Emily Mendenhall, Devon Payne-Sturges, Deborah Thomas, and Amber Wutich. I have benefited greatly from the numerous opportunities to present this work since 2014 at various conferences, institutions, and classes. I am thankful for the lovely invitations and to all those who asked questions and provided helpful suggestions that assisted in improving the quality of this work. I am also deeply indebted to the invaluable fieldwork and Spanish translation assistance provided by Emilia Guevara over several years. Her excellent ethnographic wisdom in the field as a graduate research assistant made this work possible and kept me grounded. Additionally, I am grateful to the Society for Medical Anthropology, and the members of its Critical Anthropology for Global Health Caucus, for awarding me the Rudolf Virchow Professional Award for my paper on the landscape of care. I am honored that an article exploring immigration and rural health in Maryland was recognized for its contributions to global health.

The University of North Carolina Press and my editor Lucas Church have been nothing short of incredible to work with. It means a lot to have an editorial team that is encouraging, supportive, and understanding, especially in these uncertain times. I am also indebted to the three anonymous reviewers who provided generous suggestions and comments during various rounds of reviews that vastly improved the book's cohesiveness and readability.

Most of all, I am particularly indebted to so many on the Eastern Shore who made this work possible. Tim Dunn, Veronique Felix, Sue Hagie, Fritz Jeudy, Leila Borrero Krouse, Amy Leibman, Kerry Palakanis, Nohora Rivero, Jennifer Shahan, and Danielle Weber were instrumental to my entry into the field and provided invaluable connections and resources. Many whose voices and stories are documented in the book—and have asked not to be named publicly—offered helpful advice and took the time to talk and think with me. I am truly humbled by all who taught me a great deal about rural health and immigration and forced me to think more concretely about their intimate connections. This book, in many ways, is a testament to their situated knowledge, analytical insight, and worldmaking. Thank you for allowing me to be a part of your lives even for a brief moment in time.

Finally, the support of family and friends was crucial to the development and completion of this book. Longtime writing partners, comrades, friends, and academic sisters, Adia Benton and Jennifer Liu, provided thoughtful feedback on earlier versions of the manuscript, while my family, especially my parents, Kathirethamby and Nala Sangaramoorthy, provided the comforts of home, helped out with childcare, and performed many other forms of visible and invisible labor that made writing possible. Delon and Anita Pinto, along with Sonia, Mira, and Mathew, seamlessly incorporated me and my children into their family and offered wonderful respite from the stress of solo parenting and not having a permanent place to call home; Mulu, Yonas, and many others made my transition to Addis Ababa feasible and provided the care and resources I needed to work on the book. James Cerwinski, in particular, read many versions of this manuscript and was generous in planning many distractions that helped me balance work, home, and everything in-between. My children, Ashok and Gyan, continue to be my biggest cheerleaders, not only in the process of writing this book but in life. Amid the messiness of life and work, I know that I am lucky to have such unwavering support and encouragement from people that I care about deeply.

Portions of chapters 2 and 5 have been revised from my 2019 article "Liminal Living: Everyday Injury, Disability, and Instability among Migrant Mexican Women in Maryland's Seafood Industry," in *Medical Anthropology Quarterly*. An earlier version of chapter 3 appeared in the *Journal of Immigrant and Minority Health* in 2017 (Sangaramoorthy and Guevara, "Immigrant Health in Rural Maryland: A Qualitative Study of Major Barriers to Health Care Access"). Parts of chapter 4 have also been modified from my 2018 article in *American Anthropologist*, "'Putting Band-Aids on Things That Need Stitches': Immigration and the Landscape of Care in Rural America."

I write this book as a living memorial to my grandmothers, ancestors, and fellow Eelam Tamils—all those who, despite experiencing the terror of life on the move, refuse to let grief, loss, and oppression destroy them, imagining and fighting for living and being otherwise—and to Ashok and Gyan as keepers of this remarkable legacy of people and places.

Notes

Preface

1. For additional context on Black July, see Eleanor Pavey, "The Massacres in Sri Lanka During the Black July Riots of 1983," *The Online Encyclopedia of Mass Violence*, May 13, 2008, https://www.sciencespo.fr/mass-violence-war-massacre-resistance/en/document/massacres-sri-lanka-during-black-july-riots-1983.html.

2. For more on personal reflections of Sri Lankan Civil War and connections to the Black Lives Matter movement, see Thurka Sangaramoorthy, "Black Lives Matter and Reflections from a Civil War," *Sapiens*, November 22, 2016.

3. I use Leisy Abrego's piece to think through the rendering of "out-of-place" scholars in academia, particularly women of color from working-class backgrounds whose ability to rigorously conduct research and publish impactful work is often in question. See Leisy Abrego, "Research as Accompaniment."

4. Naisargi Dave explores the moral biographies of animal activists in India and the event of witnessing after which "nothing can ever be the same." She asks why some people fall into obligation with others, of staying put rather than remaining safely enclosed in our own skins, when one would rather turn or run away. See Dave, "*Witness*," 434.

5. I draw on Deborah Thomas's notion of witnessing, a form of seeing and living witness to life that is co-performed and committed to a moral praxis. See Thomas, *Political Life in the Wake of the Plantation*.

6. Alexander Chee, "So You Want to Write?" *The Cut*, July 21, 2020.

7. Sangaramoorthy, *Treating AIDS*.

8. For additional background on immigrants in the mid-Atlantic and rural Maryland regions, see Allison Smith Gaffney, "Don't Hassle Me, I'm Local"; see also Sangaramoorthy and Guevara, "Immigrant Health in Rural Maryland."

9. Ricketts, "The Changing Nature of Rural Health Care."

10. Baba, "Anthropology and Transnational Migration."

11. For an overview of contemporary debates about whether immigrant incorporation has occurred at different levels in health care, see Marrow and Joseph, "Excluded and Frozen Out," and Joseph and Marrow, "Health Care, Immigrants, and Minorities."

Introduction

1. For an excellent manual on Maryland blue crabs, see Jamie Liu, "Maryland Crabs: A Guide to the East Coast's Essential Summer Feast," *Eater*, June 5, 2015. Also see a popular recipe for Maryland crab cakes from local rock band, Clutch in their song, Hot Bottom Feeder: https://www.youtube.com/watch?v=SOTrHrGSeNM, December 2022.

2. H-2B visas have an annual "cap" of 66,000 that is established by law. In 2018, the U.S. government introduced a randomization process and a lottery system to deal with the significant rise in H-2B applications. Some crab processing plants received a lower number of visas than what they requested due to these processes. Politicians and companies have petitioned Congress to issue additional visas on a yearly basis over the past few years. See Samantha Hawkins, "Md. Crabbing Industry Fears Long-Term Impacts of 2020 Visa Shortages," *Maryland Matters*, May 3, 2020.

3. For an overview of recent immigration trends in rural regions, see Dalla, Villarruel, Cramer, and Gonzalez-Kruger, "Examining Strengths and Challenges of Rapid Rural Immigration"; Jensen, "New Immigrant Settlements in Rural America"; Lichter, "Immigration and the New Racial Diversity in Rural America"; and McAreavey, *New Immigration Destinations*.

4. Sharp and Lee, "New Faces in Rural Places"; Lichter and Johnson, "A Demographic Lifeline?"

5. Doherty, "Life (and Limb) in the Fast-Lane"; Griffiths, "Networks of Reciprocity"; Sangaramoorthy, "Putting Band-Aids on Things That Need Stitches"; and Sangaramoorthy, "Liminal Living."

6. For an overview of Tubman's early life in Maryland, see Humez, *Harriet Tubman*.

7. For additional details on Gloria Richardson and her work with the Cambridge movement, see Fitzgerald, *The Struggle Is Eternal*.

8. Arizpe, *Migration, Women and Social Development*; Gálvez, *Eating NAFTA*.

9. The literature on race, gender, and forced migration is extensive. I draw on the following work: Castles, "Towards a Sociology of Forced Migration and Social Transformation"; Dreby and Schmalzbauer, "The Relational Contexts of Migration"; Hennebry and Preibisch, "A Model for Managed Migration?"; Hondagneu-Sotelo, *Gender and U.S. Immigration*; Massey, Durand, and Malone, *Beyond Smoke and Mirrors*; Phizacklea, *One Way Ticket*; Preibisch and Encalada Grez, "The Other Side of El Otro Lado"; Rosenbloom, *Looking for Work, Searching for Workers*; Segura and Zavella, *Women and Migration in the U.S.–Mexico Borderlands*; Valdez, "Socialism and Empire"; and Tyner, *Made in the Philippines*.

10. Goode and Maskovsky, *New Poverty Studies*; Hennebry, "Transnational Precarity"; Torres and Carte, "Migration and Development?"; and Valdez, "Socialism and Empire."

11. U.S. Bureau of Labor Statistics, "Labor Force Characteristics of Foreign-Born Workers Summary."

12. For additional context on how women have broadened and deepened their involvement in agricultural production over the last few decades as they increasingly shoulder the responsibility for household survival and respond to economic opportunities in commercial agriculture, see Katz, "The Changing Role of Women in the Rural Economies of Latin America," and Lastarria-Cornhiel, "Feminization of Agriculture."

13. Flippen and Parrado, "A Tale of Two Contexts"; U.S. Bureau of Labor Statistics, "Labor Force Characteristics of Foreign-Born Workers Summary."

14. Brettell, "Theorizing Migration in Anthropology"; Cloke, Marsden, and Mooney, *Handbook of Rural Studies*; Vertovec, "The Cultural Politics of Nation and Migration."

15. This work is broad but includes recent scholarship by several anthropologists and sociologists. Some examples include Holmes, *Fresh Fruit, Broken Bodies*; Horton,

They Leave Their Kidneys in the Fields; Marrow, *New Destination Dreaming*; Stuesse, *Scratching Out a Living*; and Vogt, "Crossing Mexico."

16. For an overview of public health work on immigration, see Castañeda et al., "Immigration as a Social Determinant of Health," and Viruell-Fuentes, Miranda, and Abdulrahim, "More than Culture."

17. Bourgois et al., "Structural Vulnerability"; Kline, *Pathogenic Policing*; Willen, "Migration, 'Illegality,' and Health."

18. My thoughts on conceptualizations of the othering of "immigrants" draw from selected writings that underscore the racialized nature of Western notions of the human. See, for example, Hartman, *Scenes of Subjection*; King, *Black Shoals*; Quashie, *Black Aliveness*; Sharpe, *In the Wake*; Wynter, "Unsettling the Coloniality of Being/Power/Truth/Freedom."

19. Sangaramoorthy and Carney, "Immigration, Mental Health and Psychosocial Well-Being."

20. Sharryn Kasmir, "Precarity," *The Cambridge Encyclopedia of Anthropology*, March 13, 2018, https://www.anthroencyclopedia.com/entry/precarity.

21. Butler, *Frames of War*, 25.

22. Anne Allison, "Precarity: Commentary by Anne Allison," *Cultural Anthropology*, 2016, https://journal.culanth.org/index.php/ca/precarity-commentary-by-anne-allison.

23. Al-Mohammad, "A Kidnapping in Basra."

24. Kathleen Stewart, "Precarity: Interview with the Authors," *Cultural Anthropology*, 2016, https://journal.culanth.org/index.php/ca/precarity-interview-with-the-authors.

25. Ethnographic writing on precarity includes varying examples of experiences, perceptions, and affective relations, including those that examine detachment and relational autonomy among *catadores* (urban poor who reclaim recyclables) in Rio de Janeiro (Millar, "The Precarious Present"), violence and mutual suffering of individuals and their loved ones in post-invasion Basra (Al-Mohammad, "A Kidnapping in Basra"), and boredom and embodied displacement among the homeless in Bucharest (O'Neill, "Cast Aside").

26. Gilmore, "Fatal Couplings of Power and Difference"; Gilroy and Gilmore, *Selected Writings on Race and Difference*.

27. Selected readings include Denzin, Lincoln, and Tuhiwai Smith, *Handbook of Critical and Indigenous Methodologies*; Hawthorne, "Black Matters Are Spatial Matters"; Kelley, *Freedom Dreams*; King, *Black Shoals*; McKittrick, *Demonic Grounds*; Simpson, *Mohawk Interruptus*.

28. I draw from Laura Pulido's work on Flint to understand the racialized devaluation of people and places. See Pulido, "Flint, Environmental Racism, and Racial Capitalism."

29. Quashie, *Black Aliveness*, 5.

30. Sangaramoorthy and Carney, "Immigration, Mental Health and Psychosocial Well-Being."

31. Sangaramoorthy and Benton, "Imagining Rural Immunity."

32. Guzman, "Household Income."

33. Md. Code Ann., Est. & Trusts § 3-203 (2016).

34. U.S. Department of Agriculture, Economic Research Service, "State Fact Sheets: Maryland."

35. Maryland Department of Health and Mental Hygiene, "2016 Primary Care Needs Assessment."

36. There is little published research that chronicles Maryland communities' connection to Appalachia. For some exceptions, see Hanna, "Finding a Place in the World-Economy," and Sangaramoorthy et al., "Place-Based Perceptions."

37. For a critical discussion of the notion of living through prolonged crisis, see Sangaramoorthy, "Chronicity, Crisis, and the 'End of AIDS'"; Scheper-Hughes, "A Talent for Life"; and Vigh, "Crisis and Chronicity."

38. This literature is extensive. Some foundational texts that I draw on include Feld and Basso, *Senses of Place*; Gupta and Ferguson, "Beyond 'Culture'"; Hirsch and O'Hanlon, *The Anthropology of Landscape*; Low, *Spatializing Culture*; Rodman, "Empowering Place"; and Rosaldo, "Ideology, Place, and People without Culture."

39. This literature is vast. Selected readings include Andaya, "The Gift of Health"; Brotherton, *Revolutionary Medicine*; Coe, "The Temporality of Care"; Gesler, "Therapeutic Landscapes"; Smith and Mbakwem, "Life Projects and Therapeutic Itineraries"; Kangas, "Therapeutic Itineraries in a Global World"; Ledeneva, *Russia's Economy of Favours*; Praspaliauskiene, "Enveloped Lives"; Rhodes, "The Shape of Action"; Rivkin-Fish, *Women's Health in Post-Soviet Russia*; Samuelsen, "Therapeutic Itineraries"; Williams, "Changing Geographies of Care"; and Wilson, "Therapeutic Landscapes and First Nations Peoples."

40. See Milligan and Wiles, "Landscapes of Care." I draw from and expand on their conceptualization.

41. Here, I draw from the work of AbdouMaliq Simone and others on "people as infrastructure," which has advanced our understandings of urban infrastructure as a modality of social practice. See Addie, "Urban Life in the Shadows of Infrastructural Death"; Doherty, "Life (and Limb) in the Fast-Lane"; and Simone, "People as Infrastructure."

42. Ricketts, *Rural Health in the United States*.

43. Stratford, *Island Geographies*.

44. McKittrick, *Demonic Grounds*.

45. Additional provisions related to this coverage expansion included prohibiting insurers from denying coverage because of preexisting health conditions, allowing young adults to be on parental health insurance policies until age 26, and establishing high-risk insurance pools to help sicker individuals obtain insurance. Another critical element of the ACA was to contain soaring health care spending and taxpayer costs and increase health care delivery efficiency, but it led to increasing corporatization of health care. Health insurance exchanges and ensuing "competition" in the market-based system, Medicare payment restructuring, and the excise tax on high-cost health care plans were more prominent measures established to contain costs. The creation of medical homes and accountable care organizations, bundled payments, and stiff penalties for hospital readmissions also aimed to increase efficiency in the health care delivery system. See Horton et al., "Critical Anthropology of Global Health 'Takes a Stand' Statement."

46. Dao and Mulligan, "Toward an Anthropology of Insurance and Health Reform"; Mulligan and Castañeda, *Unequal Coverage*; Mazurenko et al., "The Effects of Medicaid Expansion under the ACA."

47. Rao and Hellander, "The Widening U.S. Health Care Crisis."

48. Noncitizenship status is a barrier for many immigrants who do not qualify for aid or insurance. To be eligible for full Medicaid or Maryland Children's Health Program (MCHP) coverage, most noncitizens must have a "qualified" immigration status, except for pregnant women and children under age 21, who must only be lawfully present. In general, permanent resident immigrants (green card holders) are eligible for Medicaid and MCHP after five years of residence on the same basis as U.S. citizens and must meet all other program requirements. See Horton et al., "Critical Anthropology of Global Health 'Takes a Stand' Statement."

49. The 1996 federal welfare and immigration reform laws—the Personal Responsibility and Work Opportunity Reconciliation Act (PRWORA) and the Illegal Immigration Reform and Immigrant Responsibility Act (IIRIRA)—constituted a radical shift in post–World War II U.S. immigration policies that had previously increased the rights and privileges to immigrants. Before 1996, legally admitted immigrants were eligible for Medicaid and other benefits the same as citizens, but when PRWORA and IIRIRA were instated, they created a sharp divide between citizens and noncitizens, redefining the social membership of immigrants by restricting services and increasing enforcement activities. PRWORA restricts Medicaid eligibility of immigrants so that those legally admitted into the United States after August 1996 are not eligible for coverage, except for emergencies, during their first five years in the country.

50. U.S. Citizenship and Immigration Services, Department of Homeland Security, "Public Charge Ground of Inadmissibility."

51. Artiga, Garfield, and Damico, *Estimated Impacts of Final Public Charge Inadmissibility Rule*.

52. For how scholars have documented similar concerns, see Ricketts, "The Changing Nature of Rural Health Care," and Rosenbaum et al., *Community Health Centers*.

53. The literature on immigration and local context is vast. Writings that I draw from include Carney, *The Unending Hunger*; Castañeda, "Medical Humanitarianism"; Castañeda, "'Over-Foreignization' or 'Unused Potential'?"; Fassin, *Humanitarian Reason*; Sangaramoorthy and Kroeger, "Mobility, Latino Migrants, and the Geography of Sex Work"; Sargent and Larchanché, "Transnational Migration and Global Health"; Suphanchaimat et al., "Challenges in the Provision of Healthcare Services for Migrants"; Ticktin, *Casualties of Care*; and Willen, *Fighting for Dignity*.

54. For related ruminations, see Redfield, "On Band-Aids and Magic Bullets."

55. For more on informal economies and gift exchanges, see Misztal, *Informality*, and Stan, "Neither Commodities nor Gifts."

56. I draw from Julie Livingston's notion of improvisation (Livingston, *Improvising Medicine*).

Chapter One

1. Kendzior, *The View from Flyover Country*.

2. Blanchette and LaFlamme, "Introduction"; Hibbard and Römer, "Planning the Global Countryside"; Lichter and Brown, "Rural America in an Urban Society"; McCarthy, "Rural Geography"; Nelson and Nelson, "The Global Rural"; and Woods, "Engaging the Global Countryside."

3. See, for instance, Cairns, "Youth, Dirt, and the Spatialization of Subjectivity"; Cloke and Little, *Contested Countryside Cultures*; and Cloke, Marsden, and Mooney, *Handbook of Rural Studies*.

4. Pew Research Center, "Changing Patterns in U.S. Immigration and Population," and Pew Research Center, *What Unites and Divides Urban, Suburban and Rural Communities*.

5. Portes and Rumbaut, *Immigrant Américà*.

6. Baker and Hotek, "Perhaps a Blessing"; Cravey, "The Changing South"; Lichter, "Immigration and the New Racial Diversity in Rural America"; Lichter and Johnson, "A Demographic Lifeline?"; Marrow, *New Destination Dreaming*; Martin, Fix, and Taylor, *The New Rural Poverty*; and Massey and Sana, "Patterns of U.S. Migration."

7. Carr and Kefalas, *Hollowing Out the Middle*; and Gary Paul Green, "Deindustrialization of Rural America."

8. Hogan and Roberts, "Occupational Employment Projections to 2024."

9. Pulido, "Flint, Environmental Racism, and Racial Capitalism."

10. Terrazas, "Immigrants in New-Destination States."

11. Passel and Cohn, "Unauthorized Immigrant Population"; Terrazas, "Immigrants in New-Destination States."

12. U.S. Census Bureau data, including from the 2019 American Community Survey, the 2010 Census, and the 2000 Census; also 1960 to 1990 data from Gibson and Lennon, "Historical Census Statistics on the Foreign-Born Population of the United States: 1850–1990."

13. Singer, "The Rise of New Immigrant Gateways."

14. Brown and Wardwell, *New Directions in Urban–Rural Migration*; and Mathema, Svajlenka, and Hermann, *Revival and Opportunity*.

15. Massey, *New Faces in New Places*.

16. American Immigration Council, *Immigrants in Maryland*.

17. U.S. Census Bureau data from the 2019 American Community Survey, the 2010 Census, and the 2000 Census; 1960 to 1990 data Gibson and Lennon, "Historical Census Statistics on the Foreign-Born Population of the United States: 1850–1990."

18. American Immigration Council, *Immigrants in Maryland*.

19. McHugh and Morawski. *Immigrants and WIOA Services*.

20. De Leon et al., "Community-Based Organizations and Immigrant Integration."

21. U.S. Census Bureau, "State and County QuickFacts, Maryland and Washington, 2020."

22. The Eastern Shore has a long history of trying to separate from the state of Maryland, evidenced by proposals in the state's General Assembly in 1833–1835, 1852, and 1998. Earlier proposals also alluded to a separate state encompassing the Delmarva Peninsula. Although the 1998 proposal by state Senators Richard F. Colburn and J. Lowell Stoltzfus did not indicate a status for Eastern Shore's nine counties following secession, it did suggest the newly formed state could be named "Delmarva." See Michael Dresser, "Saying So Long to City Bullies Secession," *Baltimore Sun*, February 11, 1998.

23. Housing Assistance Council, "Housing for Families and Unaccompanied Migrant Farmworkers"; Maryland Advisory Committee to the U.S. Commission on Civil Rights, "Migrant Workers on Maryland's Eastern Shore."

24. State of Maryland, "U.S. Census Bureau Population Estimates."

25. This percentage is calculated by comparing census data from 2000 and 2019. Specifically, "foreign born as a percentage of total population—2000" data from the Maryland Department of Planning, Planning Data Services, "Foreign-Born in Maryland: What We Know from the Census," presentation to the Maryland Coalition for Refugees and Immigrants, June 20, 2002, https://planning.maryland.gov/MSDC/Documents /Census/Cen2000/sf3/foreign_born/Foreign-Born-Md.ppt; and U.S. Census Bureau, "State and County QuickFacts, Maryland, Foreign-Born Persons."

26. Dunn and Liebman, *Needs Assessment Report*; Dunn, Aragonés, and Shivers, "Recent Mexican Migration"; and Allison Smith Gaffney, "Don't Hassle Me, I'm Local."

27. Maryland State Archives. "Maryland at a Glance."

28. MacDonald, "Tracking the Consolidation of U.S. Agriculture."

29. Miller, Martin, and Kee, "Migrants in Delmarva Agriculture."

30. Erwin, "Grower Influence during a Participatory Project with Farmworkers"; Goldstein, "Agribusiness Lobbies for a New Temporary Foreign Worker Program."

31. National Marine Fisheries Service, *Fisheries of the United States, 2019*.

32. Paolisso, "Blue Crabs and Controversy on the Chesapeake Bay."

33. Maryland Seafood, "Crab and Oyster Processing Facilities," accessed December 2016, http://seafood.maryland.gov/crab-and-oyster-processing-facilities/.

34. American University, *Picked Apart*; John Fritze, "Court Halts Ban on Foreign Worker Visas," *Baltimore Sun*, March 18, 2015.

35. Straut-Eppsteiner, "Coming and Going."

36. American University, *Picked Apart*.

37. Delmarva Chicken Association, "Here's How the Chicken Community Is Working for Delmarva."

38. For an overview of labor in the meatpacking industry, see Freshour, "'Ain't No Life for a Mother'"; Frydenlund and Cullen Dunn, "Refugees and Racial Capitalism"; Roediger and Esch, *The Production of Difference*; and Sinclair, *The Jungle*. For a work on the local poultry industry, see Dunn, Aragonés, and Shivers, "Recent Mexican Migration." See also Horowitz and Miller, "Immigrants in the Delmarva Poultry Processing Industry."

39. Trull, "Why a Mexican Flag Flies High in a Trump County."

40. U.S. Bureau of Labor Statistics, "Occupational Employment and Wages."

41. Daniel Costa, "H-2B Crabpickers Are So Important to the Maryland Seafood Industry That They Get Paid $3 Less per Hour than the State or Local Average Wage," *Working Economics Blog*, May 26, 2017, https://www.epi.org/blog/h-2b-crabpickers -maryland-seafood-industry-paid-less-than-average/.

42. Costa, "H-2B Crabpickers."

43. American University, *Picked Apart*.

44. Sangaramoorthy, "Liminal Living."

45. I draw from Victor Ray's seminal work on racialized organizations to understand the ordinary ways in which race is constitutive of organizational foundations, hierarchies, and processes. See Ray, "A Theory of Racialized Organizations."

46. Ray, "A Theory of Racialized Organizations," 32.

47. White, "Migration, Urbanization, and Social Adjustment."

48. International Organization for Migration, *World Migration Report 2015*.

49. De Boer, "Resilience and the Fragile City."

50. Institute for Women's Policy Research, *Gender, Urbanization, and Democratic Governance*.

51. Parker et al., "Demographic and Economic Trends."

52. Dalla et al., "Examining Strengths and Challenges of Rapid Rural Immigration."

53. Broadway, "Planning for Change in Small Towns."

54. Dalla and Christensen, "Latino Immigrants Describe Residence in Rural Midwestern Meatpacking Communities"; Dalla, Ellis, and Cramer, "Immigration and Rural America."

55. I draw from Laura Pulido's work on environmental racism and racial capitalism in Flint, Michigan, and the devaluation and abandonment of people and places by both the state and capital. See Pulido, "Flint, Environmental Racism, and Racial Capitalism."

56. Singh and Siahpush, "Widening Rural–Urban Disparities in Life Expectancy."

57. Bolin et al., "Rural Healthy People 2020"; James, "All Rural Places Are Not Created Equal."

58. Hartley, "Rural Health Disparities."

59. Stein et al., "The Epidemic of Despair among White Americans."

60. Ivey-Stephenson et al., "Suicide Trends."

61. Fowler et al., "Increase in Suicides"; Luo et al., "Impact of Business Cycles on U.S. Suicide Rates"; Margerison-Zilko et al., "Health Impacts of the Great Recession."

62. National Center for Health Statistics, *Health, United States*.

63. Douthit et al., "Exposing Some Important Barriers to Health Care Access."

64. MacDowell et al., "A National View of Rural Health Workforce Issues."

65. Ricketts, "The Changing Nature of Rural Health Care."

66. Ricketts, *Rural Health in the United States*.

67. Kaufman et al., "The Rising Rate of Rural Hospital Closures." For statistics on closures since 2005, see also University of North Carolina, "Rural Hospital Closures," Cecil G. Sheps Center for Health Services Research, accessed December 2022, https://www.shepscenter.unc.edu/programs-projects/rural-health/rural-hospital -closures/.

68. Gujral and Basu, "Impact of Rural and Urban Hospital Closures on Inpatient Mortality."

69. Courtemanche et al., "Early Impacts of the Affordable Care Act."

70. Rosenbaum et al., *Community Health Centers*.

71. Sangaramoorthy and Guevara, "Immigrant Health in Rural Maryland"; Sangaramoorthy, "Putting Band-Aids on Things That Need Stitches."

72. Sangaramoorthy and Kroeger, "Mobility, Latino Migrants, and the Geography of Sex Work."

73. Lister et al., "A Systematic Review of Rural-Specific Barriers."

74. Kugel and Zuroweste, "The State of Health Care Services for Mobile Poor Populations."

75. Hogan, "Constructing the Global," 22.

76. Woods, "Engaging the Global Countryside."

Chapter Two

1. Balibar, *We, the People of Europe?*; Cohen, *The New Helots*; Negri and Hardt, *Empire*; Kalleberg and Vallas, "Probing Precarious Work"; Kalleberg, "Nonstandard Employment Relations; Lambert and Herod, *Neoliberal Capitalism and Precarious Work*; Sassen, *Globalization and Its Discontents*.

2. Binford, *Tomorrow We're All Going to the Harvest*; Gentsch and Massey, "Labor Market Outcomes for Legal Mexican Immigrants"; Otero, "Neoliberal Globalization, NAFTA, and Migration"; Preibisch, "Pick-Your-Own Labor."

3. Millar, "The Precarious Present."

4. Han, "Precarity, Precariousness, and Vulnerability"; Prentice, "Work after Precarity."

5. Quesada, Hart, and Bourgois, "Structural Vulnerability and Health."

6. Arcury and Quandt, "Delivery of Health Services to Migrant and Seasonal Farmworkers"; Holmes, *Fresh Fruit, Broken Bodies*; Horton, *They Leave Their Kidneys in the Fields*; Saxton, *The Devil's Fruit*; Smith-Nonini, "The Illegal and the Dead; Stuesse, *Scratching Out a Living*.

7. Quesada, Hart, and Bourgois, "Structural Vulnerability and Health"; Saxton and Stuesse, "Workers' Decompensation."

8. De Genova, "Migrant 'Illegality' and Deportability in Everyday Life."

9. I draw on several sources to formulate thoughts on the spatialization of racial capitalism in rural regions, including Taylor, *Race for Profit*; McKittrick, *Demonic Grounds*; and Pulido, "Flint, Environmental Racism, and Racial Capitalism."

10. Walia, *Border and Rule*.

11. McRuer, *Crip Theory*; Sandahl, "Queering the Crip or Cripping the Queer?"; Gilmore, *Golden Gulag*.

12. Anzaldúa, *Borderlands/La Frontera*; Kim, "Toward a Crip-of-Color Critique"; Lorde, *Sister Outsider*; Minich, *Accessible Citizenships*.

13. In the early 1990s, mortality from fishing pressure, disease, and environmental degradation led to a 70 percent drop in the region's blue crabs. These conditions resulted in severe losses in employment, wages, and overall economic revenue (Paolisso, "Blue Crabs and Controversy on the Chesapeake Bay"). In 2008, the federal government declared such drastic population declines a disaster. As a result, Maryland implemented severe restrictions on crabbing and established management and sustainability guidelines to improve blue crab population health (Chesapeake Bay Foundation, "Bad Water and the Decline of Blue Crabs in the Chesapeake Bay"). Since then, substantial increases in the crab population have prompted experts to predict a slow recovery among Maryland's blue crab fisheries (Fincham, "The Blue Crab Conundrum"). This recovery has foregrounded debates on the growing need for workers to sustain Maryland's crab industry. See also Griffith, "New Immigrants in an Old Industry"; Lawson, Mason, and Laporte, "The Fate and Transport of Mercury."

14. Arizpe, *Migration, Women and Social Development*; Dreby and Schmalzbauer, "The Relational Contexts of Migration"; Kossoudji and Ranney, "The Labor Market Experience of Female Migrants"; Preibisch and Hennebry, "Temporary Migration, Chronic Effects."

15. Gendered and racialized labor relations have long characterized the mid-Atlantic blue crab industry. The success of the blue crab industry in this region up until the mid-1980s rested on the comparative disadvantage of African American rural women in the formal labor market (Griffith, "New Immigrants in an Old Industry"). African American women picked crab from early spring to early fall. They relied on public benefits, transfer payments, social networks, and part-time jobs or informal economic activities to support themselves and their families during the winter months. Throughout most of the twentieth century, African American women and girls comprised the vast majority of workers in crab processing. However, the rapid decline of the African American labor force is due in part to the growth of educational and alternative employment opportunities for young African American women, reduced amounts of available work, and favoritism toward foreign workers (Griffith, *American Guestworkers*; Holt and Mattern, "Making Home"). As a result, very few African American women work in crab processing today.

16. U.S. Department of Homeland Security, "Nonimmigrant Admissions."

17. Southern Poverty Law Center, *Close to Slavery*.

18. American University, *Breaking the Shell*.

19. Southern Poverty Law Center, *Close to Slavery*.

20. Melamed, "Racial Capitalism," 78, referring to the definition of racism outlined by Ruth Wilson Gilmore. See Gilmore, "Fatal Couplings of Power and Difference."

21. In English, this translates to "When you do not have your mother, your grandmother feeds you," or "You make do with what you have." Haitians say this proverb when they do not have the right means or resources to do what needs to get done and when they have to use what is available to solve a problem or to deal with a situation.

22. Farmer, *AIDS and Accusation*; Sangaramoorthy, *Treating AIDS*.

23. The U.S. Congress created Temporary Protected Status (TPS) in the Immigration Act of 1990. TPS is a temporary immigration status provided to nationals of countries experiencing ongoing armed conflict, environmental disaster, or extraordinary but temporary conditions. It provides a work permit and stay of deportation to foreign nationals from those countries who are in the United States at the time the U.S. government makes the designation. After the 2010 earthquake, Haiti was added to the list of nations eligible for TPS, which is set to expire on August 2024. See Hallett, "Temporary Protection, Enduring Contradiction"; Paik, *Rightlessness*.

24. Tyner, *Dead Labor*; Berry, *The Price for Their Pound of Flesh*.

25. Melamed, "Racial Capitalism."

26. In 1986, the Immigration Reform and Control Act (IRCA) authorized two types of legalization programs for undocumented immigrants. One provision provided for legalization of persons who could establish entry before 1982. The other program for special agricultural workers (SAW) required these applicants to prove that they resided in the United States and had worked in agriculture for at least ninety days in the twelve months preceding application.

27. U.S. Department of Agriculture, "2017 Census of Agriculture."

28. Maryland Department of Labor, "Housing Concerns for H2A Temporary Agricultural Workers."

29. Daniel, *Bitter Harvest*.

30. Maryland Advisory Committee to the U.S. Commission on Civil Rights, "Migrant Workers on Maryland's Eastern Shore."

31. She referred to the Hilton hotel chain to indicate luxurious living conditions compared to other migrant labor camps.

32. This story is adapted from a blog entry contributed by Emilia M. Guevara; see "Health and Housing: A Tale of Two Farmworkers," *Thurka Sangaramoorthy* (blog), October 4, 2016, https://www.thurkasangaramoorthy.com/media/.

33. Addie, "Urban Life in the Shadows of Infrastructural Death"; Mitchell, "Dead Labor and the Political Economy of Landscape"; Tyner, *Dead Labor*.

34. For conceptualization of necrocapitalism, see Tyner, *Dead Labor*, xiii–xiv.

35. Bruno, The H-2B Visa and the Statutory Cap."

36. Sheppard, "Using Pain, Living with Pain."

37. De Wolfe, "Private Tragedy in Social Context?"; Vick, "Theorizing Episodic Disabilities."

38. Lightman et al., "Not Disabled Enough."

39. Rogaly, "Commentary."

40. Christina E. Green, *Journey to Banana Land*; Hahamovitch, *No Man's Land*; Preibisch and Hennebry, "Temporary Migration, Chronic Effects"; Segura and Zavella, *Women and Migration in the U.S.–Mexico Borderlands*; Torres and Carte, "Migration and Development?"

Chapter Three

1. Hunsaker and Kantayya, "Building a Sustainable Rural Health System"; Maryland Department of Health and Mental Hygiene, "2010 Primary Care Needs Assessment"; Maryland Rural Health Association, "Maryland Rural Health Plan"; Ricketts, "The Changing Nature of Rural Health Care."

2. U.S. Department of Health and Human Services, "Find Shortage Areas."

3. Salinsky, "Health Care Shortage Designations"; U.S. General Accounting Office, "Health Professional Shortage Areas."

4. Wang, "Measurement, Optimization, and Impact of Health Care Accessibility."

5. Weinhold and Gurtner, "Understanding Shortages of Sufficient Health Care in Rural Areas."

6. U.S. General Accounting Office, "Health Professional Shortage Areas."

7. There has been intense debate in the past few years about ACA's effects. The ACA made several changes to Medicaid. Perhaps the most widely discussed is expanding eligibility to adults with incomes up to 138 percent of the federal poverty level. Initially, this expansion was a requirement under the ACA. But the June 2012 U.S. Supreme Court ruling in National Federation of Independent Business v. Sebelius effectively made the Medicaid expansion an option for states. By the end of 2014, twenty-eight states and the District of Columbia expanded their Medicaid programs. As a result, qualified individuals

in these states have been eligible to purchase subsidized private health insurance cover-age since 2014 through federal and state-based marketplaces established by the ACA. However, several states that did not expand Medicaid programs contributed to a "cover-age gap" of 3.1 million people, those already with incomes too low to qualify for federal subsidies. At the end of 2021, eleven states have yet to expand Medicaid, leaving 2.2 mil-lion poor adults potentially uninsured during the COVID-19 health crisis when many have lost income and housing. States with the largest uninsured populations—almost all in the U.S. South—have a more significant number of those in the coverage gap. See Kaiser Family Foundation, "Status of State Medicaid Expansion Decisions: Interactive Map," last modified November 9, 2022, https://www.kff.org/medicaid/issue-brief /status-of-state-medicaid-expansion-decisions-interactive-map/.

8. Kaufman et al., "Medicaid Expansion Affects Rural and Urban Hospitals Differ-ently"; Mazurenko et al., "The Effects of Medicaid Expansion under the ACA."

9. Rosenbaum et al., *Community Health Centers*.

10. Sangaramoorthy and Guevara, "Immigrant Health in Rural Maryland"; Sanga-ramoorthy, "Putting Band-Aids on Things that Need Stitches."

11. Arcury and Quandt, *Latino Farmworkers in the Eastern United States*; Casey, Blewett, and Call, "Providing Health Care to Latino Immigrants"; Cervantes and Men-jívar, "Legal Violence, Health, and Access to Care"; Cristancho et al., "Listening to Ru-ral Hispanic Immigrants in the Midwest"; Heyman, Núñez, and Talavera, "Healthcare Access and Barriers for Unauthorized Immigrants in El Paso County, Texas"; Jacquez et al., "Health Care Use and Barriers"; Kozhimannil and Henning-Smith, "Racism and Health in Rural America"; and White et al., "Impact of Alabama's Immigration Law."

12. Miriam Jordan, "Migrant Workers Restricted to Farms under One Grower's Vi-rus Lockdown," *New York Times*, October 19, 2020.

13. Ricketts, "The Changing Nature of Rural Health Care."

14. Rosenbaum et al., *Community Health Centers*.

15. Institute of Medicine, *The Future of the Public's Health in the 21st Century*.

16. Deferred Action for Childhood Arrivals (DACA) is a policy that allows certain individuals who meet program requirements to request a grant of deferred action on their deportation. Individuals who are granted DACA are able to renew their grant and are eligible for work authorization.

17. Pew Research Center, "U.S. Unauthorized Immigrant Population Estimates by State."

18. Williams, Figueroa, and Tharpe, "Inclusive Approach to Immigrants Who Are Undocumented Can Help Families and States Prosper."

19. Arnold, "Racial Profiling in Immigration Enforcement."

20. Ricketts, *Rural Health in the United States*; Hartley, "Rural Health Disparities, Population Health, and Rural Culture"; Bolin et al., "Rural Healthy People 2020"; Hart et al., "Rural Health Care Providers in the United States"; Daniels et al., "Factors in Recruiting and Retaining Health Professionals for Rural Practice."

21. Castañeda et al., "Immigration as a Social Determinant of Health"; Holmes, *Fresh Fruit, Broken Bodies*; Quesada, Hart, and Bourgois, "Structural Vulnerability and Health"; Willen, "How Is Health-Related 'Deservingness' Reckoned?"

22. Jones et al., "Health Status and Health Care Access of Farm and Rural Populations"; Ziller, Lenardson, and Coburn, "Health Care Access and Use among the Rural Uninsured"; Douthit et al., "Exposing Some Important Barriers to Health Care Access."

23. Gamm et al., *Rural Healthy People 2010*; Cunningham et al., *Health Coverage and Access to Care for Hispanics*"; Derose, Escarce, and Lurie, "Immigrants and Health Care."

24. Rhodes et al., "The Impact of Local Immigration Enforcement Policies"; Martinez et al., "Evaluating the Impact of Immigration Policies"; Fuentes-Afflick and Hessol, "Immigration Status and Use of Health Services"; Toomey et al., "Impact of Arizona's SB 1070 Immigration Law"; Ortega et al., "Health Care Access, Use of Services, and Experiences"; Campbell et al., "A Comparison of Health Access"; Bustamante et al., "Variations in Healthcare Access and Utilization among Mexican Immigrants"; Maldonado et al., "Fear of Discovery among Latino Immigrants."

25. Jacobs et al., "Overcoming Language Barriers in Health Care"; Ku and Flores, "Pay Now or Pay Later"; and Karliner et al., "Do Professional Interpreters Improve Clinical Care for Patients with Limited English Proficiency?"

26. Cristancho et al., "Listening to Rural Hispanic Immigrants in the Midwest."

27. Artiga and Diaz, *Health Coverage and Care of Undocumented Immigrants*.

28. Kaiser Family Foundation. "Health Coverage of Immigrants"; Zuckerman, Waidmann, and Lawton, "Undocumented Immigrants."

Chapter Four

1. Redfield, "On Band-Aids and Magic Bullets."

2. Redfield, "On Band-Aids and Magic Bullets."

3. Kangas, "Traveling for Medical Care in a Global World"; Silva, Sancho, and Figueiredo, "Between Flows and Therapeutic Projects."

4. Leach et al., "New Therapeutic Landscapes in Africa."

5. Hampshire et al., "Out of the Reach of Children?"; Kangas, "Traveling for Medical Care in a Global World"; Samuelsen, "Therapeutic Itineraries."

6. Lewin and Altman, *America's Health Care Safety Net*; Becker, "Deadly Inequality in the Health Care 'Safety Net.'"

7. Boehm, "The Safety Net of the Safety Net"; Horton, "The Double Burden on Safety Net Providers"; Horton et al., "Transforming the Safety Net"; Lamphere, "Providers and Staff Respond to Medicaid Managed Care"; Morgen and Maskovsky, "The Anthropology of Welfare 'Reform.'"

8. Andaya, "The Gift of Health;" Benton, *HIV Exceptionalism*; Benton, Sangaramoorthy, and Kalofonos, "Temporality and Positive Living in the Age of HIV/AIDS; Brotherton, *Revolutionary Medicine*; Ledeneva, *Russia's Economy of Favours*; Prince and Marsland, *Making and Unmaking Public Health in Africa*; Rivkin-Fish, *Women's Health in Post-Soviet Russia*; Wendland, *A Heart for the Work*; Whyte et al., "Therapeutic Clientship."

9. Praspaliauskiene, "Enveloped Lives."

10. Livingston, *Improvising Medicine*.

11. Mol, Moser, and Pols, *Care in Practice*.

12. Hacker et al., "The Impact of Immigration and Customs Enforcement on Immigrant Health"; Kline, *Pathogenic Policing*; Rhodes et al., "The Impact of Local Immigration Enforcement Policies."

13. French et al., "Key Provisions of the Patient Protection and Affordable Care Act."

14. Robert Pear, "Health Law Tax Penalty? I'll Take, Millions Say," *New York Times*, October 27, 2016.

15. Nguyen, "Antiretroviral Globalism, Biopolitics, and Therapeutic Citizenship."

16. The implementation of the ACA, popularly known as "Obamacare," began in 2010 and represented the most significant change to health care funding and delivery since Medicaid and Medicare were introduced in 1965. A primary goal of the ACA was to reduce the number of uninsured Americans, which at the time stood at approximately 50 million, through the expansion of both private insurance and government-funded Medicaid (Horton et al., "Critical Anthropology of Global Health 'Takes a Stand' Statement"). Another key objective of the ACA was to contain soaring health care spending and taxpayer costs and increase efficiency in health care delivery.

17. Castañeda, "Medical Humanitarianism"; Gottlieb, Filc, and Davidovitch, "Medical Humanitarianism, Human Rights and Political Advocacy"; Larchanché, *Cultural Anxieties*; Rosenthal, "'Illegality' and Illness in the Everyday Struggles"; Willen, "Do 'Illegal' Im/migrants Have a Right to Health?"; Willen, "How Is Health-Related 'Deservingness' Reckoned?"

18. Castañeda, "Medical Humanitarianism."

19. Oberlander, "Long Time Coming."

20. Mulligan and Castañeda, *Unequal Coverage*; Rao and Hellander, "The Widening U.S. Health Care Crisis."

21. Although former President Barack Obama ("United States Health Care Reform") extolled the significant progress made by the ACA, many insist that the ACA falls far short of providing universal coverage and instead operates within a neoliberal logic, framed by less government intervention and increased deregulation and privatization in the market economy, which began to take shape during the postwar years (Adam Gaffney, "The Neoliberal Turn in American Health Care"). The so-called neoliberal turn in American health care led to significant transformations, including the rise in corporatized managed care, increased cost-sharing among insurance plans, and consumer-driven health care. Under this logic, health care is commoditized, and its distribution is determined by individual "consumers," seen as rational actors exercising their economic and political freedom in electing the quantity and quality of health care goods that they desire.

22. Bornstein and Redfield, *Forces of Compassion*; Fassin, *Humanitarian Reason*; Ticktin, *Casualties of Care*; Willen, "How Is Health-Related 'Deservingness' Reckoned?"

23. Ricketts, "The Changing Nature of Rural Health Care."

24. Ricketts, "The Changing Nature of Rural Health Care."

25. Rosenbaum et al., *Community Health Centers*.

26. Horton et al., "Critical Anthropology of Global Health 'Takes a Stand' Statement"; Joseph and Marrow, "Health Care, Immigrants, and Minorities;" Rosenbaum et al., *Community Health Centers*.

27. Pulido, "Flint, Environmental Racism, and Racial Capitalism," 8.

28. Butler, *Precarious Life*; Lorey, *State of Insecurity*.

29. Butler, *Frames of War*, 14.

30. Ferguson, "Declarations of Dependence."

31. Martínez-San Miguel and Stephens, "Introduction."

32. Huntington, *Political Order in Changing Societies*; Misztal, *Informality*; Stan, "Neither Commodities nor Gifts"; Zerilli, "Corruption, Property Restitution and Romanianness."

Chapter Five

1. Trull, "Why a Mexican Flag Flies High in a Trump County."

2. Estes, *Our History Is the Future*; Goeman, *Mark My Words*; Greer, *Black Ethnics*; Hartman, *Scenes of Subjection*; Kelley, *Freedom Dreams*; Perry, *Black Women against the Land Grab*; King, *Black Shoals*; Sharpe, *In the Wake*; and Walia, *Border and Rule*.

3. Walia, *Undoing Border Imperialism*, and Walia, *Border and Rule*.

4. Anzaldúa, *Borderlands/La Frontera*.

5. I draw inspiration from the work of Liisa Malkki and her exploration of the figure of the refugee as an object of concern and knowledge for the "international community" and for a particular variety of humanism. See Malkki, "Speechless Emissaries."

6. I am indebted to the work of Laura Pulido and Jodi Melamed in informing these analyses on racialized and spatialized ideas about risk and capital and how they mediate exclusion and belonging. See Pulido, "Geographies of Race and Ethnicity II," and Melamed, "Racial Capitalism."

7. McKittrick, *Demonic Grounds*.

8. McKittrick and Woods, *Black Geographies and the Politics of Place*, 4.

9. McKittrick and Woods, *Black Geographies and the Politics of Place*.

Bibliography

Abrego, Leisy. "Research as Accompaniment: Reflections on Objectivity, Ethics, and Emotions." In *Out of Place: Power, Person, and Difference in Socio-Legal Research*, edited by L. Chua and M. Massoud (forthcoming). Accessed December 2022, https://escholarship.org/uc/item/34v2g837.

Addie, Jean-Paul D. "Urban Life in the Shadows of Infrastructural Death: From People as Infrastructure to Dead Labor and Back Again." *Urban Geography* 42, no. 9 (2021): 1349–61.

Al-Mohammad, Hayder. "A Kidnapping in Basra: The Struggles and Precariousness of Life in Postinvasion Iraq." *Cultural Anthropology* 27, no. 4 (2012): 597–614.

American Immigration Council. *Immigrants in Maryland*. Washington, D.C.: American Immigration Council, 2015.

American University (American University and Centro de los Derechos del Migrante). *Breaking the Shell: How Maryland's Migrant Crab Pickers Continue to Be "Picked Apart."* Washington, D.C.: American University, 2020.

———. *Picked Apart: The Hidden Struggles of Migrant Worker Women in the Maryland Crab Industry*. Washington, D.C.: American University, 2010. http://www.cdmigrante.org/picked-apart-the-hidden-struggles-of-migrant-worker-women-in-the-maryland-crab-industry/.

Andaya, Elise. "The Gift of Health: Socialist Medical Practice and Shifting Material and Moral Economies in Post-Soviet Cuba." *Medical Anthropology Quarterly* 23, no. 4 (2009): 357–74.

Anzaldúa, Gloria. *Borderlands/La Frontera: The New Mestiza*. San Francisco: Aunt Lute Press, 1987.

Arcury, Thomas A., and Sarah A. Quandt. "Delivery of Health Services to Migrant and Seasonal Farmworkers." *Annual Review of Public Health* 28 (2007): 345–63.

———, eds. *Latino Farmworkers in the Eastern United States: Health, Safety and Justice*. New York: Springer, 2009.

Arizpe, Lourdes. *Migration, Women and Social Development: Key Issues*. New York: Springer, 2014.

Arnold, Carrie L. "Racial Profiling in Immigration Enforcement: State and Local Agreements to Enforce Federal Immigration Law." *Arizona Law Review* 49 (2007): 113–42.

Artiga, Samantha, and Maria Diaz. *Health Coverage and Care of Undocumented Immigrants*. Menlo Park, Calif.: Kaiser Family Foundation, 2019.

Artiga, Samantha, Rachel Garfield, and Antony Damico. *Estimated Impacts of Final Public Charge Inadmissibility Rule on Immigrants and Medicaid Coverage*. Menlo Park, Calif.: Kaiser Family Foundation, 2019.

Baba, Marietta L. "Anthropology and Transnational Migration: A Focus on Policy." *International Migration* 51, no. 2 (2013): 1–9.

Baker, Phyllis L., and Douglas R. Hotek. "Perhaps a Blessing: Skills and Contributions of Recent Mexican Immigrants in the Rural Midwest." *Hispanic Journal of Behavioral Sciences* 25, no. 4 (2003): 448–68.

Balibar, Etienne. *We, the People of Europe? Reflections on Transnational Citizenship*. Translated by J. Swenson. Princeton, N.J.: Princeton University Press, 2004.

Becker, Gay. "Deadly Inequality in the Health Care 'Safety Net': Uninsured Ethnic Minorities' Struggle to Live with Life-Threatening Illnesses." *Medical Anthropology Quarterly* 18, no. 2 (2004): 258–75.

Benton, Adia. *HIV Exceptionalism: Development through Disease in Sierra Leone*. Minneapolis: University of Minnesota Press, 2015.

Benton, Adia, Thurka Sangaramoorthy, and Ippolytos Kalofonos. "Temporality and Positive Living in the Age of HIV/AIDS: A Multisited Ethnography." *Current Anthropology* 58, no. 4 (2017): 454–76.

Berry, Daina Ramey. *The Price for Their Pound of Flesh: The Value of the Enslaved, from Womb to Grave, in the Building of a Nation*. Boston: Beacon Press, 2017.

Binford, Leigh. *Tomorrow We're All Going to the Harvest: Temporary Foreign Worker Programs and Neoliberal Political Economy*. Austin: University of Texas Press, 2013.

Blanchette, Alex, and Marcel LaFlamme. "Introduction: An Anthropological Almanac of Rural Americas." *Journal for the Anthropology of North America* 22, no. 2 (2019): 52–62.

Boehm, Deborah. "The Safety Net of the Safety Net: How Federally Qualified Health Centers 'Subsidize' Medicaid Managed Care." *Medical Anthropology Quarterly* 19, no. 1 (2005): 47–63.

Bolin, Jane N., Gail R. Bellamy, Alva O. Ferdinand, Ann M. Vuong, Bia A. Kash, Avery Schulze, and Janet W. Helduser. "Rural Healthy People 2020: New Decade, Same Challenges." *Journal of Rural Health* 31, no. 3 (2015): 326–33.

Bornstein, Erica, and Peter Redfield, eds. *Forces of Compassion: Humanitarianism between Ethics and Politics*. Santa Fe, N.Mex.: SAR Press, 2011.

Bourgois, Philippe, Seth M. Holmes, Kim Sue, and James Quesada. "Structural Vulnerability: Operationalizing the Concept to Address Health Disparities in Clinical Care." *Academic Medicine: Journal of the Association of American Medical Colleges* 92, no. 3 (2017): 299–307.

Brettell, Caroline B. "Theorizing Migration in Anthropology." *Migration Theory* 2 (2000): 97–137.

Broadway, Michael J. "Planning for Change in Small Towns or Trying to Avoid the Slaughterhouse Blues." *Journal of Rural Studies* 16 (2000): 37–46.

Brotherton, Sean P. *Revolutionary Medicine: Health and the Body in Post-Soviet Cuba*. Durham, N.C.: Duke University Press, 2012.

Brown, David L., and John M. Wardwell, eds. *New Directions in Urban–Rural Migration: The Population Turnaround in Rural America*. New York: Academic Press, 2013.

Bruno, Andorra. "The H-2B Visa and the Statutory Cap: In Brief." *Congressional Research Service*, April 17, 2018. https://fas.org/sgp/crs/homesec/R44306.pdf.

Burroughs, Edgar Rice. *The Land That Time Forgot*. New York: Grosset and Dunlap, 1924.

Bustamante, Arturo Vargas, Hai Fang, Jeremiah Garza, Olivia Carter-Pokras, Steven P. Wallace, John A. Rizzo, and Alexander N. Ortega. "Variations in Healthcare Access and Utilization among Mexican Immigrants: The Role of Documentation Status." *Journal of Immigrant and Minority Health* 14, no. 1 (2012): 146–55.

Butler, Judith. *Frames of War: When Is Life Grievable?* London: Verso Books, 2016.

———. *Precarious Life: The Powers of Mourning and Violence*. London: Verso Books, 2006

Cairns, Kate. "Youth, Dirt, and the Spatialization of Subjectivity: An Intersectional Approach to White Rural Imaginaries." *Canadian Journal of Sociology* 38, no. 4 (2013): 623–46.

Campbell, Ruth M., A. G. Klei, Brian D. Hodges, David Fisman, and Simon Kitto. "A Comparison of Health Access between Permanent Residents, Undocumented Immigrants and Refugee Claimants in Toronto, Canada." *Journal of Immigrant and Minority Health* 16, no. 1 (2014): 165–76.

Carney, Megan. *The Unending Hunger: Tracing Women and Food Insecurity across Borders*. Berkeley: University of California Press, 2015.

Carr, Patrick J., and Maria J. Kefalas. *Hollowing Out the Middle: The Rural Brain Drain and What It Means for America*. Boston: Beacon Press, 2009.

Casey, Michella M., Lynn A. Blewett, and Kathleen T. Call. "Providing Health Care to Latino Immigrants: Community-Based Efforts in the Rural Midwest." *American Journal of Public Health* 94, no. 10 (2004): 1709–11.

Castañeda, Heide. "Medical Humanitarianism and Physicians' Organized Efforts to Provide Aid to Unauthorized Migrants in Germany." *Human Organization* 70 (2011): 1–10.

———. "'Over-Foreignization' or 'Unused Potential'? A Critical Review of Migrant Health in Germany and Responses toward Unauthorized Migration." *Social Science & Medicine* 74, no. 6 (2012): 830–38.

Castañeda, Heide, Seth M. Holmes, Daniel S. Madrigal, Maria-Elena DeTrinidad Young, Naomi Beyeler, and James Quesada. "Immigration as a Social Determinant of Health." *Annual Review of Public Health* 36 (2015): 375–92.

Castles, Stephen. "Towards a Sociology of Forced Migration and Social Transformation." *Sociology* 37, no. 1 (2003): 13–34.

Cervantes, Andrea Gómez, and Cecilia Menjívar. "Legal Violence, Health, and Access to Care: Latina Immigrants in Rural and Urban Kansas." *Journal of Health and Social Behavior* 61, no. 3 (2020): 307–23.

Chesapeake Bay Foundation. "Bad Water and the Decline of Blue Crabs in the Chesapeake Bay," December 2008. https://www.conservationgateway.org/Documents/CBF-BadWatersReport.pdf.

Cloke, Paul J., and Jo Little, eds. *Contested Countryside Cultures: Otherness, Marginalisation, and Rurality*. London: Routledge, 1997.

Cloke, Paul, Terry Marsden, and Patrick Mooney, eds. *Handbook of Rural Studies*. London: Sage, 2006.

Coe, Cati. "The Temporality of Care: Gender, Migration, and the Entrainment of Life-Courses." In *Anthropological Perspectives on Care*, edited by E. Alber and H. Drotbohm, 181–205. New York: Palgrave Macmillan, 2015.

Cohen, Robin. *The New Helots: Migrants in the International Division of Labour*. Hants, U.K.: Gower Publishing, 1987.

Corchado, Alfredo. "The Mexican Revival of Small-Town America." *New York Times*, June 2, 2018.

Costa, Daniel. "H-2B Crabpickers Are So Important to the Maryland Seafood Industry that They Get Paid $3 Less per Hour than the State or Local Average Wage." *Working Economics Blog*, May 26, 2017. https://www.epi.org/blog/h-2b -crabpickers-maryland-seafood-industry-paid-less-than-average/.

Courtemanche, Charles, James Marton, Benjamin Ukert, Aaron Yelowitz, and Daniela Zapata. "Early Impacts of the Affordable Care Act on Health Insurance Coverage in Medicaid Expansion and Non-Expansion States." *Journal of Policy Analysis and Management* 36, no. 1 (2017): 178–210.

Cravey, Altha J. "The Changing South: Latino Labor and Poultry Production in Rural North Carolina." *Southeastern Geographer* 37, no. 2 (1997): 295–300.

Cristancho, Sergio D., Marcela Garces, Karen E. Peters, and Benjamin C. Mueller. "Listening to Rural Hispanic Immigrants in the Midwest: A Community-Based Participatory Assessment of Major Barriers to Health Care Access and Use." *Qualitative Health Research* 18, no. 5 (2008): 633–46.

Cunningham, Peter J., Michelle Banker, Samantha Artiga, and Jennifer Tolbert. *Health Coverage and Access to Care for Hispanics in "New Growth Communities" and "Major Hispanic Centers."* Menlo Park, Calif.: Kaiser Family Foundation.

Dalla, Rochelle L., and April Christensen. "Latino Immigrants Describe Residence in Rural Midwestern Meatpacking Communities: A Longitudinal Assessment of Social and Economic Change." *Hispanic Journal of Behavioral Sciences* 27, no. 1 (2005): 23–42.

Dalla, Rochelle L., Amy Ellis, and Sheran C. Cramer. "Immigration and Rural America: Latinos' Perceptions of Work and Residence in Three Meatpacking Communities." *Community, Work and Family* 8, no. 2 (2005): 163–85.

Dalla, Rochelle L., Francisco Villarruel, Sheran C. Cramer, and Gloria Gonzalez-Kruger. "Examining Strengths and Challenges of Rapid Rural Immigration." *Great Plains Research* (2004): 231–51.

Daniel, Cletus E. *Bitter Harvest: A History of California farmworkers, 1870–1941.* Berkeley: University of California Press, 1982.

Daniels, Zina M., Betsy J. Vanleit, Betty J. Skipper, Margaret L. Sanders, and Robert L. Rhyne. "Factors in Recruiting and Retaining Health Professionals for Rural Practice." *Journal of Rural Health* 23, no. 1 (2007): 62–71.

Dao, Amy, and Jessica Mulligan. "Toward an Anthropology of Insurance and Health Reform: An Introduction to the Special Issue." *Medical Anthropology Quarterly* 30, no. 1 (2016): 5–17.

Dave, Naisargi N. "Witness: Humans, Animals, and the Politics of Becoming." *Cultural Anthropology* 29, no. 3 (2014): 433–56.

Davis, Angela Y. *Freedom Is a Constant Struggle: Ferguson, Palestine, and the Foundations of a Movement*. Chicago: Haymarket Books, 2016.

De Boer, John. "Resilience and the Fragile City." *Stability: International Journal of Security and Development* 4, no. 1 (2015).

De Genova, Nicholas. "Migrant 'Illegality' and Deportability in Everyday Life." *Annual Review of Anthropology* 31, no. 1 (2002): 419–47.

De Leon, Erwin, Matthew Maronick, Carol J. DeVita, and Elizabeth T. Boris. "Community-Based Organizations and Immigrant Integration in the Washington, D.C., Metropolitan Area." Washington, D.C.: The Urban Institute, 2009.

Delmarva Chicken Association. "Here's How the Chicken Community Is Working for Delmarva," 2019. https://www.dcachicken.com/facts/facts-figures.cfm.

Denzin, Norman K., Yvonna S. Lincoln, and Linda Tuhiwai Smith, eds. *Handbook of Critical and Indigenous Methodologies*. Thousand Oaks, Calif.: Sage, 2008.

Derose, Kathryn P., José J. Escarce, and Nicole Lurie. "Immigrants and Health Care: Sources of Vulnerability." *Health Affairs* 26, no. 5 (2007): 1258–68.

De Wolfe, Patricia. "Private Tragedy in Social Context? Reflections on Disability, Illness and Suffering." *Disability & Society* 17 (2002): 255–67.

Doherty, Jacob. "Life (and Limb) in the Fast-Lane: Disposable People as Infrastructure in Kampala's Boda Industry." *Critical African Studies* 9, no. 2 (2017): 192–209.

Douthit, Nathan, Sakal Kiv, Tzvi Dwolatzky, and Seema Biswas. "Exposing Some Important Barriers to Health Care Access in the Rural USA." *Public Health* 129, no. 6 (2015): 611–20.

Dreby, Joanna, and Leah Schmalzbauer. "The Relational Contexts of Migration: Mexican Women in New Destination Sites." In *Sociological Forum* 28, no. 1 (2013): 1–26.

Dunn, Timothy J., Ana María Aragonés, and George Shivers. "Recent Mexican Migration in the Rural Delmarva Peninsula: Human Rights versus Citizenship Rights in a Local Context." In *New Destinations: Mexican Immigration in the United States*, edited by Víctor Zúñiga and Rubén Hernández-León, 155–83. New York: Russell Sage Foundation, 2005.

Dunn, Timothy, and Amy Liebman. *Needs Assessment Report of Hispanic Immigrants on the Eastern Shore of Maryland for the Eastern Shore Regional Library*. Salisbury, Md.: Eastern Shore Regional Library, 2004.

Erwin, Anna. "Grower Influence during a Participatory Project with Farmworkers." *Geoforum* 130 (2022): 69–77.

Estes, Nick. *Our History Is the Future: Standing Rock versus the Dakota Access Pipeline, and the Long Tradition of Indigenous Resistance*. Brooklyn: Verso, 2019.

Farmer, Paul. *AIDS and Accusation: Haiti and the Geography of Blame*. Berkeley: University of California Press, 2006.

Fassin, Didier. *Humanitarian Reason: A Moral History of the Present*. Berkeley: University of California Press, 2011.

Feld, Steven, and Keith H. Basso, eds. *Senses of Place*. Santa Fe, N. Mex.: SAR Press, 1996.

Ferguson, James. "Declarations of Dependence: Labour, Personhood, and Welfare in Southern Africa." *Journal of the Royal Anthropological Institute* 19, no. 2 (2013): 223–242.

Fincham, Michael W. "The Blue Crab Conundrum." *Chesapeake Quarterly* 11 (2012): 1–8.

Fitzgerald, Joseph R. *The Struggle Is Eternal: Gloria Richardson and Black Liberation.* Lexington: University Press of Kentucky, 2018.

Flippen, Chenoa A., and Emilio A. Parrado. "A Tale of Two Contexts: U.S. Migration and the Labor Force Trajectories of Mexican Women." *International Migration Review* 49, no. 1 (2015): 232–59.

Fowler, Katherine A., Matthew Gladden, Kevin J. Vagi, Jamar Barnes, and Leroy Frazier. "Increase in Suicides Associated with Home Eviction and Foreclosure during the U.S. Housing Crisis: Findings from 16 National Violent Death Reporting System States, 2005–2010." *American Journal of Public Health* 105, no. 2 (2015): 311–16.

French, Michael T., Jenny Homer, Gulcin Gumus, and Lucas Hickling. "Key Provisions of the Patient Protection and Affordable Care Act (ACA): A Systematic Review and Presentation of Early Research Findings." *Health Services Research* 51, no. 5 (2016): 1735–71.

Freshour, Carrie Rebecca. "'Ain't No Life for a Mother': Racial Capitalism and the Making of Poultry Processing Workers in Northeast Georgia." PhD diss., Cornell University, 2018.

Frey, William H. "Three Americas: The Rising Significance of Regions." *Journal of the American Planning Association* 68, no. 4 (2002): 349–55.

Frydenlund, Shae, and Elizabeth Cullen Dunn. "Refugees and Racial Capitalism: Meatpacking and the Primitive Accumulation of Labor." *Political Geography* 95 (2022): 1–8..

Fuentes-Afflick, Elena, and Nancy A. Hessol. "Immigration Status and Use of Health Services among Latina Women in the San Francisco Bay Area." *Journal of Women's Health* 18, no. 8 (2009): 1275–80.

Gaffney, Adam. "The Neoliberal Turn in American Health Care." *International Journal of Health Services* 45, no. 1 (2015): 33–52.

Gaffney, Allison Smith. "Don't Hassle Me, I'm Local: The Integration of Latin American Settlers in the Delmarva Peninsula." Working Paper 152. Center for Iberian and Latin American Studies and Center for Comparative Immigration Studies, University of California-San Diego, 2007.

Gálvez, Alyshia. *Eating NAFTA: Trade, Food Policies, and the Destruction of Mexico.* Berkeley: University of California Press, 2018.

Gamm, Larry D., Linnae L. Hutchison, Betty J. Dabney, and Alicia M. Dorsey, eds. *Rural Healthy People 2010: A Companion Document to Healthy People 2010,* Vol. 2. College Station: Texas A&M University System Health Science Center, 2003. https://srhrc.tamhsc.edu/docs/rhp-2010-volume2.pdf.

Gentsch, Kerstin, and Douglas S. Massey. "Labor Market Outcomes for Legal Mexican Immigrants under the New Regime of Immigration Enforcement." *Social Science Quarterly* 92, no. 3 (2011): 875–93.

Gesler, Wilbert M. "Therapeutic Landscapes: Medical Issues in Light of the New Cultural Geography." *Social Science & Medicine* 34, no. 7 (1992): 735–46.

Gibson, Campbell J., and Emily Lennon. "Historical Census Statistics on the Foreign-Born Population of the United States: 1850–1990." Working Paper 29. U.S. Census Bureau Population Division, February 1999.

Gilmore, Ruth Wilson. "Fatal Couplings of Power and Difference: Notes on Racism and Geography." *The Professional Geographer* 54, no. 1 (2002): 15–24

———. *Golden Gulag: Prisons, Surplus, Crisis, and Opposition in Globalizing California.* Berkeley: University of California Press, 2007.

Gilroy, Paul, and Ruth Wilson Gilmore. *Selected Writings on Race and Difference.* Durham, N.C.: Duke University Press, 2021.

Gladwell, Malcolm. *The Tipping Point: How Little Things Can Make a Big Difference.* New York: Little, Brown, 2002.

Goeman, Mishuana. *Mark My Words: Native Women Mapping Our Nations.* Minneapolis: University of Minnesota Press, 2013.

Goldstein, Bruce. "Agribusiness Lobbies for a New Temporary Foreign Worker Program." *In Defense of the Alien* 20 (1997): 86–110.

Goode, Judith G., and Jeff Maskovsky, eds. *New Poverty Studies: The Ethnography of Power, Politics, and Impoverished People in the United States.* New York: NYU Press, 2001.

Gottleib, Nora, Dani Filc, and Nadav Davidovitch. "Medical Humanitarianism, Human Rights and Political Advocacy: The Case of the Israeli Open Clinic." *Social Science & Medicine* 74 (2012): 839–45.

Green, Christina E. *Journey to Banana Land: Race and Gender in Afro-Caribbean Labor Migration to Honduras and the United States.* Berkeley: University of California, 2017.

Green, Gary Paul. "Deindustrialization of Rural America: Economic Restructuring and the Rural Ghetto." *Local Development & Society* 1 (2020): 15–25.

Greer, Christina M. *Black Ethnics: Race, Immigration, and the Pursuit of the American Dream.* Oxford: Oxford University Press, 2013.

Griffith, David. *American Guestworkers: Jamaicans and Mexicans in the U.S. Labor Market.* University Park: Penn State University Press, 2006.

———. "New Immigrants in an Old Industry: Mexican H-2B Workers in the Mid-Atlantic Blue Crab Processing Industry." Conference paper presented at Immigration and the Changing Face of Rural America: Focus on the Mid-Atlantic and Southeastern States, Newark, Delaware, September 11–13, 1997.

Griffiths, Michael. "Networks of Reciprocity: Precarity and Community Social Organisations in Rural Myanmar." *Journal of Contemporary Asia* 49, no. 4 (2019): 602–25

Gujral, Kritee, and Anirban Basu. "Impact of Rural and Urban Hospital Closures on Inpatient Mortality." NBER Working Paper 26182. National Bureau of Economic Research, 2019.

Gupta, Akhil, and James Ferguson. "Beyond 'Culture': Space, Identity, and the Politics of Difference." *Cultural Anthropology* 7, no. 1 (1992): 6–23.

Guzman, Gloria G. "Household Income: 2019, American Community Survey Briefs." U.S. Census Bureau, 2020.

Hacker, Karen, Jocelyn Chu, Carolyn Leung, Robert Marra, Alex Pirie, Mohamed Brahimi, Margaret English, Joshua Beckmann, Dolores Acevedo-Garcia, and Robert P. Marlin. "The Impact of Immigration and Customs Enforcement on Immigrant Health: Perceptions of Immigrants in Everett, Massachusetts, USA." *Social Science & Medicine* 73, no. 4 (2011): 586–94.

Hahamovitch, Cindy. *No Man's Land: Jamaican Guestworkers in America and the Global History of Deportable Labor*. Princeton, N.J.: Princeton University Press, 2014.

Hallett, Miranda Cady. "Temporary Protection, Enduring Contradiction: The Contested and Contradictory Meanings of Temporary Immigration Status." *Law & Social Inquiry* 39, no. 3 (2014): 621–42.

Hampshire, Kate, Gina Porter, Samuel Asiedu Owusu, Augustine Tanle, and Albert Abane. "Out of the Reach of Children? Young People's Health-Seeking Practices and Agency in Africa's Newly-Emerging Therapeutic Landscapes." *Social Science & Medicine* 73 (2011): 702–10.

Han, Clara. "Precarity, Precariousness, and Vulnerability." *Annual Review of Anthropology* 47 (2018): 331–43.

Hanna, Stephen P. "Finding a Place in the World-Economy: Core-Periphery Relations, the Nation-State and the Underdevelopment of Garrett County, Maryland." *Political Geography* 14, no. 5 (1995): 451–72.

Hart, L. Gary, Edward Salsberg, Deborah M. Phillips, and Denise M. Lishner. "Rural Health Care Providers in the United States." *Journal of Rural Health* 18 Suppl (2002): 211–32.

Hartley, David. "Rural Health Disparities, Population Health, and Rural Culture." *American Journal of Public Health* 94, no. 10 (2004): 1675–78.

Hartman, Saidiya V. *Scenes of Subjection: Terror, Slavery, and Self-Making in Nineteenth-Century America*. Oxford: Oxford University Press, 1997.

Hawthorne, Camilla. "Black Matters Are Spatial Matters: Black Geographies for the Twenty-First Century." *Geography Compass* 13, no. 11 (2019). https://doi.org/10.1111/gec3.12468.

Hennebry, Jenna L. "Transnational Precarity: Women's Migration Work and Mexican Seasonal Agricultural Migration." *International Journal of Sociology* 44, no. 3 (2014): 42–59.

Hennebry, Jenna L., and Kerry Preibisch. "A Model for Managed Migration? Re-Examining Best Practices in Canada's Seasonal Agricultural Worker Program." *International Migration* 50 (2012): e19–e40.

Heyman, Josiah McC., Guillermina Gina Núñez, and Victor Talavera. "Healthcare Access and Barriers for Unauthorized Immigrants in El Paso County, Texas." *Family & Community Health* 32, no. 1 (2009): 4–21.

Hibbard, Michael, and Claudia Römer. "Planning the Global Countryside: Comparing Approaches to Teaching Rural Planning." *Journal of Planning Education and Research* 19, no. 1 (1999): 87–92.

Hirsh, Eric, and Michael O'Hanlon, eds. *The Anthropology of Landscape: Perspectives on Place and Space*. Oxford: Oxford University Press, 1995.

Hogan, Andrew, and Brian Roberts. "Occupational Employment Projections to 2024." *Monthly Labor Review*, December 2015.

Hogan, Jackie. "Constructing the Global in Two Rural Communities in Australia and Japan." *Journal of Sociology* 40 (2004): 21–40.

Holmes, Seth M. *Fresh Fruit, Broken Bodies: Migrant Farmworkers in the United States.* Berkeley: University of California Press, 2013.

Holt, Alejandra Okie, and Evelyn Mattern. "Making Home: Culture, Ethnicity, and Religion among Farmworkers in the Southeastern United States." In *The Human Cost of Food*, 22–53. Austin: University of Texas Press, 2021.

Hondagneu-Sotelo, Pierrette, ed. *Gender and U.S. Immigration: Contemporary Trends.* Berkeley: University of California Press, 2003.

Horowitz, Roger, and Mark J. Miller. "Immigrants in the Delmarva Poultry Processing Industry: The Changing Face of Georgetown, Delaware and Environs." East Lansing: Julian Samora Research Institute, Michigan State University, 1999.

Horton, Sarah. "The Double Burden on Safety Net Providers: Placing Health Disparities in the Context of the Privatization of Health Care in the U.S." *Social Science & Medicine* 63, no. 10 (2006): 2702–14

———. *They Leave Their Kidneys in the Fields: Illness, Injury, and Illegality among U.S. Farmworkers.* Berkeley: University of California Press, 2016.

Horton, Sarah, Cesar Abadía, Jessica Mulligan, and Jennifer Jo Thompson. "Critical Anthropology of Global Health 'Takes a Stand' Statement: A Critical Medical Anthropological Approach to the U.S.'s Affordable Care Act." *Medical Anthropology Quarterly* 28 (2014): 1–22.

Horton, Sarah, Joanne McCloskey, Caroline Todd, and Marta Henriksen. "Transforming the Safety Net: Responses to Medicaid Managed Care in, Rural and Urban New Mexico." *American Anthropologist* 103, no. 3 (2001): 733–46.

Housing Assistance Council. "Housing for Families and Unaccompanied Migrant Farmworkers," 1997.

Humez, Jean M. *Harriet Tubman: The Life and the Life Stories.* Madison: University of Wisconsin Press, 2006.

Hunsaker, Matthew, and Vivek S. Kantayya. "Building a Sustainable Rural Health System in the Era of Health Reform." *Disease-a-month* 56, no. 12 (2010): 698–705.

Huntington, Samuel P. *Political Order in Changing Societies.* New Haven, Conn.: Yale University Press, 1968.

Institute for Women's Policy Research. *Gender, Urbanization, and Democratic Governance.* Washington, D.C.: National Democratic Institute, 2015.

Institute of Medicine. *The Future of the Public's Health in the 21st Century.* Washington, D.C.: National Academies Press, 2003.

International Organization for Migration (IOM). *World Migration Report 2015.* Geneva: IOM, 2015.

Ivey-Stephenson, Asha Z., Alex E. Crosby, Shane P. Jack, Tadesse Haileyesus, and Marcie-jo Kresnow-Sedacca. "Suicide Trends among and within Urbanization Levels by Sex, Race/Ethnicity, Age Group, and Mechanism of Death—United States, 2001–2015." *MMWR Surveillance Summaries* 66, no. 18 (2017): 1–16.

Jacobs, Elizabeth A., Donald S. Shepard, Jose A. Suaya, and Esta-Lee Stone. "Overcoming Language Barriers in Health Care: Costs and Benefits of Interpreter Services." *American Journal of Public Health* 94, no. 5 (2004): 866–69.

Jacquez, Farrah, Lisa Vaughn, Jenny Zhen-Duan, and Camille Graham. "Health
Care Use and Barriers to Care among Latino Immigrants in a New Migration
Area." *Journal of Health Care for the Poor and Underserved* 27, no. 4 (2016): 1761–78.

James, Wesley L. "All Rural Places Are Not Created Equal: Revisiting the Rural
Mortality Penalty in the United States." *American Journal of Public Health* 104,
no. 11 (2014): 2122–29.

Jensen, Leif. "New Immigrant Settlements in Rural America: Problems, Prospects,
and Policies." *Reports on Rural America* 1, no. 3 (2006).

Jones, Carol Adaire, Timothy S. Parker, Mary Ahearn, Ashok K. Mishra, and
Jayachandran N. Variyam. "Health Status and Health Care Access of Farm and Rural
Populations." Economic Information Bulletin No. 57, Economic Research Service,
U.S. Department of Agriculture, 2009.

Joseph, Tiffany D., and Helen B. Marrow. "Health Care, Immigrants, and Minorities:
Lessons from the Affordable Care Act in the U.S." *Journal of Ethnic and Migration
Studies* 43, no. 12 (2017): 1965–84.

Kaiser Family Foundation. "Health Coverage of Immigrants," April 6, 2022.
https://www.kff.org/racial-equity-and-health-policy/fact-sheet/health-coverage
-of-immigrants/.

Kalleberg, Arne L. "Nonstandard Employment Relations: Part-Time, Temporary and
Contract Work." *Annual Review of Sociology* 26, no.1 (2000): 341–65.

Kalleberg, Arne L., and Stephen P. Vallas. "Probing Precarious Work: Theory,
Research, and Politics." *Research in the Sociology of Work* 31, no. 1 (2018): 1–30.

Kangas, Beth. "Therapeutic Itineraries in a Global World: Yemenis and Their Search
for Biomedical Treatment Abroad." *Medical Anthropology* 21, no. 1 (2002): 35–78.

———. "Traveling for Medical Care in a Global World." *Medical Anthropology* 29
(2010): 344–62

Karliner, Leah S., Elizabeth A. Jacobs, Alice Hm Chen, and Sunita Mutha. "Do
Professional Interpreters Improve Clinical Care for Patients with Limited English
Proficiency? A Systematic Review of the Literature." *Health Services Research* 42,
no. 2 (2007): 727–54.

Katz, Elizabeth. "The Changing Role of Women in the Rural Economies of Latin
America." In *Current and Emerging Issues for Economic Analysis and Policy Research
(CUREMIS II). Volume I: Latin America and the Caribbean*, edited by B. Davis,
31–66. Rome: Food and Agriculture Organization of the United Nations (FAO),
2003.

Kaufman, Brystana G., Kristin L. Reiter, George H. Pink, and George M. Holmes.
"Medicaid Expansion Affects Rural and Urban Hospitals Differently." *Health
Affairs* 35, no. 9 (2016): 1665–72.

Kaufman, Brystana G., Sharita R. Thomas, Randy K. Randolph, Julie R. Perry,
Kristie W. Thompson, George M. Holmes, and George H. Pink. "The Rising Rate
of Rural Hospital Closures." *Journal of Rural Health* 32, no. 1 (2016): 35–43.

Kelley, Robin D. G. *Freedom Dreams: The Black Radical Imagination*. Boston: Beacon
Press, 2002.

Kendzior, Sarah. *The View from Flyover Country: Dispatches from the Forgotten America*.
New York: Flatiron Books, 2018.

Kim, Jina B. "Toward a Crip-of-Color Critique: Thinking with Minich's 'Enabling Whom?'" *Lateral* 6, no. 1 (2017).

King, Tiffany Lethabo. *Black Shoals: Offshore Formations of Black and Native Studies.* Durham, N.C.: Duke University Press, 2019.

Kline, Nolan. *Pathogenic Policing: Immigration Enforcement and Health in the U.S. South.* New Brunswick, N.J.: Rutgers University Press, 2019.

Kossoudji, Sherrie, and Susan Ranney. "The Labor Market Experience of Female Migrants: The Case of Temporary Mexican Migration to the U.S." *International Migration Review* 18, no. 4 (1984): 1120–43.

Kozhimannil, Katy B., and Carrie Henning-Smith. "Racism and Health in Rural America." *Journal of Health Care for the Poor and Underserved* 29, no. 1 (2018): 35–43.

Ku, Leighton, and Glenn Flores. "Pay Now or Pay Later: Providing Interpreter Services in Health Care." *Health Affairs* 24, no. 2 (2005): 435–44.

Kugel, Candace, and Edward L. Zuroweste. "The State of Health Care Services for Mobile Poor Populations: History, Current Status, and Future Challenges." *Journal of Health Care for the Poor and Underserved* 21, no. 2 (2010): 421–29.

Lambert, Rob, and Andrew Herod, eds. *Neoliberal Capitalism and Precarious Work: Ethnographies of Accommodation and Resistance.* Cheltenham, UK: Edward Elgar Publishing, 2016.

Lamphere, Louise. "Providers and Staff Respond to Medicaid Managed Care: The Unintended Consequences of Reform in New Mexico." *Medical Anthropology Quarterly* 19, no. 1 (2005): 3–25

Larchanché, Stephanie. *Cultural Anxieties: Managing Migrant Suffering in France.* New Brunswick, N.J.: Rutgers University Press, 2020.

Lastarria-Cornhiel, Susana. "Feminization of Agriculture: Trends and Driving Forces." Washington, DC: World Bank, 2008.

Lawson, Nicole, Robert Mason, and Jean-Michel Laporte. "The Fate and Transport of Mercury, Methylmercury, and Other Trace Metals in Chesapeake Bay Tributaries." *Water Research* 35, no. 2 (2001): 501–15.

Leach, Melissa, James Fairhead, Dominique Millimouno, and Alpha Ahmadou Diallo. "New Therapeutic Landscapes in Africa: Parental Categories and Practices in Seeking Infant Health in the Republic of Guinea." *Social Science & Medicine* 66 (2008): 2157–67.

Ledeneva, Alena V. *Russia's Economy of Favours: Blat, Networking and Informal Exchange.* Cambridge: Cambridge University Press, 1998.

Lewin, Marion Ein, and Stuart Altman, eds. *America's Health Care Safety Net: Intact but Endangered.* Washington, D.C.: National Academies Press, 2000.

Lichter, Daniel T. "Immigration and the New Racial Diversity in Rural America." *Rural Sociology* 77, no. 1 (2012): 3–35.

Lichter, Daniel T., and David L. Brown. "Rural America in an Urban Society: Changing Spatial and Social Boundaries." *Annual Review of Sociology* 37 (2011): 565–92.

Lichter, Daniel T., and Kenneth M. Johnson. "A Demographic Lifeline? Immigration and Hispanic Population Growth in Rural America." *Population Research and Policy Review* 39, no. 5 (2020): 785–803.

Lightman, Ernie, Andrea Vick, Dean Herd, and Andrew Mitchell. "'Not Disabled Enough': Episodic Disabilities and the Ontario Disability Support Program." *Disability Studies Quarterly* 29, no. 3 (2009).

Lister, Jamey J., Addie Weaver, Jennifer D. Ellis, Joseph A. Himle, and David M. Ledgerwood. "A Systematic Review of Rural-Specific Barriers to Medication Treatment for Opioid Use Disorder in the United States." *American Journal of Drug and Alcohol Abuse* 46, no. 3 (2020): 273–88.

Livingston, Julie. *Improvising Medicine: An African Oncology Ward in an Emerging Cancer Epidemic*. Durham, N.C.: Duke University Press, 2012.

Lorde, Audre. *Sister Outsider: Essays and Speeches*. Berkeley, Calif.: Crossing Press, 1984.

Lorey, Isabell. *State of Insecurity: Government of the Precarious*. Translated by Aileen Derieg. London: Verso Books, 2015.

Low, Setha M. *Spatializing Culture: The Ethnography of Space and Place*. London: Routledge, 2016.

Luo, Feijun, Curtis S. Florence, Myriam Quispe-Agnoli, Lijing Ouyang, and Alexander E. Crosby. "Impact of Business Cycles on U.S. Suicide Rates, 1928–2007." *American Journal of Public Health* 101, no. 6 (2011): 1139–46.

MacDonald, James M. "Tracking the Consolidation of U.S. Agriculture." *Applied Economic Perspectives and Policy* 42, no. 3 (2020): 361–79.

MacDowell, Martin, Michael Glasser, Mike Fitts, Kimberly Nielsen, and Matthew Hunsaker. "A National View of Rural Health Workforce Issues in the USA." *Rural and Remote Health* 10, no. 3 (2010): 1531.

Maldonado, Cynthia Z., Robert M. Rodriguez, Jesus R. Torres, Yvette S. Flores, and Luis M. Lovato. "Fear of Discovery among Latino Immigrants Presenting to the Emergency Department." *Academic Emergency Medicine* 20, no. 2 (2013): 155–61.

Malkki, Liisa H. "Speechless Emissaries: Refugees, Humanitarianism, and Dehistoricization." *Cultural Anthropology* 11, no. 3 (1996): 377–404.

Margerison-Zilko, Claire, Sidra Goldman-Mellor, April Falconi, and Janelle Downing. "Health Impacts of the Great Recession: A Critical Review." *Current Epidemiology Reports* 3, no. 1 (2016): 81–91.

Marrow, Helen. *New Destination Dreaming: Immigration, Race, and Legal Status in the Rural American South*. Stanford, Calif.: Stanford University Press, 2011.

Marrow, Helen B., and Tiffany D. Joseph. "Excluded and Frozen Out: Unauthorized Immigrants' (Non) Access to Care after U.S. Health Care Reform." *Journal of Ethnic and Migration Studies* 41, no. 14 (2015): 2253–73

Martin, Philip, Michael Fix, and J. Edward Taylor, *The New Rural Poverty: Agriculture and Immigration in California*. Washington, D.C.: Urban Institute Press, 2006.

Martinez, Omar, Elwin Wu, Theo Sandfort, Brian Dodge, Alex Carballo-Dieguez, Rogeiro Pinto, Scott Rhodes, Eva Moya, and Silvia Chavez-Baray. "Evaluating the Impact of Immigration Policies on Health Status among Undocumented Immigrants: A Systematic Review." *Journal of Immigrant and Minority Health* 17, no. 3 (2013): 1–24.

Martínez-San Miguel, Yolanda, and Michelle Stephens. "Introduction: 'Isolated Above but Connected Below': Toward New, Global, Archipelagic Linkages." In

Contemporary Archipelagic Thinking: Toward New Comparative Methodologies and Disciplinary Formations, edited by Michelle Stephens and Yolanda Martínez-San Miguel, 1–44. London: Rowman and Littlefield, 2020.

Maryland Advisory Committee to the U.S. Commission on Civil Rights. "Migrant Workers on Maryland's Eastern Shore." ERIC No. ED279436, June 1983.

Maryland Department of Health and Mental Hygiene. "2010 Primary Care Needs Assessment," October 28, 2011.

———. "2016 Primary Care Needs Assessment," March 31, 2016.

Maryland Department of Labor. "Housing Concerns for H2A Temporary Agricultural Workers." Accessed December 2018, https://mda.maryland.gov /about_mda/Documents/H2A_Workers_DLLR.pdf.

Maryland Rural Health Association. "Maryland Rural Health Plan," October 2018. https://www.mdruralhealth.org/maryland-rural-health-plan/.

Maryland State Archives. "Maryland at a Glance: Agriculture." Accessed September 2020, https://msa.maryland.gov/msa/mdmanual/01glance/html/agri.html

Massey, Douglas S., ed. *New Faces in New Places: The Changing Geography of American Immigration*. New York: Russell Sage Foundation, 2008.

Massey, Douglas S., Jorge Durand, and Nolan J. Malone. *Beyond Smoke and Mirrors: Mexican Immigration in an Era of Economic Integration*. New York: Russell Sage Foundation, 2002.

Massey, Douglas S., and Mariano Sana. "Patterns of U.S. Migration from Mexico, the Caribbean, and Central America." *Migraciones Internacionales* 2, no. 2 (2003): 5–39.

Mathema, Silva, Nicole Prchal Svajlenka, and Anneliese Hermann. *Revival and Opportunity: Immigrants in Rural America*. Washington, D.C.: Center for American Progress, 2018.

Mazurenko, Olena, Casey P. Balio, Rajender Agarwal, Aaron E. Carroll, and Nir Menachemi. "The Effects of Medicaid Expansion under the ACA: A Systematic Review." *Health Affairs* 37, no. 6 (2018): 944–50.

McAreavey, Ruth. *New Immigration Destinations: Migrating to Rural and Peripheral Areas*. London: Taylor & Francis, 2017.

McCarthy, James. "Rural Geography: Globalizing the Countryside." *Progress in Human Geography* 32, no. 1 (2008): 129–37.

McHugh, Margie, and Madeline Morawski. *Immigrants and WIOA Services: Comparison of Sociodemographic Characteristics of Native- and Foreign-Born Adults in the United States*. Washington, D.C.: Migration Policy Institute, 2016.

McKittrick, Katherine. *Demonic Grounds: Black Women and the Cartographies of Struggle*. Minneapolis: University of Minnesota Press, 2006.

McKittrick, Katherine, and Clyde Adrian Woods, eds. *Black Geographies and the Politics of Place*. Boston: South End Press, 2007.

McRuer, Robert. *Crip Theory: Signs of Queerness and Disability*. New York: NYU Press, 2006.

Melamed, Jodi. "Racial Capitalism." *Critical Ethnic Studies*, no. 1 (2015): 76–85.

Millar, Kathleen M. "The Precarious Present: Wageless Labor and Disrupted Life in Rio de Janeiro, Brazil." *Cultural Anthropology* 29, no. 1 (2014): 32–53.

Miller, Mark J., Philip L. Martin, and Ed Kee. "Migrants in Delmarva Agriculture." Unpublished conference paper prepared for the Changing Face of Delmarva, University of Delaware, Newark, September 11, 1997.

Milligan, Christine, and Janine Wiles. "Landscapes of Care." *Progress in Human Geography* 34, no. 6 (2010): 736–54.

Minich, Julie. *Accessible Citizenships: Disability, Nation, and the Cultural Politics of Greater Mexico*. Philadelphia: Temple University Press, 2014.

Misztal, Barbara A. *Informality: Social Theory and Contemporary Practice*. London: Routledge, 2000.

Mitchell, Don. "Dead Labor and the Political Economy of Landscape: California Living, California Dying." In *Handbook of Cultural Geography*, edited by Kay Anderson, Mona Domosh, Steve Pile, and Nigel Thrift, 233–48. London: Sage, 2003.

Mol, Annemarie, Ingunn Moser, and Jeannette Pols, eds. *Care in Practice: On Tinkering in Clinics, Homes, and Farms*. Bielefeld: Verlag, 2015.

Morgen, Sandra, and Jeff Maskovsky. "The Anthropology of Welfare 'Reform': New Perspectives on U.S. Urban Poverty in the Post-Welfare Era." *Annual Review of Anthropology* 32, no. 1 (2003): 315–38.

Mulligan, Jessica M., and Heide Castañeda, eds. *Unequal Coverage: The Experience of Health Care Reform in the United States*. New York: NYU Press, 2017.

National Center for Health Statistics (NCHS). *Health, United States: Urban and Rural Health Chartbook*. Hyattsville, Md.: NCHS, 2001.

National Marine Fisheries Service. *Fisheries of the United States, 2019*. Silver Spring, Md.: U.S. Department of Commerce, National Oceanic and Atmospheric Administration (NOAA), 2021. https://www.fisheries.noaa.gov/national/sustainable-fisheries/fisheries-united-states.

Negri, Antonio, and Michael Hardt. *Empire*. Cambridge, Mass.: Harvard University Press, 2001.

Nelson, Lise, and Peter B. Nelson. "The Global Rural: Gentrification and Linked Migration in the Rural USA." *Progress in Human Geography* 35, no. 4 (2011): 441–45.

Nguyen, Vinh-Kim. "Antiretroviral Globalism, Biopolitics, and Therapeutic Citizenship." In *Global Assemblages: Technology, Politics, and Ethics as Anthropological Problems*, edited by Aihwa Ong and Stephen Collier, 124–44. Malden, Mass.: Blackwell, 2005.

Obama, Barack. "United States Health Care Reform: Progress to Date and Next Steps." *JAMA* 316, no. 5 (2016): 525–32.

Oberlander, Jonathan. "Long Time Coming: Why Health Reform Finally Passed." *Health Affairs* 29, no. 6 (2010): 1112–16.

O'Neill, Bruce. "Cast Aside: Boredom, Downward Mobility, and Homelessness in Post-Communist Bucharest." *Cultural Anthropology* 29, no. 1 (2014): 8–31.

Ortega, Alexander N., Hai Fang, Victor H. Perez, John A. Rizzo, Olivia Carter-Pokras, Steven P. Wallace, and Lillian Gelberg. "Health Care Access, Use of Services, and Experiences among Undocumented Mexicans and Other Latinos." *Archives of Internal Medicine* 167, no. 21 (2007): 2354–60.

Otero, Gerardo. "Neoliberal Globalization, NAFTA, and Migration: Mexico's Loss of Food and Labor Sovereignty." *Journal of Poverty* 15, no. 4 (2011): 384–402.

Paik, A. Naomi. *Rightlessness: Testimony and Redress in U.S. Prison Camps since World War II*. Chapel Hill: University of North Carolina Press, 2016.

Paolisso, Michael. "Blue Crabs and Controversy on the Chesapeake Bay: A Cultural Model for Understanding Watermen's Reasoning about Blue Crab Management." *Human Organization* 61, no. 3 (2002): 226–39.

Parker, Kim, Juliana Menasce Horowitz, Anna Brown, Richard Fry, D'Vera Cohn, and Ruth Igielnik. "Demographic and Economic Trends in Urban, Suburban and Rural Communities." In *What Unites and Divides Urban, Suburban and Rural Communities*, 16–28. Washington, D.C.: Pew Research Center, 2018.

Passel, Jeffrey S., and D'Vera Cohn. *Unauthorized Immigrant Population: National and State Trends, 2010*. Washington, D.C.: Pew Hispanic Center, 2011.

Perry, Keisha-Khan Y. *Black Women against the Land Grab: The Fight for Racial Justice in Brazil*. Minneapolis: University of Minnesota Press, 2013.

Pew Research Center. "Changing Patterns in U.S. Immigration and Population," December 18, 2014.

———. "U.S. Unauthorized Immigrant Population Estimates by State, 2016," February 5, 2019. https://www.pewresearch.org/hispanic/interactives/u-s -unauthorized-immigrants-by-state/.

———. *What Unites and Divides Urban, Suburban and Rural Communities*. Washington, D.C.: Pew Research Center, 2018.

Phizacklea, Annie, ed. *One Way Ticket: Migration and Female Labour*. London: Routledge, 1983.

Portes, Alejandro, and Rubén G. Rumbaut. *Immigrant Amèricà*. Berkeley: University of California Press, 2014.

Praspaliauskiene, Rima. "Enveloped Lives: Practicing Health and Care in Lithuania." *Medical Anthropology Quarterly* 30, no. 4 (2016): 582–98.

Preibisch, Kerry. "Pick-Your-Own Labor: Migrant Workers and Flexibility in Canadian Agriculture." *International Migration Review* 44, no. 2 (2010): 404–41.

Preibisch, Kerry, and Evelyn Encalada Grez. "The Other Side of El Otro Lado: Mexican Migrant Women and Labor Flexibility in Canadian Agriculture." *Signs* 35, no. 2 (2010): 289–316.

Preibisch, Kerry, and Jenna Hennebry. "Temporary Migration, Chronic Effects: The Health of International Migrant Workers in Canada." *Canadian Medical Association Journal* 183, no. 9 (2011): 1033–38.

Prentice, Rachel. "Work after Precarity: Anthropologies of Labor and Wageless Life." *Focaal* 88 (2020): 117–24.

Prince, Ruth, and Rebecca Marsland, eds. *Making and Unmaking Public Health in Africa: Ethnographic and Historical Perspectives*. Athens: Ohio University Press, 2013.

Pulido, Laura. "Flint, Environmental Racism, and Racial Capitalism." *Capitalism Nature Socialism* 27, no. 3 (2016): 1–16.

———. "Geographies of Race and Ethnicity II: Environmental Racism, Racial Capitalism and State-Sanctioned Violence." *Progress in Human Geography* 41, no. 4 (2017): 524–33.

Quashie, Kevin. *Black Aliveness, or a Poetics of Being*. Durham, N.C.: Duke University Press, 2021.

Quesada, James, Laurie Kain Hart, and Philippe Bourgois. "Structural Vulnerability and Health: Latino Migrant Laborers in the United States." *Medical Anthropology* 30, no. 4 (2011): 339–62.

Rao, Birju, and Ida Hellander. "The Widening U.S. Health Care Crisis Three Years after the Passage of 'Obamacare.'" *International Journal of Health Services* 44 (2014): 215–32.

Ray, Victor. "A Theory of Racialized Organizations." *American Sociological Review* 84, no. 1 (2019): 26–53.

Redfield, Peter. "On Band-Aids and Magic Bullets." *Limn* 5 (2017).

Rhodes, Lorna A. "The Shape of Action." In *Knowledge, Power and Practice: The Anthropology of Medicine and Everyday Life*, edited by Shirley Lindenbaum and Margaret Lock, 129–44. Berkeley: University of California, 1993.

Rhodes, Scott, Lilli Mann, Florence Simán, Eunyoung Song, Jorge Alonzo, Mario Downs, Emma Lawlor et al. "The Impact of Local Immigration Enforcement Policies on the Health of Immigrant Hispanics/Latinos in the United States." *American Journal of Public Health* 105, no. 2 (2015): 329–37.

Ricketts, Thomas C. "The Changing Nature of Rural Health Care." *Annual Review of Public Health* 21, no. 1 (2000): 639–57.

———, ed. *Rural Health in the United States*. Oxford: Oxford University Press, 1999.

Rivkin-Fish, Michelle. *Women's Health in Post-Soviet Russia: The Politics of Intervention*. Indianapolis: Indiana University Press, 2005.

Rodman, Margaret C. "Empowering Place: Multilocality and Multivocality." *American Anthropologist* 94, no. 3 (1992): 640–56.

Roediger, David R., and Elizabeth D. Esch. *The Production of Difference: Race and the Management of Labor in U.S. History*. Oxford: Oxford University Press, 2012.

Rogaly, Ben. "Commentary: Agricultural Racial Capitalism and Rural Migrant Workers." *Journal of Rural Studies* 88 (2021): 527–31.

Rosaldo, Renato. "Ideology, Place, and People without Culture." *Cultural Anthropology* 3, no. 1 (1988): 77–87.

Rosenbaum, Sara, Julia Paradise, Anne Markus, Jessica Sharac, Chi Tran, David Reynolds, and Peter Shin. *Community Health Centers: Recent Growth and the Role of the ACA*. Menlo Park, Calif.: Kaiser Family Foundation, 2017.

Rosenbloom, Joshua. *Looking for Work, Searching for Workers: American Labor Markets During Industrialization*. Cambridge: Cambridge University Press, 2002.

Rosenthal, Anat. "'Illegality' and Illness in the Everyday Struggles of Undocumented HIV+ Migrant Workers in Tel Aviv." *International Migration* 45, no. 3 (2007): 134–56.

Salinsky, Eileen. "Health Care Shortage Designations: HPSA, MUA, and TBD." Background Paper 75. National Health Policy Forum, George Washington University, June 4, 2010.

Samuelsen, Helle. "Therapeutic Itineraries: The Medical Field in Rural Burkina Faso." *Anthropology & Medicine* 11 (2004): 27–41.

Sandahl, Carrie. "Queering the Crip or Cripping the Queer? Intersections of Queer and Crip Identities in Solo Autobiographical Performance." *GLQ: A Journal of Gay and Lesbian Studies* 9, no. 1–2 (2003): 25–26.

Sangaramoorthy, Thurka. "Chronicity, Crisis, and the 'End of AIDS.'" *Global Public Health* 13, no. 8 (2018): 982–96.

———. "Liminal Living: Everyday Injury, Disability, and Instability among Migrant Mexican Women in Maryland's Seafood Industry." *Medical Anthropology Quarterly* 33, no. 4 (2019): 557–78.

———. "'Putting Band-Aids on Things That Need Stitches': Immigration and the Landscape of Care in Rural America." *American Anthropologist* 120, no. 3 (2018): 487–99.

———. *Treating AIDS: Politics of Difference, Paradox of Prevention*. New Brunswick, N.J.: Rutgers University Press, 2014.

Sangaramoorthy, Thurka, and Adia Benton. "Imagining Rural Immunity." *Anthropology News* 61, no. 3 (2020): 28–30.

Sangaramoorthy, Thurka, and Megan A. Carney. "Immigration, Mental Health and Psychosocial Well-Being." *Medical Anthropology* 40, no. 7 (2021): 591–97.

Sangaramoorthy, Thurka, and Emilia Guevara. "Immigrant Health in Rural Maryland: A Qualitative Study of Major Barriers to Health Care Access." *Journal of Immigrant and Minority Health* 19, no. 4 (2017): 939–46.

Sangaramoorthy, Thurka, Amelia M. Jamison, Meleah D. Boyle, Devon C. Payne-Sturges, Amir Sapkota, Donald K. Milton, and Sacoby M. Wilson. "Place-Based Perceptions of the Impacts of Fracking along the Marcellus Shale." *Social Science & Medicine* 151 (2016): 27–37.

Sangaramoorthy, Thurka, and Karen Kroeger. "Mobility, Latino Migrants, and the Geography of Sex Work: Using Ethnography in Public Health Assessments." *Human Organization* 72, no. 3 (2013): 263–72.

Sargent, Carolyn, and Stephanie Larchanché. "Transnational Migration and Global Health: The Production and Management of Risk, Illness, and Access to Care." *Annual Review of Anthropology* 40 (2011): 345–61.

Sassen, Saskia. *Globalization and Its Discontents: Essays on the New Mobility of People and Money*. New York: New Press, 1998.

Saxton, Dvera. *The Devil's Fruit: Farmworkers, Health, and Environmental Justice*. New Brunswick, N.J.: Rutgers University Press, 2021.

Saxton, Dvera, and Angela Stuesse, "Workers' Decompensation: Engaged Research with Injured Im/migrant Workers." *Anthropology of Work Review* 39, no. 2 (2018): 65–78.

Scheper-Hughes, Nancy. "A Talent for Life: Reflections on Human Vulnerability and Resilience." *Ethnos* 73, no. 1 (2008): 25–56.

Segura, Denise A., and Patricia Zavella, eds. *Women and Migration in the U.S.–Mexico Borderlands: A Reader*. Durham, N.C.: Duke University Press, 2007.

Sharp, Gregory, and Barrett A. Lee. "New Faces in Rural Places: Patterns and Sources of Nonmetropolitan Ethnoracial Diversity Since 1990." *Rural Sociology* 82, no. 3 (2017): 411–43.

Sharpe, Christina. *In the Wake: On Blackness and Being*. Durham, N.C.: Duke University Press, 2016.

Sheppard, Emma. "Using Pain, Living with Pain." *The Feminist Review* 120 (2018): 54–69.

Silva, Neide Emy Kurokawa, Leyla Gomes Sancho, and Wagner dos Santos Figueiredo. "Between Flows and Therapeutic Projects: Revisiting the Notions of Lines of Care in Health and Therapeutic Itineraries." *Ciência & Saúde Coletiva* 21 (2016): 843–52.

Simone, AbdouMaliq. "People as Infrastructure: Intersecting Fragments in Johannesburg." *Public Culture* 16, no. 3 (2004): 407–29.

Simpson, Audra. *Mohawk Interruptus: Political Life across the Borders of Settler States*. Durham, N.C.: Duke University Press, 2014.

Sinclair, Upton. *The Jungle*. Charleston, S.C.: CreateSpace Independent Publishing Platform, 2014. First published in 1906 by Doubleday.

Singer, Audrey. "The Rise of New Immigrant Gateways." Washington, D.C.: Brookings Institution, 2004.

Singh, Gopal K., and Mohammad Siahpush. "Widening Rural–Urban Disparities in Life Expectancy, U.S., 1969–2009." *American Journal of Preventive Medicine* 46, no. 2 (2014): e19–e29.

Smith, Ben. "A Voice from the Floor on Illegal Immigrants: 'You Lie.'" *Politico*, September 9, 2009.

Smith, Daniel Jordan, and Benjamin C. Mbakwem. "Life Projects and Therapeutic Itineraries: Marriage, Fertility, and Antiretroviral Therapy in Nigeria." *AIDS* 21 (2007): S37–S41.

Smith-Nonini, Sandy. "The Illegal and the Dead: Are Mexicans Renewable Energy?" *Medical Anthropology* 30, no. 5 (2011): 454–74.

Southern Poverty Law Center (SPLC). *Close to Slavery: Guestworker Programs in the United States*. Montgomery, Ala.: SPLC, 2013.

Stan, Sabina. "Neither Commodities nor Gifts: Post-Socialist Informal Exchanges in the Romanian Healthcare System." *Journal of the Royal Anthropological Institute* 18, no. 1 (2012): 65–82.

State of Maryland. "U.S. Census Bureau Population Estimates for Maryland's Jurisdictions: 2019." Accessed May 2019, https://planning.maryland.gov/MSDC/Pages/pop_estimate/InterCensalPopEst-cnty.aspx.

Stein, Elizabeth M., Keith P. Gennuso, Donna C. Ugboaja, and Patrick L. Remington. "The Epidemic of Despair among White Americans: Trends in the Leading Causes of Premature Death, 1999–2015." *American Journal of Public Health* 107, no. 10 (2017): 1541–47.

Stratford, Elaine, ed. *Island Geographies: Essays and Conversations*. London: Routledge, 2017.

Straut-Eppsteiner, Holly. "Coming and Going: Mexican Women Guestworkers in the U.S. Crab Industry." *Latino Studies* 14 (2016): 482–503.

Stuesse, Angela. *Scratching Out a Living: Latinos, Race, and Work in the Deep South*. Berkeley: University of California Press, 2016.

Suphanchaimat, Rapeepong, Kanang Kantamaturapoj, Weerasak Putthasri, and Phusit Prakongsai. "Challenges in the Provision of Healthcare Services for

Migrants: A Systematic Review through Providers' Lens." *BMC Health Services Research* 15, no. 1 (2015): 1–14.

Taylor, Keeanga-Yamahtta. *Race for Profit: How Banks and the Real Estate Industry Undermined Black Homeownership*. Chapel Hill: University of North Carolina Press, 2019.

Terrazas, Aaron. *Immigrants in New-Destination States*. Washington, D.C.: Migration Policy Institute, 2011.

Thomas, Deborah A. *Political Life in the Wake of the Plantation: Sovereignty, Witnessing, Repair*. Durham, N.C.: Duke University Press, 2019.

Ticktin, Miriam. *Casualties of Care: Immigration and the Politics of Humanitarianism in France*. Berkeley: University of California Press, 2011.

Toomey, Russell B., Adriana J. Umaña-Taylor, David R. Williams, Elizabeth Harvey-Mendoza, Laudan B. Jahromi, and Kimberly A. Updegraff. "Impact of Arizona's SB 1070 Immigration Law on Utilization of Health Care and Public Assistance among Mexican-Origin Adolescent Mothers and Their Mother Figures." *American Journal of Public Health* 104 Suppl (2014): S28–S34.

Torres, Rebecca M., and Lindsey Carte. "Migration and Development? The Gendered Costs of Migration on Mexico's Rural 'Left Behind.'" *Geographical Review* 106, no. 3 (2016): 399–420.

Trull, Armando. "Why a Mexican Flag Flies High in a Trump County." *WAMU 88.5*, May 21, 2017.

Tyner, James A. *Dead Labor: Toward a Political Economy of Premature Death*. Minneapolis: University of Minnesota Press, 2019.

———. *Made in the Philippines*. London: Routledge, 2004.

U.S. Bureau of Labor Statistics. "Labor Force Characteristics of Foreign-Born Workers Summary." News release USDL-22-0902, May 18, 2022.

———. "Occupational Employment and Wages, May 2019: 51-3022 Meat, Poultry, and Fish Cutters and Trimmers," July 6, 2020. https://www.bls.gov/oes/2019/may/oes513022.htm.

U.S. Census Bureau. "State and County QuickFacts, Maryland, Foreign-Born Persons, Percent 2015–2019." Accessed December 2020, https://www.census.gov/quickfacts/fact/table/MD/PST045219.

———. "State and County QuickFacts, Maryland and Washington, 2020." https://www.census.gov/quickfacts/fact/table/MD/PST045219.

U.S. Citizenship and Immigration Services, Department of Homeland Security. "Public Charge Ground of Inadmissibility," February 24, 2022. https://www.govinfo.gov/content/pkg/FR-2022-02-24/pdf/2022-03788.pdf.

U.S. Department of Agriculture. "2017 Census of Agriculture," April 11, 2019. https://www.nass.usda.gov/Publications/AgCensus/2017/index.php#full_report.

U.S. Department of Agriculture, Economic Research Service. "State Fact Sheets: Maryland," November 1, 2021.

U.S. Department of Health and Human Services. "Find Shortage Areas: HPSA by State and County, 2015." http://hpsafind.hrsa.gov/.

U.S. Department of Homeland Security. "Nonimmigrant Admissions by Selected Classes of Admission and Sex and Age: Fiscal Year 2021." Accessed December

2022, https://www.dhs.gov/immigration-statistics/readingroom/NI/Nonimmigrant COAsexage.

U.S. General Accounting Office. "Health Professional Shortage Areas: Problems Remain with Primary Care Shortage Area Designation System," Accessed May 2006. https://www.govinfo.gov/content/pkg/GAOREPORTS-HEHS-95-200 /html/GAOREPORTS-HEHS-95-200.htm.

Valdez, Inés. "Socialism and Empire: Labor Mobility, Racial Capitalism, and the Political Theory of Migration." *Political Theory* 49, no. 6 (2021): 902–33.

Vertovec, Steven. "The Cultural Politics of Nation and Migration." *Annual Review of Anthropology* 40 (2011): 241–56.

Vick, Andrea. "Theorizing Episodic Disabilities: The Case for an Embodied Politics." *Canadian Social Work Review* 29, no. 1 (2012): 41–60.

Vigh, Henrik. "Crisis and Chronicity: Anthropological Perspectives on Continuous Conflict and Decline." *Ethnos* 73, no. 1 (2008): 5–24.

Viruell-Fuentes, Edna A., Patricia Y. Miranda, and Sawsan Abdulrahim. "More than Culture: Structural Racism, Intersectionality Theory, and Immigrant Health." *Social Science & Medicine* 75, no. 12 (2012): 2099–106.

Vogt, Wendy A. "Crossing Mexico: Structural Violence and the Commodification of Undocumented Central American Migrants." *American Ethnologist* 40, no. 4 (2013): 764–80.

Walia, Harsha. *Border and Rule: Global Migration, Capitalism, and the Rise of Racist Nationalism*. Chicago: Haymarket Books, 2021.

———. *Undoing Border Imperialism*. Oakland, Calif.: Ak Press, 2013.

Wang, Fahui. "Measurement, Optimization, and Impact of Health Care Accessibility: A Methodological Review." *Annals of the Association of American Geographers* 102, no. 5 (2012): 1104–12.

Weinhold, Ines, and Sebastian Gurtner. "Understanding Shortages of Sufficient Health Care in Rural Areas." *Health Policy* 118, no. 2 (2014): 201–14.

Wendland, Claire. *A Heart for the Work: Journeys through an African Medical School*. Chicago: University of Chicago Press, 2010.

White, Karie, Valerie A. Yeager, Nir Menachemi, and Isabel C. Scarinci. "Impact of Alabama's Immigration Law on Access to Health Care among Latina Immigrants and Children: Implications for National Reform." *American Journal of Public Health* 104, no. 3 (2014): 397–405.

White, Michael J. "Migration, Urbanization, and Social Adjustment." Policy Brief 1. Presented at the Wilson Center, Washington, D.C., February 8–9, 1999.

Whyte, Susan, Michael Whyte, Lotte Meinert, and Jenipher Twebaze. "Therapeutic Clientship: Belonging in Uganda's Projectified Landscape of AIDS Care." In *When People Come First: Critical Studies in Global Health*, edited by João Biehl and Adriana Petryna, 140–65. Princeton, N.J.: Princeton University Press, 2013.

Willen, Sarah. "Do 'Illegal' Im/migrants Have a Right to Health? Engaging Ethical Theory as Social Practice at a Tel Aviv Open Clinic." *Medical Anthropology Quarterly* 25 (2011): 303–30.

———. *Fighting for Dignity: Migrant Lives at Israel's Margins*. Philadelphia: University of Pennsylvania Press, 2021.

———. "How Is Health-Related 'Deservingness' Reckoned? Perspectives from Unauthorized Im/migrants in Tel Aviv." *Social Science & Medicine* 74, no. 6 (2012): 812–21.

———. "Migration, 'Illegality,' and Health: Mapping Embodied Vulnerability and Debating Health-Related Deservingness." *Social Science & Medicine* 74, no. 6 (2012): 805–11.

Williams, Allison. "Changing Geographies of Care: Employing the Concept of Therapeutic Landscapes as a Framework in Examining Home Space." *Social Science & Medicine* 55, no. 1 (2002): 141–54.

Williams, Erica, Eric Figueroa, and Wesley Tharpe. "Inclusive Approach to Immigrants Who Are Undocumented Can Help Families and States Prosper." Washington D.C.: Center on Budget and Policy Priorities, December 2019.

Wilson, Kathleen. "Therapeutic Landscapes and First Nations Peoples: An Exploration of Culture, Health and Place." *Health & Place* 9, no. 2 (2003): 83–93.

Woods, Michael. "Engaging the Global Countryside: Globalization, Hybridity and the Reconstitution of Rural Place." *Progress in Human Geography* 31, no. 4 (2007): 485–507.

Wynter, Sylvia. "Unsettling the Coloniality of Being/Power/Truth/Freedom: Towards the Human, After Man, Its Overrepresentation—An Argument." *CR: The New Centennial Review* 3, no. 3 (2003): 257–337.

Zerilli, Filippo. "Corruption, Property Restitution and Romanianness." In *Corruption: Anthropological Approaches*, edited by Dieter Haller and Cris Shore, 83–100. Ann Arbor, Mich.: Pluto Press, 2005.

Ziller, Erika C., Jennifer D. Lenardson, and Andrew F. Coburn, "Health Care Access and Use among the Rural Uninsured." *Journal of Health Care for the Poor and Underserved* 23, no. 3 (2012): 1327–45.

Zuckerman, Stephen, Timothy A. Waidmann, and Emily Lawton, "Undocumented Immigrants, Left out of Health Reform, Likely to Continue to Grow as Share of the Uninsured." *Health Affairs* 30 no. 10 (2011): 1997–2004.

Index

Affordable Care Act (2010, ACA, Patient Protection and Affordable Care Act), xiii, 17–18, 40, 41, 67, 75, 78–79, 89–90, 101, 104, 134n46, 138n69, 143n13, 144n16, 144n21; aim of, 17, 134n45; increased capacity of health centers, 110; limits of, 67, 89, 101, 105, 108, 113; Medicaid expansion option, 75; Obamacare, 66, 144n16; political debate on, 141–42nn7–8; reduced the uninsured, 108–9; requirements of, 104; sustained inequitable health, 108–9. *See also* landscapes of care

agricultural work, xv, 4, 19, 25, 31, 32, 33, 36, 45, 50, 51, 54, 56–60, 62, 65, 68, 93, 117, 123, 132n12, 133n34, 137nn28–29, 140nn26–29; April to October, 107; ethnic succession in, 57; Haitians, 103; immigrants, xv; historical labor camp, 59–60; Latinx, 103; Mexico, 7; occupational segregation, 36, 37; peak season (June to August), 4; seek more foreign workers, 36. *See also* crab processing work; Haitians; Mexicans; migrant temporary contract labor

Asians, 8; Asia, 122; South Asians, xii

Band-Aid care, 19, 20, 91, 93–114, 95, 132n5, 135n54, 138n71, 142n10, 143nn1–2; bastardized care, 19, 96; diabetes case, 94; enveloped care, 98, 134n39, 143n9. *See also* landscapes of care; neoliberalism; Redfield, Peter

belonging, xi–xii, xix, 4, 13, 24, 25, 37, 53, 70, 120, 123, 124, 125, 145n6; alienation, difference and, 120; being and, 112; health care and, 88; legal, 10; legal and social, 109; politics of,

xvii, 3; possibilities of, 76; racialized, 43; right to, 52; social, economic and political, 41; social connections and, 111; struggle for, 125. *See also* marginalization; racialization

Butler, Judith, 112, 124, 133n21, 144nn28–29; precarity defined, 12. *See also* precarity

Caribbean, xv, 12, 28, 29, 31, 38, 50, 56, 57, 69, 118, 122; Jamaicans, 31, 57. *See also* Haitians

Central Americans, xv, xvi, xvii, 34; Guatemalans, 31, 34; Hondurans, 77; Panamanians, 77; Salvadorians, 31, 57

colonialism, 69, 120, 123, 133n18; coloniality, xii; Haiti, 50, 54, 55; settler, 121. *See also* othering; racial capitalism

crab processing work: coercive plant care, 66; compensation, gratitude, and sacrifice discourse, 118; daily quota of twenty-four pounds, 9; eight to nine hours shifts, 8; employers seek more foreign workers, 36; mainly poor Mexican women, 35; Mexican women's work abilities, 64; monitoring of production, 9; negative health impacts, 6; occupational segregation, 36, 37; peak season (June to August), 4; predominance of Mexican women (H-2B), 33; profit from workers, 35; succession from African American to Mexican women, 1; termination of workers not meeting the quota, 9; women's internalization of work ideologies, 65; worker suffering, 9. *See also* immigrants/immigration; Mexicans; migrant temporary contract labor dead labor, 61, 140n24, 141nn33–34; explained, 61. *See also* disposability; precarity

Deferred Action for Childhood Arrivals (DACA), 80, 142n16

deservingness, xvii, xviii, xix, 4, 11, 98, 142n21, 144n17, 144n22. *See also* belonging; othering

disposability, xiv, 37, 45, 48, 56, 61, 111; dead labor, 61; essential workers and, 68; uncertainty and, 123. *See also* Melamed, Jodi; precarity

enslavement, 5, 30, 39, 51, 54–56, 120, 123, 140n17, 140n19; colonialism and, 50, 123; Haitians view of poultry processing as, 51, 55, 64; imperialism and, 123

essential workers, 68–69; described, 68; disposability of, 68; paradox of, 68; popular use, 68; racialization of, 68. *See also* disposability; precarity

federally designated health professional shortage areas (HPSAs), 66, 73, 74; described, 73. *See also* landscapes of care; medically underserved areas/medically underserved populations (MUAs/MUPs),

federally qualified health centers (FQHC), 4, 14, 17, 65, 66, 67, 73–78, 81, 83, 84, 85, 89, 90, 103, 110; discriminate against uninsured, 84. *See also* landscapes of care; medically underserved areas/medically underserved populations (MUAs/MUPs)

gendering, xviii, 7, 28, 35, 69, 119, 120, 132n9, 138n50, 140n15; bias, 52; disablement, 69; hierarchies, 120, 122; ideologies, 64. *See also* crab processing work; place/placemaking; racialization; racism

Gilmore, Ruth Wilson, 56, 133n26, 139n11; coupling of power and difference, 133n26, 140n20

Haiti, xii, xv, xvii, 23, 24, 31, 34, 49, 56, 57, 77; earthquake (2010), 49, 55, 140n23; Kreyòl language, xvi, 32, 86, 89; military coup, xiii; Temporary Protected Status (TPS), 55, 140n23. *See also* Haitians; poultry processing work

Haitians, xii, xiii, xv, xvi, 23, 24, 31, 34, 35, 36, 47, 48–49, 54–56, 67, 84, 103, 104, 121, 122, 140nn21–22; discrimination against, xii, 36; disliked, 56; disposable at poultry plants, 48; expendable at poultry plants, 36; humiliated at poultry plants, 56; inhumane treatment of, 50; marginalization of, xv; most vulnerable, 31; no Kreyòl translators, 86; racial hierarchies in poultry jobs, 35–36, 50; racial hierarchy with African American supervisors, 48; racialization, xv; social separateness, 56; Temporary Protected Status (TPS), 55, 140n23. *See also* Haiti; poultry processing work; Temporary Protected Status (TPS)

Illegal Immigration Reform and Immigrant Responsibility Act (1996, IIRIRA), 109, 135n49. *See also* Personal Responsibility and Work Opportunity Reconciliation Act (1996, PRWORA)

immigrants/immigration: anti-immigrant rhetoric, 3; confounding of immigration and legal status, 10; cooperation with ICE, 85; dead labor, 61; debates on place, identity, and belonging, 25; deportability and exploitation, 50; five-year bar on public benefits, 17, 89–90; global restructuring and, 26; H-2B visa vital to seafood economy, 2; in rural communities, 26–29; in rural Maryland, 29–32; invisible injuries, 63, 64; limited access to health care, 42; limits of legality framework, 11; mitigation of rural decline, 3; polarizing issue in Maryland, 2; poor treatment of, 3; positive and negative effects of, 24; racialized labor conditions, 67; racialized others, 37; rural residents depend on but resent, 38; surge in undocumented, 28; work conditions and disciplining of, 60–61. *See also* belonging; place/placemaking; public charge migrant rules

Immigration Act (1990): creation of TPS, 140n23

Immigration Reform and Control Act (1986, IRCA): legalization, 140n26

landscapes of care, xvi, 16, 20, 42, 43, 79, 85, 88–90, 94–96, 99, 101–2, 109, 112–13, 114, 119, 123, 125; alternate geography, 125; barriers to health care, 83; beyond Maryland, 19; coercive care, 66; contested space, 17, 125; explained, xiv, 16; federal and state policy alignment, 87–88; fraction of residents reached, 42; goodwill, 105–07; informal transaction, 99–107, 113–14; interdependence and personhood, 112; Milligan, Christine and Janine Wiles formulation of, 134n40; not only spatial, 125; positive care in Maryland, 87; possibilities of belonging, 76, 123, 125; provider's personal funding, 6; racial and spatial exclusion in, 20, 103–5; racial inequities in, 74; racially discriminatory policies, 75; rural health abandoned by the state, 40, 79, 82, 110; struggling abandoned system, 82; use of emergency rooms for medical care, 84; violent cycle, 89; willful noncompliance, 96, 103–5, 113. *See also* federal qualified health centers (FQHC); federally designated health professional shortage areas (HPSAs); medically underserved areas/medically

underserved populations (MUAs/MUPs); precarity; racialization; scarcity; uncertainty

Latin America, xv, 12, 28, 29, 31, 34, 38, 50, 56, 69, 118, 122, 132n12. *See also* Central Americans; Mexicans

Latinx, xv, 11. 31, 41, 50; Central American, Hispanic, Latino, Mexican, xvi; documented, 103; immigrants, 89; permanent settlement of, 31; undocumented, 31, 50, 103. *See also* Central Americans; Maryland Eastern Shore; Mexicans

marginalization, xix, 49; cultural, political and social, xv; economic and social, 11; economic, exploitation, and political, 98; economic, political, and social, 41; feelings of, xix; immigrant, 10; uncertainty and, 13. *See also* precarity; racialization

Maryland's Eastern Shore: hatred of Hispanic residents, 38–39; hidden population of Black immigrants, 31; key economic sectors, 30; Nanticoke people original inhabitants of, 5; new receiving destination, 29; nine counties in, 3, 29; physical remoteness of, 3; politically conservative, xiii, 2, 25, 38–39, 117; support for Trump, 21, 117, 137n39, 145n1; support of anti-immigrant discourse, 3, 117; the land that time forgot, 5; violent legacy of anti-Black racism, 30. *See also* agricultural work; crab processing work; poultry processing work

medically underserved areas/medically underserved populations (MUAs/MUPs), 74, 89; described, 73. *See also* federally designated health professional shortage areas (HPSAs); federally qualified health centers (FQHC); landscapes of care

Melamed, Jodi, 45, 56, 140n20, 140n25, 145n6. *See also* racial capitalism

Mexicans, xv, xvi, 2, 8, 34, 52–55, 57, 117, 122, 137n26, 137nn38–39, 139n2, 143n24; estrangement from family and friends, 53; Island of Mexican Women (*Islas de las Mexicanas*), 54, 117; Mexican Americans, 21; migrants, 21. *See also* agricultural work; crab processing work; Latinx; Mexico; migrant temporary contract labor

Mexico, xv, xvii, 1, 7, 8, 9, 11, 28, 31, 33, 34, 50, 53, 63, 64, 81, 87, 107, 117, 132n9, 132n15, 141n40; flag of, 117, 118, 145n1; *gorgojos chinos* herb (Chinese weevils), 101; material benefits from remittances, 118; migration from, 56, 77; neoliberalism in, 7; Oaxacan tea, 101; precarity in, 52, 82. *See also* crab processing work; Mexicans; migrant temporary contract labor

migrant temporary contract labor, xv, 69; collusion to ignore regulations, 57; continued precarity, 58; guest workers, 69; health insurance, 67; H–2A visa, 35, 52, 53, 57, 58, 67; H–2B visa, 2, 33, 35, 52, 53, 67, 117, 122, 132n2, 137nn41–42, 141n35. *See also* agricultural work; crab processing work; Mexicans

neoliberalism, 11, 28, 97, 108, 113, 123, 139nn1–2, 144n21; Affordable Care Act, 108; capitalism, 139n1; coerced migration, 49; democratic capitalism, 53; empire, 120; exclusion and inequality, 113, 114; exploitation, 38; Haitian colonialism, 55; link to racism, 38; makes work more precarious, 49; precarity, 49, 112; structural violence, 50; white settler states, 121; white supremacy, 123. *See also* Pulido, Laura; racial capitalism; racism

new receiving destinations, 25, 26–27, 28, 132n15, 136n6, 136nn10–11; emerging destinations, 25; traditional destinations, 27

othering, 11, 37, 133n18. *See also* colonialism; racial capitalism; racialization; racism

Personal Responsibility and Work Opportunity Reconciliation Act (1996, PRWORA), 109, 135n4. *See also* Illegal Immigration Reform and Immigrant Responsibility Act (1996, IIRIRA)

place/placemaking, xviii, 10, 12, 13, 15–16, 21, 25, 29, 43, 73, 114, 125, 133n28, 134n36, 134n38, 138n55, 145n8; belonging and, 125; capital forms and, 89; degrading of labor and, 53; displacement, 12, 13, 42, 120, 133n25; keep in their place, 51, 59; migrants as placeless, 10, 11; out-of-place, xii, 131n3; people and, 56, 113, 121; personhood and, 99, 114; placed-base health care, 15; politics of, 25; power and, 123; profit from abandoned, 76; racialized workplace, 50, 55; risk and, 80; space and, xviii, ; surplus, 28, 61; values of, 99. *See also* belonging

poultry processing work, xv–xvi, 19, 32, 33–34, 35, 36, 37, 47, 48, 49, 50, 51, 5456, 58, 61, 64, 66, 67, 68, 93, 103, 104, 123, 137nn38–39; African American supervisors, 48; daily indignities, 49; dependence on racialized and immigrant labor, 34; employers seek more foreign workers, 36; English-language disadvantage, 48; exposure to physical harm, 49; occupational segregation, 36, 37; Purdue Farms, 33; racial hierarchies, 35; succession from African American to migrant labor, 34; traumatic, 47. *See also* Haitians

precarity, xiii, xiv, xv, xvii, xviii, xix, 3–4, 8, 10, 11, 12–15, 19, 20, 39, 40, 41, 43, 49, 51, 52, 58, 67, 69, 73, 76, 88, 94, 96, 99, 109, 111–12, 113, 114, 119, 122, 123–24, 132n10, 133nn20–22, 133nn24–25, 139n4; border imperialism, 51; capital abandonment, 39;

collective livingness, 13; defined, xiv; economic, 54, 57; despair deaths, 40; embodiment of, 119; health, xvii; in Mexico, 52; field of relations, xiv; infrastructural abandonment, 40; mediated, xiv; normalized, 68; shared precarity, 3; socioeconomic abandonment, 13, 14, 15, 76; state abandonment, 39, 79; structural abandonment, 38; under neoliberalism, 112. *See also* Butler, Judith; disposability; racial capitalism; uncertainty

public charge migrant rules, xiv, 18, 135nn50–51; discouraged use of public health care, 18

Puerto Ricans, 57

Pulido, Laura, 28, 111, 133n28, 136n9, 138n55, 139n9, 144n27, 145n6. *See also* racial capitalism

racial capitalism, xviii, 3, 12, 19, 45, 53, 61, 67, 70, 121, 123, 133n28, 136n9, 137n38, 138n55, 139n9, 140n20, 140n25, 144n27, 145n6; class, 12, 28, 35, 119, 120; experienced as ordinary, 51; exploitation, 12, 69; globalized, 121; migrant labor, 50; social inequalities, 50; social separateness, 56; tool of antirelationality, 56; violence in, 43. *See also* colonialism; Melamed, Jodi; neoliberalism; Pulido, Laura; white supremacy

racialization, xiv, xv, xviii, 9–11, 14, 19, 24, 30, 33, 34, 37, 38, 39, 43, 50, 51–52, 55, 60, 61, 64, 65, 67, 68–70, 80, 88–89, 111, 113, 119, 120, 121, 122, 132n3, 133n18, 133n28, 136n6, 140n15, 145n6; defined, xv; devaluation, 13, 28; disablement, 69; geographies, 18, 50, 114; organizations, 11, 16, 137nn45–46; racial capitalist logics, 16; racial logics, xv, xix, 11, 20, 119, 123; spaces and, 13; violence, 50; work regimes, 13. *See also* racial capitalism; racism; white supremacy

racism, xi, xii, 3, 12, 15, 16, 20, 24, 25, 27, 28, 30, 31, 35, 35–36, 37, 38, 42, 43, 45, 48, 50, 54, 56, 75, 89, 90, 94, 96, 103, 107, 111, 112, 119, 120, 121, 123, 133n28, 136n9; environmental, 138n55, 139n9, 140n20, 142n11, 142n19, 144n27; Jim Crow, 30; racial articulations, xviii; racial equity, xviii, xix; racial inequalities, xviii, 74; structural, 68. *See also* colonialism; enslavement; neoliberalism; racial capitalism; racialization; white supremacy

Redfield, Peter, 91, 95, 135n54, 143nn1–2, 144n22. *See also* Band-Aid care

scarcity, 4, 11, 23, 79, 100, 102, 111; environmental and socioeconomic, 40; defines rural health care, 122. *See also* landscapes of care; precarity; racialization; uncertainty

seafood processing. *See* crab processing work

selective blindness, 20

Temporary Protected Status (TPS), 55; explained, 55; Haitians, 55, 104, 140n23; Salvadorians, 57

therapeutic itineraries/landscapes, 15, 97–98, 99, 101, 102, 107, 108, 134n39, 143nn4–5; defined, 97; therapeutic citizenship, 144n14; therapeutic clientship, 143n8

uncertainty, xiv, xix, 12–13, 51, 52, 56, 57, 58, 59, 69, 82, 85, 98, 99, 112, 123; chronic, 54; economic, 49; economic, existential and political, 11; everyday, 12, 69; fear, 18; time, 12. *See also* disposability; precarity

white supremacy, xiii, 3, 38, 121, 123; roots of anthropology, xiii; shapes precarity, 3. *See also* racial capitalism; racialization; racism